T0339710

THE BATTLE FOR COMPASSION

The Battle for Compassion

Ethics in an Apathetic Universe

Jonathan Leighton

Algora Publishing
New York

Library of Congress Cataloging-in-Publication Data —

Leighton, Jonathan, 1966-
   The battle for compassion: ethics in an apathetic universe / Jonathan Leighton.
      p. cm.
   Includes bibliographical references and index.
      ISBN 978-0-87586-870-7 (soft cover: alk. paper) — ISBN 978-0-87586-871-4
(hard cover: alk. paper) — ISBN 978-0-87586-872-1 (ebook) 1. Compassion. 2. Ethics,
Evolutionary. I. Title.
      BJ1475.L46 2011
      177.7—dc22

                              2011014288

Printed in the United States

And the Earth spins round
While the people fall down
And the world stands still
Not a sound, not a sound
There is love, there is love
To be found
In the worst way, in the worst way
In the worst way

—Lisa Germano, American singer/songwriter,

"From a Shell"

ACKNOWLEDGMENTS

Over the course of this project's evolution, my sometimes wavering conviction that the kernel of a book with something worth saying could be distilled out of a pile of late night scribblings and journal notes was sustained by the enthusiasm of the many friends, family members and acquaintances with whom I discussed the project and sometimes shared excerpts, and to whom I would like to express my gratitude. Irene Schmid, one of my biggest cheerleaders since the beginning and a stimulating intellectual sparring partner, offered detailed comments early on. Patricia Goldschmid, with whom I have had numerous philosophical discussions, has been a great source of encouragement and provided helpful comments on the manuscript. Liz Miller, the other member of the very unofficial Lausanne Philosophy Association, also provided detailed comments and suggestions on part of the manuscript. Aïda Muro was a supportive witness and a catalyst for the generation of several of the initial ideas. I would also like to specifically mention Cathy Henzelin, Olivier Baenninger, David Merillet, Anett Juhasz, Vivian Oyarbide, Sean Blix and Don Antunes for their contributions, whether specific suggestions or valued support for the project along the way. Samah Atout reinforced my hope that open-minded, creative people may yet achieve peace in the Middle East, and that the notion of universal humanitarian values has a role to play. Dave Pearce's writings were an inspiration, as was his enthusiasm about this project, even though he would have liked me to take a stronger stance in favor of veganism. My parents were also a patient and appreciated source of support as they waited with interest to see the result of my writing. Finally, I would like to thank Kaisa for causing me to sometimes doubt one of the premises of this book, which is that the universe has no purpose.

TABLE OF CONTENTS

1. PROLOGUE

I am sitting on the beach on a stretch of coastline in southern Spain, gazing at a sublime sunset. Normally, as most people do, I instinctively appreciate sunsets at face value, entranced by the pastel hues with which the reddish sun bathes the sky as it slowly drops into the sea. I know, of course, that it is the Earth rotating on its axis that causes the sun to set, but it is almost always the geocentric perspective that dominates, the sun like a decorative element moving towards the horizon. But this time, I suddenly see things differently. I find myself gazing across the blue, watery surface of a planet towards the star it revolves around, millions of miles away in the distance, with nothing in between but empty space. As if I have suddenly been transported into a life-size version of one of those old solar system charts for schoolchildren showing the sun and its 9 planets, and I am viewing the sun from atop one of those spheres.[1] I find the perspective striking, almost vertiginous. What is striking is not anything I have learned from the situation that I hadn't already known, but how surprisingly different it feels, as the result of a subtle shift in mental perspective, to be looking at this familiar scene. This perspective has its own arresting beauty. And it does not prevent me from reverting to the usual perspective. But it impresses on me, once again, how conditioned we are to seeing the world in a

---

[1] The solar system is now down to 8 planets since Pluto was demoted to a dwarf planet in 2006. For a chart of the solar system see www.kidsastronomy.com/solar_system.htm.

certain way, and how dramatic an experience it can be to change the way we think about everyday things. Six hundred years after Copernicus presented his revolutionary and heretical heliocentric theory, a sunset can still look unexpectedly new.

What if the fate of our world depended on a similar shift in perspective?

2. Introduction

We are living in an unprecedented, uniquely critical sliver of time in the Earth's existence, possibly even in that of the universe. Sir Martin Rees, a recent president of the Royal Society and an influential voice among the world's scientists, has estimated the chance of our civilization surviving this century at no greater than 50%. An accumulation of distinct threats stemming from human activity, runaway or malevolently used technology and the forces of nature risk turning all the sublime beauty we are capable of experiencing into a short-lived blip of intense meaning in the workings of a vast, inanimate cosmos. While the precise figure cited can obviously be debated, the profound significance of a catastrophe that destroys humanity, and the rarity with which this issue has been so bluntly confronted, are indicative of our broader inability to scale up our level of concern with the challenges we face.

Yet once we stop to contemplate deeply the threats to our existence and what they mean, we are obliged to turn our attention to the present and reflect on what it is that we really care about preserving, and why. The beauty many of us experience often comes at a terrible price. Massive, intense suffering continues to occur in countless places on our planet, often out of view to those of us living comfortable lives, but as real as anything else that exists in this universe. Much of it is potentially preventable. The poverty, malnutrition and disease that continue to plague the developing world. The precarious existence of huge numbers of marginalized shantytown dwellers. The deaths and injuries resulting from war, sectarian violence, terrorist attacks, massacres and genocides. Humans locked up in remote dungeons because of their beliefs, ethnic origin or peaceful self-expression, many subjected to excruciating physical and psychological torture. The millions condemned to meaningless lives behind bars for crimes they committed out of hopelessness. The thousands still executed by their own governments every year. And, shifting our gaze beyond the boundary of our species, the incalculable number of animals made to suffer horrifically at human hands.

Although many of us realize that it is literally the case, we still fail fully to come to grips with the fact that no one is in charge, running the show and managing the details. That we are all part of a giant, unplanned and unguided "experiment" with an uncertain outcome. Perhaps we never fully escape a subconscious longing for the protective balm of childhood. As a result, there is a diffuse sense that it is up to someone else to try to solve these problems. While these issues are on the minds of large numbers of people and organizations working to mitigate them, as a species, we just don't seem to care enough.

The threats to our existence and the persistence of intense suffering are closely intertwined issues with similar underlying causes. Addressing them honestly requires us to reflect deeply and detachedly on who we are, probe the boundaries of ethical thinking, and ask some really big questions. What are the basic forces driving our species' trajectory, and where are they leading us? What really matters at the most fundamental level, and how much does it all matter? And what, consequently, would it realistically take for us to align our world with what matters and preserve a future worth living in?

This book is a reflection on these pivotal questions and an attempt to offer some answers. While our instincts usually serve us well in our daily lives, they have also created a terrible mess of our world. Just as the beauty of a sunset blinds us to the actual mechanics of the phenomenon, our illusions and preconceptions subtly but significantly distort our understanding of the nature of our relationship to the world and hide a larger sense of meaning. In these pages, I take a big-picture look at the human condition and explore the relationship between the subjective and objective aspects of it, i.e. how things actually feel and the physical reality dictating it all. Ideally, by shifting the perspective from which we understand our existence, we may find a way to reconcile our desire to enjoy life in an intuitive way with these existential considerations, and use this understanding to have a positive impact on the world.

One cannot deny that our situation as a species is rather grim, and it is hard to be wildly optimistic about our collective ability to sort ourselves out, even if it is a battle worth valiantly fighting. The scale of suffering and cruelty on this planet, and the recurrence of conflict, seem as inevitable as the rising and setting of the sun, an inextricable aspect of life on Earth, with most initiatives to bring relief just a form of damage control in an endless Sisyphean[2] effort. Perhaps, like Sisyphus, we really are condemned, eternally seeking concrete solutions we are incapable of finding. At the very least, we can go down with the ship knowing what's happening to us. But if we want to have any chance at all of preserving the fragile future and making it livable for many more of us, it is likely that more people will need to break taboos in their thinking and reflect deeply and analytically about the big questions and their practical implications.

This book attempts, in a relatively short space, to cover a wide range of topics from metaphysics to international relations. But I think it is a worthwhile and perhaps even necessary endeavour. We compartmentalize disciplines instead of grasping how they relate to each other. Philosophical reflections about freedom, identity and morality are only practically useful if an attempt is made to tie them to the real world. When the reflections result in conclusions that are unexpected or counterintuitive, it is all the more important to see how they play out in reality.

The ultimate impetus for this book is still a passionate hope for action. It is not filled with empirical data or detailed analyses of the specific issues facing humanity.[3] Nor is it a comprehensive review of past philosophical thinking about ethics and related subjects, although ethics is a central theme. It is, rather, an attempt to distill out a few essential ideas about our existence that are not always apparent and to show how they are linked, to

---

2   Sisyphus was a figure in Greek mythology who, as punishment for stepping on certain divine toes, was forced to push a boulder up a hill for eternity, the boulder continually rolling back down before he could reach the top.

3   James Martin's *The Meaning of the 21th Century* and Martin Rees's *Our Final Hour* (UK edition: *Our Final Century*) are two books that offer a broad look at the range of very real existential challenges we are and will increasingly be confronted with. The websites and reports of organizations like Amnesty International (www.amnesty.org) and Human Rights Watch (www.hrw.org) provide detailed descriptions of some of the worst forms of preventable suffering, the human rights abuses still being committed worldwide.

place brutal realism at the service of idealism, and to inspire more people to reflect open-mindedly about our conundrum as a species—and, with a large dose of optimism, about the kind of approaches and initiatives that just might make a difference.

3. A Step Back

> We shall require a substantially new manner of thinking if humanity is to survive.
>
> —Albert Einstein (physicist)

Our Biased View of Reality

A starting point in this endeavor is to properly shake up our instinctive sense that how we perceive the world is how it really "is" and that what we think matters represents an absolute truth. Life is admittedly most fun, rich and meaningful when we go with the flow, regarding it as a playground, embracing our illusions, taking things at face value and acting instinctively in our interactions with others, rather than analyzing everything in an attempt to understand what's really going on behind the scenes. If following our instincts were enough, we wouldn't need to look further. But it isn't. The world is much stranger than we usually realize, and we know a lot less than we think we do about the underlying nature of reality. We seldom stop to think deeply about our relationship to the rest of the world, the causes of our actions, and the ambiguity of such fundamental concepts as freedom, identity, responsibility and morality. We don't fully perceive the large-scale trends that are taking place at the level of the planet and our species. And we are mostly unaware of the huge range of people's states-of-mind and experiences. These all represent layers of understanding that are usually hidden from view. It is a little like looking at a painting by a 17th century Dutch master, unaware that the outer layers of paint conceal an earlier, very different painting underneath. Or, to take another example, going about our daily routine, oblivious to the tremendous complexity of life cohabiting with us on a much smaller scale that entirely escapes our perception, revealed in fascinating documentaries such as "Microcosmos".

The 20th century psychologist and Nobel laureate Konrad Lorenz, tainted though he was by some unsavory associations and writings about race during the Nazi period, is best known for his classic demonstration of a phenomenon known as imprinting. Newborn geese for which Lorenz was the first moving object they laid eyes on followed him around faithfully, presumably never suspecting that this old man with a goatee was anything other than Mother Goose. This is a useful metaphor for a phenomenon that occurs in all human societies. Cultural imprinting biases us from an early age against thinking objectively and openly about the nature of the world, the different levels of reality, and the values instilled in us.

We perceive the world through filters we are not even aware of, our sense of normality and of what matters strongly influenced by what we see and hear in our everyday lives. Much of the information we are exposed to today is delivered through the mass media, increasingly focused on whatever will attract readers or viewers. The pressure of society and the weight of governments, corporations and interest groups, whose agendas are often dominated directly or indirectly by the goals of power and income generation, restrict the focus of our attention and cause our thought patterns to hover over the same, limited range of ideas. It can take years of independent reflection as an adult to escape the constrained perspectives we grew up with, to see reality more broadly and to realize, to put it simply, that there's a lot more going on than meets the eye.

Our bias in the way we view the world can be compared to the Newtonian physics many of us learned in high school. The simple mathematical formulas developed by Isaac Newton work fine when applied to our everyday world of moving objects, whether an apple falling out of a tree or a Lotus accelerating on a highway. But they completely break down at the two extremes of subatomic and cosmic scales, where the very strange laws of quantum mechanics and general relativity, respectively, are needed to explain how matter actually behaves. In a very similar way, our innate perceptions of the world, reinforced by the society we grew up in, allow us to adapt to our surroundings and function on a daily basis. Our sense of

reality is like a cocoon, built up and cultivated through the addition of layers of meaning and complexity to our lives, sheltering us from some of the
cold facts about the universe and human nature. Yet the underlying reality
is still very much there. And it reveals itself when we dig a little by asking
questions persistently, when we stray from our immediate environment and
try to solve larger problems, or when the world changes around us and we
find ourselves faced with monumental threats. The veneer of suaveness and
comfort is rapidly shed, and life can appear very strange and highly unintuitive. As the old expression goes, it may feel we're not in Kansas anymore.
The tragic events of 9/11 and the oft-repeated reference to the deceptive
beauty of the clear, blue sky that morning are both a powerful reminder and
a metaphor for the fact that, at various levels, there may be invisible forces
operating of which we are unaware.

For those who don't bask in professional kudos from carrying it out
as a career, coming to terms with the physical basis of reality and how it
steers human nature can potentially lead to a somber and alienating view
of life. Although science can reveal the beauty of complexity in the world
and patterns in nature that escape the naked eye, when human relationships and behavior are observed through high-powered scientific lenses and
subjected to philosophical ruminations, the magic and mystery can fade. A
little like when the lights are turned on in a nightclub at 5am. Party's over.

In fact, if we persistently try to understand the connections between
things and the patterns and processes inherent to objective reality, it all
seems to come down to mathematical equations—a theme of the Darren
Aronofsky film "Pi". And the more we analyze life and human behavior in
terms of physical processes and numbers, the more readily it can interfere
with our ability to interact naturally and emotionally with others and with
our environment. At this level of understanding, the absurdity of life comes
more clearly into focus, and our instinctive sense of what it really means to
be human can seem awfully fragile. Rational thinking, when pursued sys-
tematically, forces us to confront such facts as the lack of external validity
of our value system, our regular misattribution of causes to the things we or
others do, and the underlying forces ultimately driving our behavior.

There is a great paradox in the duality of wanting to understand the big
picture and simultaneously continue to enjoy playing the game. Feminist
Gloria Steinem used to say, "The truth will set you free. But first, it will
piss you off." It's a challenge to think hard about existence while staying on

"this" side of the sanity barrier. Staying sane requires us to be able to snap back to our intuitive, instinctive view of the world most of the time.

Fortunately, this is something we tend to do naturally. In fact, the extent to which people align themselves with their society and culture's world view and value system suggests that the much greater challenge is retaining a more detached perspective. It's very much like travelling abroad. Vacations during which you explore distant cultures can open your mind, allowing you to gain insights into other ways of living and realize how profoundly different life can feel. Yet once you return home to the old routine, these feelings and insights can fade very quickly. It's very difficult to latch onto specific states-of-mind indefinitely.

Cultural imprinting and, more generally, the diversion of our attention by the mass of information we are exposed to have significant consequences for our priorities. Let me provide another analogy. Compression is a processing technique in music production that reduces the increase in output in response to an increased signal, in order to avoid distortion. In other words, even when all the instruments and voices are played at maximum volume, the recording level is compressed to keep it below the red distortion zone. The concept of compression can similarly be applied to how we make sense of the world, because the amount of attention we focus on an issue and how much we care about it usually do not scale up with its deeper meaning or broader significance to people's lives. The news items of the day, whether an international conflict, a humanitarian disaster or the latest escapades of a neurotic Hollywood star, are granted similarly bold headlines and roughly comparable amounts of media coverage. Everything simply happens *now*. Minor happenings are sometimes delivered with an air of hysteria, and often what is communicated is a mood rather than information. Current events are commented on with a short-sighted perspective, without any attempt to put them into a larger context, to convey an understanding of the underlying processes at work and an indication of where things are likely heading, or to provide some guidance as to what issues matter most. While compression in music production avoids a distorted sound, compression as a societal phenomenon severely distorts our sense of what matters, usually without our even realizing the extent of the distortion.

Under everyday circumstances, there is only so much we can care about things, and partly as a result, we end up "maxing out" on trivialities. In a cycle of consumption, people become absorbed in the details, their attention focused on whatever subjects news producers and talk show hosts choose to cover, and on products dangled in front of them by advertising executives—all of these in turn influenced by what people are likely to consume. The sheer amount of information we are confronted with, often coming to us in fragments, makes it very difficult for people to make sense of it and prioritize: there is never the time and detachment to connect the dots and draw the right conclusions. Extending the concept of compression, the phenomenon whereby our attention is diverted towards the little things while we overlook the things that really matter can be aptly described as "inversion".

With the explosion of blogging, social networks and user-generated content, while there is an even greater diversity of ideas available, the average individual is all the more easily overwhelmed by details and the reactions of others, rather than guided towards detached analysis and reflection. Philosopher Daniel Dennett has written about how there just doesn't seem to be enough room in our collective brains to contain the explosion of memes[4]. We juggle ideas, never grasping all the key ones at any one instant. And we lose a sense of perspective.

This loss of perspective matters a lot. If we don't take the time to step outside the box and reflect on it all, our behaviors will be determined by our collective instincts in response to a glut of information, rather than by anything more meaningful. Politicians, pundits, corporate leaders, opinion leaders and anyone with a laptop bombard us with contradictory prescriptions about how we should act, all confidently implying that they have the right answers. If we think independently and rationally, repeatedly ask "why" and apply an analytical, questioning approach to our most basic assumptions, we may find out that the real answers are, in fact, very different.

The Role of Philosophy

Philosophy is perhaps the most essential discipline there is, striving to answer fundamental questions about existence, meaning and knowledge. It relates in some way to the life of every human being on the planet. Philoso-

---

4   The term "meme" was originally coined by scientist Richard Dawkins to describe self-replicating information, such as an idea or cultural concept that spreads in a population, analogously to a gene. Daniel Dennett's essay "There Aren't Enough Minds to House the Population Explosion of Memes" appears in the book *What Is Your Dangerous Idea?*, a superb collection of essays by leading thinkers.

phers have been instrumental in guiding attempts to create a just society, and their writings have influenced the thinking of countless leaders and politicians over the millennia. Some of the themes addressed in this book have already been explored deeply by generations of philosophers and writers. When it comes to the big issues, a lot has been said over the past few centuries and, especially, in recent decades, with every philosophy professor and graduate student having had a chance to mull over age-old questions and look for a fresh tack that leads to virgin terrain. Some of the roads might appear to have been followed about as far as they will lead. There seems, at least on the surface, to be very little uncharted territory left when it comes to the questions about the existence of free will and the origin of consciousness, the relationship between objective and subjective reality, the nature of identity and the basis of ethics, even though many of these subjects still remain lively philosophical playgrounds, and science continues to feed us fresh new details about how the brain works. In a world with billions of inhabitants, each of whom is confronted with the mystery of existence and increasing numbers of whom have the opportunity to express and spread their thoughts in writing, brand new ideas about the big questions are becoming rarer.

In fact, the more you read about people's and cultures' attempts to understand existence, the more you discover the extent to which different ideas connect and, indeed, overlap. Philosopher Ken Wilber has, for example, attempted to incorporate the wisdoms of many different cultural and spiritual traditions, the ideas of many philosophers and the findings from various scientific disciplines into a single "Integral Theory".[5] Although his ideas are controversial, and not all of his assertions, such as about the mechanics of evolution, are consistent with scientific evidence, his attempt to relate apparently disparate concepts within a single conceptual framework is illuminating.

And yet, there hardly seems to be a consensus on some of the most fundamental questions. One of the reasons, as expounded by the great philosopher Ludwig Wittgenstein, is that many philosophical debates are, when it comes down to it, actually about the meaning of words. The tantalizing slipperiness of some of the issues that philosophers have tried to tackle over the millennia is often the result of imprecisions about terminology that lead to extremely intricate arguments that can never be satisfactorily resolved. A

---

5   See, for example, his book *A Brief History of Everything*.

lot of very smart people have had opposing views about basic philosophical questions, and it seems clear that, in many cases, they have been arguing about different things all along.

But there is another, related reason. I am persuaded, though many would ardently disagree, that, subject to the cultural imprinting of their own discipline, many philosophers are not prepared to confront some of our deepest taboos in thinking about existence and to persist in repeatedly asking "why". Much of philosophy is therefore akin to a mathematical puzzle where some of the underlying assumptions have not been clearly spelled out. And as a result, many philosophical arguments arrive at conclusions that are not logically solid. Expressing a similar idea, philosopher Teed Rockwell has written, "Philosophical dead ends almost always arise when philosophers try to resolve a paradox on its own terms, rather than question the presuppositions that make the paradox unavoidable."[6] Breaking taboos in our thinking about some traditional philosophical themes bears a similarity to taking on the role of the little boy in the classic Hans Christian Andersen fable who, seeing the naked emperor, exclaims, "But he hasn't got anything on!" While the answers to some of the essential questions about existence may be very difficult to come to terms with—and in that respect, they remain paradoxes—, the actual reasoning needed to arrive at answers that make sense may often be a lot more straightforward than the volumes of commentary that have been generated might suggest.

Philosophical reflections are fascinating for their inherent intellectual interest but, as suggested in the introduction, they ultimately matter most if they are translated into actions that have a positive impact on people's lives. Ethics in particular has a critical role to play today, but less for the theoretical exploration of ideas as for the argumentation it can bring to justify the prevention of suffering and the preservation of a future worth living in. This vision, however idealistic, is one of the guiding principles behind this book.

---

6   Teed Rockwell, *Neither Brain Nor Ghost* (Cambridge, Massachusetts: MIT Press, 2005), 48.

4. Blueprint for a Brain

How We Got Here: The Evolution of Extreme Complexity

To fully understand who we are, we need to go back to the beginning and consider how we got here, starting from events that took place a very long time ago, when the universe was just a tiny little thing with lots of pent-up energy. Because some of the processes that led to the present state of the world provide tremendous insight into our own existence, why we act as we do, where we might be headed, and what kinds of actions we may need to undertake to avert disaster.

Our brains and bodies developed to interact with the visible world, hunt food and make more brains and bodies, not to probe the workings of the universe, and there are aspects of reality that we still—and may ever—only have inklings about. However, it turns out that when the best of our brains are properly fed and looked after, they can turn their attention to these other questions, apply the scientific method, and come up with some solid explanations for what they observe.

We now know from incontrovertible scientific evidence—based on the same kind of observations and logical thinking that have fuelled recent technological progress—that our universe came into being about 14 billion years ago in an event of literally unimaginable proportions. Astronomers can erect telescopes on mountaintops in Chile and detect light from long ago in an attempt to learn more about what happened, but *why* it happened and where it all came from are questions that even scientists cannot answer to everyone's full satisfaction. There are limits to what even the scientific method can tell us, and we have to acknowledge that there are things we may never know or that our brains may never be able to understand.

Physicists continue to gain great insight into the fundamental building blocks of matter, in part by using advanced technology to smash particles into each other and see what happens. Intriguingly, much simpler experiments have led some physicists to conclude that there are countless parallel universes co-existing with our own which are only detectable under limited conditions. Although this "multiverse" theory is still controversial, if it is true it is profoundly important for what it says about existence. And yet this is the kind of truth that, even if you accept it, easily slips away from your attention because it seems both too abstract to fully grasp and irrelevant to your daily life. Although it's not immediately obvious just how much we need to know about broader reality in order to improve life here and now, we gain a more complete perspective on our existence as new pieces are continually added to the puzzle.

Since the Big Bang occurred, matter and energy have spent 14 billion years going about their business while unfailingly respecting the laws of physics, which scientists are still trying to consolidate into one "Theory of Everything". One of the things that happened is that our planet slowly came into existence through the concentration of dust and gas, 4.5 billion years ago. Although this is also a long time ago, and a lot has happened since then, it is still on a scale that is intuitively understandable. For example, the dinosaurs, although extinct, are a very real part of our natural history. The footprints we can visit at a natural historical site are stunning visual proof of the path an individual Allosaurus literally took in search of breakfast one fine morning 150 million years ago. The Earth came into being about 30 times longer ago. If—disregarding the signs in the museum—you were to touch the smooth contours of a petrified dinosaur skeleton, you would be in direct contact with the remains of a flesh and blood creature that lived 1/30 of the way back in time towards the creation of the Earth, and 1/90 of the way back to a moment when the entire universe, with its billions of galaxies' worth of mass, was contained in a volume much smaller than a grain of table salt. If you're feeling contemplative, that perspective can make it seem almost eerily close. But it's still a very long while back, to a degree that our existence has a tremendously important significance, as I will now come to.

Another wildly important thing that happened is that, as a consequence of various random events, the details of which we remain ignorant, life originated, eventually leading to highly organized, complex chemical entities that bear DNA and reproduce. This seems to have been a fairly—perhaps even extremely—infrequent event as far as the universe goes, requiring just the right conditions. Gradually, over eons, life became increasingly complex and sophisticated.[7] And here we are today, intelligent, curious beings, some of whom are highly aware that we are rare and, for all practical purposes, alone, at a peculiarly precise and critical moment in the history of the Earth, and perhaps even at a potential turning point in the history of the universe, where, after billions of years, the decisions we make within just the next few *decades* may determine whether intelligent life on Earth will have been a short-lived, inconsequential accident or a momentous occurrence for the universe.

The appearance of human beings in this remote corner of the universe, as magical as it seems, can be understood as the consequence of the laws of physics; the universe's constituents, matter and energy; the occurrence of very low probability events; and Mother Nature with a lot of time on her hands. The process of evolution that has been acting on reproducing organisms since they first emerged and which is responsible for the diversity of life that has since developed is not inherently "good", although it is what led to our existence. At its core, it means that change happens and only the "strong"—more precisely, those best adapted to a particular environmental niche—survive and reproduce.

Mention of the word "evolution" makes the hairs stand on end of many people who feel threatened in their religious convictions by a description of mechanical processes taking place here and, perhaps, in other parts of the universe. Putting aside the considerable hostility of some religious teachings that discourage open-minded thinking, perceived to be threatening to the dogma, the concept of evolution can be intellectually challenging all by itself. This is not because it is complicated, but precisely because its incredible simplicity seems incompatible with the immense complexity of the result. Indeed, evolutionary theory is beautiful because it is both so simple and so vast in its explanatory power.

---

7   Bill Bryson's *A Short History of Nearly Everything* brings those eons to life.

Evolution can be broken down into two processes, the generation of diversity through mutations, and the selection of useful mutations. The second concept is perhaps more readily intuitive: if you have variety in a group, the individuals that are more successful at surviving and reproducing will tend to dominate. It is the first concept which might seem more problematic. Although most people would have little trouble with the idea that random mutations can create variety, it can seem improbable to the point of impossibility that they can produce incredibly complex, functional organisms.

It is here that, once again, we come up against the average human's difficulty in grasping very large numbers, and their effect in turning very low probability events into things that actually happen. If you took a single-celled organism and let it divide with a low mutation rate and create offspring over billions of years, and for pure argument's sake, the amount of matter available was not a limiting factor and each of the offspring survived, the resulting "family" tree would yield an inconceivably large number of creatures, some of them extremely complex—more complex than us, even—and most of them simply a mess. A few billion years' worth of splitting and, eventually, sex gives you more potential variety than you could possibly imagine. Of course, reality places huge constraints on this process—there wouldn't be nearly enough atoms in the universe, never mind enough space or resources, for all of even just the functional offspring to survive. But if you continually, ruthlessly trimmed away the rubbish, some very interesting things would be left to develop. By contrast, that clichéd army of monkeys typing randomly on typewriters (or computers—let's at least give them the benefits of technology) would never in a billion years yield a novel or play worth reading, unless a very patient and long-lived editor, presumably armed with more than a few truckloads of bananas, continually sorted through their work and allowed them to randomly build on the more promising samples.

Once you have life that reproduces, changes that are beneficial to survival and reproduction in a particular environment will tend to dominate. That in itself is not a particularly counterintuitive concept. But the breathtaking complexity this principle can produce when repeated over and over and over again is. Every one of us is, in fact, the result of a very long and exceedingly improbable string of random mutations that took place over the course of billions of years, each one a success. From our present vantage point, it is as if someone had been flipping a coin and only got tails—millions of times in a row. But then, to complete the analogy, we need to keep in mind that many more people were also flipping coins and getting heads as well—it's just that they are all forgotten in the end.

Even to a scientist used to thinking abstractly, the diversity and complexity that have emerged spontaneously through the repeated application of a relatively simple algorithm can seem incredible. To someone who hasn't really thought about the process, it can stretch the imagination to the point of snapping. How can a primordial bacterium—its own microscopic complexity a source of wonder—evolve over time to yield Scarlett Johansson? And yet, it happened. Over a much shorter stretch of time, cavemen eventually put themselves on the moon. Strange and astonishing things happen in this universe if you wait long enough.

Viruses, tiny packages of genes and proteins which by traditional definition are not technically alive yet which replicate and have the potential to wreak havoc, are a good illustration of the basic principles behind evolution. Whatever personal beliefs you may have about meaning and higher purpose, viruses really do not appear to have any utility except to themselves—they just emerged. As mutations increased diversity, those that were better at reproducing in the various environments they happened to find themselves in came to dominate. Over time, viruses have developed impressive degrees of sophistication and efficiency. Today, health organizations and ministries are vigilantly watching for the emergence of any newly evolved virus strains with potentially deadly properties.

The point here is clearly not to spell out all the arguments that support evolution, for which there are plenty of dedicated books that lay out the overwhelming evidence and reasoning.[8] So anyone who dismisses it out of conviction is unlikely to change their opinion as a result of anything I write here. But there is one other important point I would like to make about evolutionary processes and, more broadly, about the development of complexity. One of the basic laws of thermodynamics is that systems tend to become increasingly disordered: overall, things become more random over time. For example, two solutions of different colors put in contact with each other will mix spontaneously, but they will never spontaneously separate out again into their original colors. This principle might at first glance seem incompatible with complexity ever emerging spontaneously. However, if one

---

8   See, in particular, Richard Dawkins's book *The Greatest Show on Earth*.

part of a system becomes more disordered, *local* order can still develop elsewhere within the system if there is a transfer of energy. The energy pumped out by the sun and absorbed by the Earth is part of the whole system in which evolution occurs, allowing the creation of order and complexity on Earth. It is in the nature of things, a property of the cosmos, that local complexity can emerge when energy is provided.[9]

By the way, the process of natural selection continues to operate today in a variety of ways that may be subtly altering gene pools, as humans continue to be subjected to environmental pressures, and those with certain genes tend to have fewer or more offspring. The distribution of genes is affected by fertility rates, which in turn are influenced by a variety of societal factors and behaviors which themselves may be partly genetically determined. In particular, the relationship between wealth and number of children has become more complex. The poorest now tend to have more babies than the richest and thus contribute disproportionately to the gene pool, while the richest tend to consolidate economic power. One can only speculate on the consequences in the coming years and decades as the future of our species is influenced by a combination of economic and demographic forces.

As the effective masters of the Earth, bumbling as we may be and perhaps not even likely to survive our term in office, we have an innate tendency to think of ourselves as the pinnacle of evolution, the point of it all. This is perfectly understandable: our starting point for making sense of the world is our own perceptions. In fact, one of the oldest philosophical problems is to know how we can know that anything outside of ourselves really exists. (An answer, in a nutshell, is that this is by far the simplest explanation.[10]) The idea that events could easily have taken a very different course usually escapes our imagination. If not for the solitary asteroid that is now accepted to have wiped out the dinosaurs (and more than half of all other species) 65 million years ago, they might still be around. In which case, one can speculate that *Homo sapiens* might never have evolved. Perhaps the pros-

---

9   For an interesting article describing the development of complexity and how it relates to the bigger picture, see Fred Spier, "How Big History Works: Energy Flows and the Rise and Demise of Complexity", *Social Evolution & History*. Volume 4, Number 1 (March 2005), 87-135. This article is available at www.socionauki.ru/journal/articles/128203. See also his book *Big History and the Future of Humanity* (Chichester, UK: Wiley-Blackwell, 2010).

10   As explicated by physicist David Deutsch in his book *The Fabric of Reality*.

pect of confronting Allosauruses would have kept any subsequent primate-like potential ancestors of ours comfortably lodged in their trees.

Nonetheless, in a very real way, we *are* the pinnacle of evolution to date. We are the first species to carry out highly complex thought, to understand its own functioning, and to possess the ability to utterly transform the planet. We are the vehicle of a tremendous acceleration in complexity taking place at this very moment that has never been remotely approached in the history of the Earth. We need make no apologies for being who we are and acknowledging our unique powers. What we need to hold ourselves accountable for is what we do with it all.

Understanding the process of evolution is of far more than just academic interest. Evolution is commonly regarded as a narrowly applicable theory that specifically explains the emergence of species, and which in some societies with a fundamentalist religious current finds itself pitted against the rigid dogma of creationism. But evolution is more than just an explanation of how we got here: it provides perhaps the single most powerful explanation of the forces that continue to shape our destiny as a species. Competition among organisms striving—explicitly or implicitly—to maximize their chances of survival and reproduction remains the defining principle of how our world works. Grasping our evolutionary relationship to the past is essential both for fully understanding the pressing issues facing us in the present, namely the welfare of humans as well as other creatures that evolved on this planet, and for more intelligently influencing our future. The implications are discussed further in the next sections.

Human Behavior

Human behavior sometimes seems limitless in its diversity, and there are countless levels of understanding and ways of making sense of it. But the evolutionary processes through which we got here—the closest equivalent to a blueprint for our brain and body—provide tremendous insight into the underlying, basic principles dictating our behavior, allowing us to understand much of why we act as we do and what higher level trends are occurring at the level of the species. They also provide plausible, consistent explanations for human characteristics, including seemingly irrational behavior that departs from conventional economic theory.

Trying to explain any particular behavior by a purported evolutionary advantage it once conferred on our ancestors is often more an exercise in cleverness than solid science, and the difficulty with which such claims can be verified subjects them to legitimate attacks by scientific purists. However, this does not diminish the validity of seeing the operation of natural selection as the overriding force that designed the human brain (within the limits of physical and chemical constraints), even though not every structure that emerged represented a useful adaptation, and even though many of the specific behaviors that the brain actually carries out are not of any discernible benefit to its owner.[11] Recognizing the goals for which the human brain was "programmed" is the most fundamental and insightful level at which to understand our sometimes frightful behavior and how we can possibly deal with the ethical and existential challenges we face.

POWER AND STATUS

Those of us alive today are here because all our ancestors, stretching back billions of years, managed to survive and reproduce in a succession of hostile environments. The *only* thing that mattered from the point of view of evolution was survival and reproduction. This rule has been applied repeatedly over eons, and traits that promoted health and attracted fertile mates who would yield healthy offspring and help provide for them were continuously selected for as environments changed.[12] Although we tend to be most comfortable among others who are most like us, it has always been mutants who were the vanguard of evolution and who more closely resembled the future—approached little by little, one mutation at a time. The operation of this very basic principle accounts for the wide variety of traits and behaviors that emerged. While physicists continue to search for an elusive theory that explains how the entire physical world works, natural selection already provides biologists with one that works exceedingly well for the emergence of human nature.

Although we have manipulated and dramatically changed the world we live in over a very short period of time, our brains have remained relatively unchanged since about 60,000 years ago, when significant migration out of Africa is believed to have occurred that led to a subsequent divergence of populations. Natural selection has continued to operate since then, and different physical and character traits and cognitive skills have been selected

---

11 For some extreme examples of self-destructive stupidity, see the Darwin Awards at www.darwinawards.com.

12 See Geoffrey Miller's *The Mating Mind: How Sexual Choice Shaped the Evolution of Human Nature.*

for as humans have found themselves in very different environments and societies over the millennia, resulting in some limited degree of genetic divergence. But if you plucked out of their environment the child of an early European caveman or dweller of the African plains from tens of thousands of years ago and brought her up today in a developed country, she would not be in any way remarkable compared with any of her classmates, especially in a country with a multicultural heritage or recent immigration. To a close approximation, we *are* the same as our common ancestors, living in different times and responding to a different world with caveman brains. To be sure, our brains do exhibit plasticity, and a stimulating environment can cause some rewiring of neural circuits. But the fundamental architecture remains, and we tend to seek the same general kinds of things as our most recent common ancestors did.

Much of our behavior is therefore the reflection of a deep-seated craving for power that facilitates access to what we desire: to accumulate resources and material wealth, influence and gain the respect of others, and ultimately, attract mates. There is probably no concept more essential to understanding human nature than this quest for power and status. This is not to say that *every individual* thirsts for great wealth or explicitly seeks a large degree of power. There is a wide spectrum of personality types, and people also adjust their expectations and needs to their situation and abilities. A local village mayor may be quite content with the respect and challenges that his situation confers on him and not seek to rule the world. A highly ambitious, power-driven business executive may be happily married and not looking for new mates. And an artist might willingly embrace a low-budget bohemian lifestyle that offers unparalleled freedom. But the underlying drivers of behavior persist. Most people seek some degree of status and respect, and strive to get what they need to attain it, even if just within their immediate social circle. This often requires competing against others in the professional world and for attractive mates. Those with the strongest innate desire for power tend to have the greatest influence on the lives of others, whether within a society or on a global dimension.

Indeed, much of international relations can be seen as the same basic human drives at work on a larger scale, with individual politicians seeking to expand their influence and power, and countries taking on many of these same characteristics. As historian Jared Diamond detailed in his book *Guns, Germs, and Steel*, the history of humanity is one of conquests by those civilizations able to carry them out. The peaceful equilibrium that exists in much of the Western world today, as in Europe, is in large part due to the creation of a system that makes conflict a highly unattractive proposition. In parts of the world where such an equilibrium does not exist, powerful cultures—often essentially large-scale clans with a common heritage—dominate and extinguish less powerful ones through the appropriation of resources, deprivation of freedoms, massacres, assimilation and population transfers.

Evolution has not made humans constitutively ecstatic, even though it would have been a relatively trivial matter from a technical point-of-view—some minor manipulation of the neurochemical wiring. Happiness tends to come from nearing goals traditionally related to survival and reproduction, such as physical security, the strengthening of supportive networks and external displays of success. If humans were always as happy as can be regardless of their material situation, they would not have felt a longing for anything else, much less any drive to accumulate power, and would eventually have died out from competition from more ambitious peers. Even in a hypothetical world of unbounded resources, mate selection would remain an inherently competitive process. It is for this reason that there is an inborn striving to stand out from the pack, often through the accumulation of more and more "stuff", regardless of whether one's material needs have been met, and through other signs of biological fitness. Our primitive, potentially violent sides lie scarily close to the surface and can be exposed in an instant when provoked or otherwise triggered.

COOPERATION AND ALTRUISM

From a broad perspective, humans are all very distant cousins of each other, descendants of siblings and cousins who dispersed and settled in diverse places and today, countless generations later, find themselves fighting over land and resources. The boundary between "us" and "them" shifts as a function of context. Although at our core, most of us are, to a rough approximation, "self-maximizers", trying to further our own interests, and the conflicts that sometimes result from this innate urge cause untold suffering, in practice, we spend much of our time cooperating with each other. When there are ample resources for all, we are more likely to behave like long lost brothers, though still subject to sibling rivalry.

Since evolution functions through the passing on of genes that best promote the survival of the organisms that contain them, helping out people who are genetically most closely related to us has emerged, through a process known as "kin selection", as a deeply hardwired behavior. Relatives with a genetically rooted tendency to be altruistic towards each other were more successful at surviving and reproducing, thereby passing on genes connected with altruism. Furthermore, from a purely self-interested standpoint, cooperation with strangers often provides the best outcome for all. Those who had a tendency to forge alliances with others who had shared goals, or more generally, to cooperate where there was a net benefit to be gained, were more successful at surviving and reproducing, and this behavior also became hardwired. The inclinations to cooperate and even act altruistically therefore exist alongside the drive to compete.

Cooperation between unrelated people requires mutual trust, which may be nothing more than a reciprocal realization that continued cooperation is in both parties' best interest. Because we can only judge people on the basis of their actions, trust tends to be built up over time, although it can be destroyed in an instant. This fact is one of the greatest challenges in international politics and, in particular, in conflict resolution, even when an objective assessment would show that cooperation is in all parties' interests, however defined.

An innate tendency to come to the aid of others sometimes extends as far as helping strangers in need, with no expectation of any reward. The status-driven corporate executive may still act instinctively and risk throwing away everything he has to save the life of a perfect stranger in danger of drowning. Altruism towards strangers has a less obvious net benefit to any genes that encode this behavior than altruism towards family members, and there is still no clear consensus on the mechanisms that caused it to appear. Its possible emergence through the phenomenon of "group selection", whereby groups containing altruistic individuals are better able to compete, though a controversial theory, has received renewed support, including recent evidence that it is actually mathematically equivalent to kin selection.[13] Alternative theories suggest that it may simply be part of a spectrum of altruistic tendencies that, on average, benefit one's own genes, or a product of other evolved psychological mechanisms, such as the longing for social interaction.

---

13   "'Nature' Paper Refigures the Evolution of Altruism," *PhysOrg.com* (26 February 2010), www.physorg.com/news186416144.html.

A branch of mathematics called game theory is often used in economics to study the optimal choices that would be made by rational self-maximizers in various competitive situations. In practice, people's actual behavior is often found to differ from what theory would predict, showing that economists' traditional assumption that people act as pure self-maximizers, as narrowly defined by absolute wealth, is not quite accurate. There are many other things that matter to people than just accumulating as much stuff as possible. Our latent capacity for altruism is likely part of the explanation.

Regardless of the exact mechanism by which altruism towards strangers emerged as a part of the human behavioral repertoire, it is a relatively weak force compared with the altruism towards family members that can cause someone to jump on a plane and travel half-way around the world to be with a sick relative. Understanding it and triggering it wisely and effectively is a critical but unfortunately rare and difficult skill.

That a behavior ultimately emerged through the evolutionary advantage it conferred does not automatically imply that it is consciously being carried out for reasons of pure self-interest, nor even that there *is* any self-interest in carrying it out. Many human interactions, such as acts of kindness, are accompanied by genuinely positive thoughts and not by cynical intentions to manipulate. Furthermore, we pursue many of our goals, including seducing members of the opposite sex, because we think they will make us happy, not because we care about spreading our genes. Evolutionary psychologists such as Steven Pinker take pains to clarify this distinction between "ultimate" and "proximate" causes of behavior,[14] and being aware of the distinction between these two levels of explanation matters for the sake of intellectual clarity.

And yet, for much of our behavior, the principle of self-interest is often in silent, subconscious operation, and the ultimate causes may still offer a deeper underlying explanation with greater predictive power. Our ability to function normally and not cede to a creeping cynicism regarding others' ultimate intentions therefore requires us to focus on the proximate causes of people's behavior in everyday interactions, rather than to see everything in terms of personal gain.

---

14 See his book *The Blank Slate.*

5. SUBJECTIVE EXPERIENCE: THE HIDDEN SIDE OF REALITY

Those who hear not the music think the dancers mad.
—Unknown

CONSCIOUSNESS

The emergence of consciousness, the one phenomenon we are all most intimately familiar with, remains one of the most puzzling aspects of the universe and continues to perplex most scientists and philosophers who consider it.[15] The perception of color and smells, the experience of emotions and pain, of complex thoughts and ideas, of intangible but vivid states-of-mind: these all continue to elude an intuitively satisfying explanation. Neuroscientists have made remarkable progress in understanding the details of the brain's wiring and functioning, and how these correlate with some aspects of consciousness[16], but the philosophically most problematic question—how physical material, stuff we can touch[17], creates subjective sensations—looms aloofly out of reach. Scientists have observed the world and developed and refined theories about how it works, but still remain mysti-

---

15 Philosopher David Chalmers has compiled a collection of papers on the subject: http://philpapers.org/browse/hard-and-easy-problems.

16 See Christof Koch's *The Quest for Consciousness*.

17 In a TED conference presentation, neuroscientist Jill Bolte Taylor both literally touches the stuff of consciousness and describes the powerful insights she gained from the inside into the brain's functioning, and the distinct characters of the left and right hemispheres, through the experience of having a stroke: www.ted.com/talks/jill_bolte_taylor_s_powerful_stroke_of_insight.html.

fied by a phenomenon that isn't satisfactorily accounted for by these theories. We are habituated to think of physical matter as having many tangible properties, of which consciousness is not one, and yet we are faced with the evidence that, when it is organized in at least some specific ways, it does indeed yield consciousness. In a very simplified way, it is a little like putting a bunch of Lego blocks together and finding that the whole construction has suddenly acquired feelings. Those philosophers who dismiss this as a non-problem posed by a brain trying to understand itself have, I believe, failed to provide a convincing and sufficiently satisfying explanation of this point-of-view. Consciousness seems, on the contrary, to tell us something profound about the universe that we are unable to fully grasp, scratching as we seem to be at the edge of knowable reality.

Consciousness in the form that we know it appears to be dependent on life and therefore to have emerged through the process of natural selection. People who cannot feel pain tend to harm themselves more readily—a disadvantage if they are keen on survival. From the perspective of an organism's subjective experience, the conscious sensation of pain is therefore useful. The same is probably true for most other aspects of consciousness, including the complex thought that is unique to humans. This implies that consciousness—in parallel to something that is intimately associated with it, namely the physical structures and activities that correlate with it at the neuronal level—conferred an advantage on creatures that had it, and that sensations such as pain and pleasure are, at this level of understanding, necessary for carrying out the behaviors that they lead to, and are not merely irrelevant by-products of brain activity.

However—and this is a subtle but critical point—consciousness is not a phenomenon that exists apart from the physical world and acts on it, but rather is a phenomenon that is *intrinsic* to the physical world and which, in parallel, also offers simpler, holistic explanations for behaviors that could also be explained at a more reductionist level. Reflecting on how mental processes are intertwined with behavior, we are forced to come to the conclusion that pain, emotions and thoughts are not so much caused by but actually *equivalent* to the processes they are associated with. The subjective and objective aspects of our existence are like two, inseparable sides of the same coin. Two aspects of the same persona, intimately bound up in the same fate, although one never quite manages to spot them both together at the same exact moment, like Superman and his alter ego Clark Kent. As I will argue, it is the subjective side that *matters*, but the objective side that gives us critically important information about how things work.

The point I have tried to express in the last paragraph is perhaps one of the most important in this whole book. Although its essence is implicitly taken for granted by most scientists and philosophers—while they may argue about details, few contemporary philosophers still maintain that a separate mind acts upon a physical brain—, the implications seem not often to have been followed through as far as they will go. I am convinced that a more widespread understanding of what this notion really implies would provide useful insight for dealing with humanity's problems today, on a large scale. The chapter on determinism and free will explores this idea at greater length.

Also unique and intrinsic to the phenomenon of consciousness is the fact that it can only be definitively known in oneself, through one's own experience. Consciousness can only be inferred to exist in other human beings through the admittedly safe assumption that they are built like us and therefore function essentially like we do. And even then, simply knowing that other humans are conscious does not go very far in telling us what their consciousness is *like*. I will come back to this point shortly.

With animals, we must take a further leap in assuming that, because they are built similarly to us and exhibit some comparable types of behavior, they therefore have some form of consciousness. As the similarity decreases as we follow the branches of the evolutionary tree backward to our common ancestors and then forward again to the present, and compare ourselves not just with apes but with dogs, mice, birds, fish, ants or earthworms, it becomes increasingly uncertain what the consciousness is like or even whether it is present altogether. However, if one considers aspects of consciousness that don't involve complex thought, there seems to be no reason why much lower organisms—perhaps even ants, for example—don't have some form of it. Even the comparatively simple ant brain is capable of carrying out rapid calculations in order to negotiate terrain and respond to the environment. We don't know what the minimum requirements are for some form of subjective experience, but it is far from unreasonable to at least posit that an ant has some "sense" of what is going on around it, rather than just being a complex, mindless calculator on legs. It seems that some scientists are more prepared to take seriously the notion of a conscious computer than of a conscious ant. But if, as is apparently the case, consciousness is a property of the universe that depends on the organization of matter, and if it conferred survival value in one of its most basic forms, pain, then it seems more than likely that it might have existed some time much earlier during the 14 billion years it took for humans to arrive on the scene.

One of the great explorers of animal consciousness, Irene Pepperberg, devoted decades to teasing out the remarkable linguistic potential of an ordinary African grey parrot named Alex.[18] In addition to being able to name numerous objects, shapes and colors as well as quantities up to six, understand basic abstract concepts such as "same" and "different" and converse in simple sentences using a vocabulary of about 150 English words, Alex regularly used words to express his personality and emotional states. One intriguing anecdote is that, on one occasion, he displayed his apparent boredom with a task by contrarily giving all the wrong answers to a puzzle except the right one, a feat statistically unlikely to occur by chance that subtly but dramatically hints at the internal emotional world of a being whose last common ancestor with humans lived about 300 million years ago.

Funding for Pepperberg's research was hard won, and she has had to rely heavily on private donations. It is somehow baffling that, with all the money spent globally on the most obscure research topics, there should be so little financial support for understanding the minds and not just the movements of the billions of other creatures we share the planet with. Undoubtedly, the fact that we are so used to regarding them as objects to be exploited and eaten, or to serve our entertainment, biases us against considering them as conscious beings with cognitive skills and emotions worthy of exploration—a contradiction that could lead us to major cognitive dissonance.[19]

As consciousness can inherently only be directly known through subjective experience, it is by no means inconceivable that other, possibly very different, forms of consciousness exist that we are unaware of and that are, perhaps, far more widespread than we realize. Perhaps there are even separate modes of consciousness generated by our brains, such as what we call our subconscious, which cannot communicate with the rest of the world

---

18 See her book *Alex & Me*.

19 Cognitive dissonance is an important, influential concept in psychology that suggests that people try to avoid having conflicting beliefs, and will either change their beliefs or actions or else rationalize them in order to give a semblance of consistency. The avoidance of cognitive dissonance provides an explanation for how we subjugate the truth for our mental well-being.

except via a transfer of information to what we consider the conscious brain. It is not impossible that other consciousnesses could thus exist in parallel, intimately intertwined with "our" consciousnesses and yet hidden from view, locked in and unable to communicate with the outside world. I say this to make the point that, even if this is unlikely to be true, it could be and we—the collection of "classical" consciousnesses that read, write and speak—wouldn't know it if it were. For example, an entry on one neuroscientist's blog stated as a matter of fact that the cerebellum—a part of the brain responsible for coordination and motor control—is not conscious. It may very well not be, as it is not directly associated with the cognitive functions we can measure, and may not even have the right kind of wiring to create subjective experience, but I don't think this statement can be made with absolute certainty. Even if its wiring were sufficient to create subjective experience, it would have no way of telling us.[20]

What is likely to cause consciousness, in the sense that we generally understand the word? It does certainly seem to involve a specific organizational complexity and dynamics—perhaps the movement of electrical charges. We still don't know the exact requirements for human-type consciousness, but the specific building blocks of the human body and brain may not be critical. In the end, the phenomenon is created out of nuclei and electrons, and the actual kinds of atoms and molecules may not matter. So, in theory and perhaps one day in practice—if it has not already happened without our realizing it—, consciousness could be created artificially using other materials.

As long as we use our own subjective experience as the defining, anthropocentric model for what consciousness necessarily resembles and what its requirements are, we may never be able to recognize its possible existence outside the animal kingdom. I assume (and would sincerely hope) that my text editing program, which stubbornly places squiggly lines under what it suspects are grammatical errors in a sentence in progress, is not conscious, but I cannot be absolutely sure.

Even whether a stone has some form of consciousness[21], despite its structural simplicity, may never be known. The fact that consciousness ex-

---

20 Susan Blackmore's *Consciousness: An Introduction* covers a wide range of issues and seeming paradoxes associated with consciousness that researchers have tried to address.

21 This seemingly bizarre suggestion, reflecting the doctrine of panpsychism, was made by Rudy Rucker in his essay "Mind is a Universally Distributed Quality"

ists and is not explained by the currently accepted laws of physics, nor even within the scope of what physics tries to explain, means we know a lot less about the properties of matter, and of complexity, than we think. Furthermore, whether consciousness is an inherent property of all matter or, as far more widely believed, dependent on complexity, it might also exist at a macroscopic level—perhaps on the scale of the universe. It is not entirely inconceivable that the universe as a whole, or a larger multiverse, is conscious, although perhaps on a much slower timescale. In a strange, unexpected way, maybe the most secular, rational scientific pursuits could come around full circle and discover a large-scale God. Of course, this idea could well be debated on purely theoretical grounds. But as mentioned earlier, respected physicists, mathematicians and cosmologists are already making serious predictions about infinite parallel universes and other bizarre phenomena that would imply that we have no clue just how weird "things"— referring to "the world" or even "the universe" does not even suffice—really are.

The universe, capable of spawning consciousness and subjectively experienced meaning, is, to a human mind, wondrous and mysterious. Conceiving of someone in charge, continuously carrying out infinite calculations in order to get things just right, is intellectually untenable. But feeling part of an unimaginably large pool of energy with properties we can only have a minute grasp of can be quite a strain on the imagination as well. Calling the whole system "God" is as good a label as anything, as long as we don't get so wrapped up in a sense of awe that we decline to actually use our brains to find out as much as we can about how it works and how to improve it. Because in a very real sense, the surge in complexity here on this planet, manifested in the sprouting of higher intelligence and such banal personifications of it as an ordinary guy named Joe frying eggs in his kitchen on a Sunday morning, is about as concrete a manifestation of an intelligent God as the Earth or perhaps even the universe has yet seen—albeit a wildly schizophrenic God, as seen in the diversity of thoughts and behaviors that exist. Seeing ourselves in this way in no way undermines a rational view of reality, but this perspective confers us with a heightened sense of responsibility to act humanistically and preserve the future.

in *What Is Your Dangerous Idea?*

SUFFERING: THE DARK SIDE OF CONSCIOUSNESS

Suffering, both of the physical and the psychological varieties, emerged through evolution because it was useful, in small doses, as an indicator to organisms that they were doing something "wrong" that, if continued, would reduce their genes' survival chances. For example, sitting too close to the fire, challenging stronger rivals, leaving their children in dangerous situations, or dawdling in the meadow pondering life instead of going out hunting mammoths with the boys and consequently going hungry. For an organism unable to escape the warning signs or dealt severe injury, the phenomenon of suffering can be extremely intense. This is certainly the greatest downside of having a brain. There is nothing particularly nice about this— except, admittedly, for the fact that some degree of suffering allows us to appreciate the good moments even more. Suffering is one of the things that the universe does, an effective solution happened upon by Mother Nature who, as rightly affirmed in one of Murphy's Laws, is a bitch.

Although we may admire the detail and seeming perfection of the animal kingdom, including the precise engineering of animal species, nature represents the result of countless generations of trying and testing, with huge numbers of poorly adapted "guinea pigs" of all species sacrificed along the way, often painfully. The development of modern day humans occurred against a continuous backdrop of mutations that caused a small fraction of individuals to become more successful in their environment while the vast majority remained unaffected or were dealt a genetic blow. This situation remains true today, with millions of people suffering from genetic disorders that cause suffering and early death.

The broader point is that the process of evolution has never "cared" about collateral pain it caused, even when this had no direct use. If pain does not pose a problem to survival and reproduction, evolution has not even had any qualms about embracing it and firmly integrating it into the lifecycle of a species. For example, childbirth without some form of anesthetic is notoriously painful in humans, who have a proportionately narrower pelvis than other animals. But childbirth occurs long after the act that causes it, and so there is little opportunity on this basis for the creation of negative associations that would significantly undermine sexual attraction. Only today do we have the technology to routinely ease or even circumvent the natural route of delivery and avoid pain.

From a minimalist philosophical perspective, one might say that the only fundamental rule governing nature is that "what is, is", and that complexity of various kinds tends sometimes to emerge, including consciousness, intelligence and suffering. Consciousness and accompanying suffering are scattered throughout the ecosphere of our planet's surface, organized into a complex web of predation. Fear of having one's life or well-being taken away, and the physical pain caused by other creatures or chance, are the ugly side of the universe. Those harmless subatomic particles that scientists study in colliders have the potential to create so much cruelty and pain when, given enough time, they combine in large numbers under the right conditions. The Big Bang contained the seeds of Auschwitz. Sacrilegious as it may sound to say so, the universe is in some ways a terrible place, profoundly unkind in bundling together extreme suffering with the extreme beauty it seemingly proffers as a justification for existence. It is at least more bearable to view our situation as a mysterious puzzle we have inherited, rather than as the intention of a conscious, intelligent force that actively willed all this suffering into existence. While we may not be able to change the nature of the universe, we can harness the power of our evolved intelligence and try to reduce suffering, at least within the limits that the universe theoretically allows. Exploring this idea is the ultimate theme of this book.

The Opacity of Subjective Experience

For all our tremendous capabilities and means of making sense of the world, we are lacking a sense of consciousness: we can only perceive it indirectly through our other senses. This fact is deceptively obvious, to the point of banality. In practice, if not reminded of it, we forget that what we see on the surface is not the same as what is going on inside. While some spend much of their lives trying, with varying degrees of success, to get into other people's bodies, accessing other people's consciousness is where the real difficulty lies, and we often mistakenly think we are there when we are, in fact, miles away.

Others' consciousness is the best kept secret in the universe, masquerading in the form of physical gestures and sounds. How easily we are fooled is illustrated, for example, by the toy pets and substitute companions that the Japanese develop, emitting sounds and displaying external movements that simulate those of conscious beings and draw people into the illusion.

In fact, it seems virtually impossible to understand how other people feel, or how they perceive or experience the world, without having been in similar circumstances oneself or having had similar states-of-mind. Even placed in the same situation or confronted with the same external stimuli, people can have dramatically different subjective experiences, for a wide variety of reasons, including entirely different associations due to unique past experiences. A simple example and metaphor for the difficulty of accessing others' subjective experience would be the attempt to fully explain what blue is like to someone who is color blind. The subtle significance of the famous phrase from Antoine de Saint-Exupéry's children's book *The Little Prince*, "One only sees clearly with the heart, the essential is invisible to the eyes," is probably lost on most of the children who read it.

Even in a close relationship, such as with a life partner, we tend to react to external displays of emotion without necessarily considering what is going on inside. How many couples have regular arguments because neither is sufficiently able to access the other's internal world, despite the fact that they are sharing their lives and know each other well? We may reassure our partner if they are worried, feel sad and console them if they cry, feel sheepish or combative if they are angry, and rapidly adapt the flight response when dishes become airborne. With time, we may adjust our behavior to accommodate the other's character and thereby also influence their behavior in a way that is better for both. But all along, we cannot know *how it really feels* to be them at that moment, and we may not even *realize* that we are missing something essential in our assessment of the situation.

It is a tremendous challenge to bring people to relax the tethers to their own system of beliefs and perceptions and try to explore others' views and experience of the world, and the challenge is even greater in dealing with people we know less well, or from different cultures. Although much of human experience and emotions is universal across cultures and time, so much is unique in a way that defies even attempts at comprehension. Words and gestures offer a glimpse, but talking to another person cannot tell you everything about how it really is to be them: we simply do not have full access to the complexity of other people's inner experiences. All of us, some sensitive types more than others, are highly tuned in to the many subtle variations in expression that a face can generate, and we attempt to gain insight into the underlying state-of-mind. The more inspired may go a step further and actively try to imagine themselves in the circumstances of the other person and how it would feel to them. This attempt at creating bridges with another person's inner world is the basis of empathy and the closest we can get to understanding another person emotionally. But we are using ourselves as a model and assuming that the other is like us. In reality, there are so many variables that make a person feel how they do, and there are an infinite number of states-of-mind, of subtly different ways of looking at things, of perceiving the world and of experiencing life.

The chasm between how other people experience the world and how we imagine they do bears some similarity to the gap between how we actually felt at a time in the past and how we remember things later. We naturally pay attention to our present mental state and forget past ones. If you were to keep a journal and re-read it occasionally, you might re-discover and possibly re-stir emotions you had forgotten you had had. To take a concrete example that many of us are familiar with, in the days, weeks and months following a painful break-up, one is acutely aware of the intensity and complexity of the emotions associated with the relationship. But the intensity fades with time, to the point where former complicit soulmates can sometimes meet for a pleasant drink without the unwelcome interference of past emotions. In fact, one can forget *what it really felt like*, just remembering in vague terms that the feelings were strong.

Smells are notoriously effective at triggering memories and eliciting emotions. You may occasionally experience the specific mindscape elicited by the whiff of a long-forgotten perfume in the wind, and the associated vivid memory, such as a past romance. You can communicate part of the experience by describing the physical aspects and other elements of the situation that others may relate to, using words as evocatively as possible within the limits of language—like Marcel Proust and his iconic madeleine. But without the same set of memories and way of looking at the world as you, others may not be able to create even a similar mental experience.

The only state-of-mind we reliably know in all its intensity is our own at the present instant. The difficulty of vividly evoking a different state-of-mind from the one that we are currently experiencing is an obstacle to projecting ourselves into the future and then taking steps to put ourselves into new, potentially happier situations. Whenever we contemplate issues that involve our or others' happiness and well-being, there will often be something fundamental lacking in our understanding.

Because we only perceive the world of our senses, it naturally escapes us that perhaps the most interesting part of the world external to us is the subjective experience of billions of similar creatures, and that real meaning exists at the interface of thoughts, sensations and memories in people's minds. And it often eludes our full awareness that others' suffering is a very real and concrete phenomenon and not a mere projection onto others of whatever emotions a disturbing sight makes us experience.

If you yourself have been in many different states-of-mind and have trouble remembering or accessing some of them on demand, you cannot possibly expect someone else to know exactly how you feel at any particular time. Yet we are usually only vaguely aware, if at all, that there is something essential lacking in our understanding of a situation. This misevaluation of reality, which recalls a once-popular school of thought in psychology known as "behaviorism" that brushed aside the relevance of internal mental states, is of critical but dramatically underestimated importance. We respect words, actions, visible accomplishments. We are even fascinated by virtual reality technology that mimics our interaction with the external world. But others' internal experience of reality is like an aside rather than the point of it all. This also means that people who make decisions, including at the highest political levels, are not only lacking key information but are in some way *unaware* that the information is lacking.

That people can be enamored by authors' or artists' works without really seeking or being able to understand what went on in their minds shows how much we are often missing. We admire the colorful paintings of a psychologically complex artist like Van Gogh for their originality and what they "do" for us, we read a few snippets about his life, and we think we know the essential about him, when in fact we have little conception of how he actually experienced the world, his tormented state of mind, and how the paintings were experienced as they were being created. Art can be interpreted and appreciated in many ways and create sensations in the observer, but as a form of self-expression, as a catharsis of inner torment, the meaning may be lost to others.

Art can, however, create effective bridges between people's consciousnesses by generating powerful, similar experiences in many people's minds simultaneously. Music is especially effective in this regard. Any other means of expression, or an emotionally powerful event, such as the fall of the Berlin Wall, can be similarly effective in resonating with observers and causing them to sense, often with justification, that others are experiencing a similar state-of-mind at the same time.

Often, of course, we are implicitly thankful that our minds are opaque. Having others be able to read our thoughts against our will would deprive us of our most essential intimacy and destroy that critical frontier between thoughts and action that enables us to enjoy a sense of freedom. Unfortunately, even this intimacy risks eventually being lost. What has always been a clear, untouchable demarcation is now showing signs of vulnerability to the encroachment of new technologies, ostensibly intended to protect us.[22] Elements of our subjective experience risk eventually becoming most accessible to those who attribute low priority to our individual freedoms.

THE LIMITS OF LANGUAGE

Because language provides labels for categories of concepts or states-of-mind that are universally comprehensible within the same community, it is often grossly inadequate for communicating specific thoughts and experiences that are too abstract or rare to be given specific words, and which live fleeting existences in the unique habitat represented by an individual's brain. Our words for emotions are just crude approximations. All the nuances of our mindscape, what it *really feels like*, are lost in translation, so to speak, although we are easily fooled into thinking that language captures abstract ideas, emotions and states-of-mind as well as it does more concrete, tangible concepts. Sometimes the words used are so general and imprecise that they are ultimately meaningless. With so much of subjective experience ephemeral and unique, describing it more precisely would require us to put people into specific situations and teach them new, invented words to label their perceptions. We sometimes hear the expression "there are no words to describe it", without grasping the full significance of the reality we are missing.

Even when a word or phrase provides a fairly exact label for a mental state, that mental state may not be evoked in a very meaningful way. If you read about someone having suffered excruciating pain, you may understand this intellectually and abstractly without attributing much emotional weight to it. An article in Slate described "the absolute interiority of pain"

22 Michael Tarm, "Mind-Reading Systems Could Change Air Security," *The Huffington Post* (8 January 2010), www.huffingtonpost.com/2010/01/08/wecu-mind-reading-systems-_n_416123.html.

as an explanation for why it is such a difficult state to express, including for many writers plagued by illness.[23]

To return to the world of smell, in the same way that perfumers prepare new combinations from a library of natural and synthetic ingredients to create perfumes with a new identity and distinct olfactive character, combinations of thoughts, memories and sensory experiences can create wholly new, if often short-lived, experiences in an individual's mind that are impossible to fully explain to another person. And in the same way that the descriptors commonly used by perfumers—for example, "citrus, fresh, green"—give you a general sense of the type of perfume and what it has in common with other perfumes, rather than what makes it unique, words can give only a general sense of how a complex emotion is experienced rather than a detailed impression.

In this specific respect, every man is, in fact, an island, alone with thoughts and feelings that he can precisely communicate to no one. The message that is expressed is often far more interesting than the one that is received. So much of the meaning that exists in the universe, concentrated on our planet, remains invisible, and the same is true for so much of the suffering. And it is very difficult to care about something you do not sense.

---

23 Amanda Fortini, "Pain Beyond Words," *Slate* (7 July 2008), www.slate.com/id/2194830.

6. Determinism: The Universe's Marionette Show

The Free Will Paradox

We have seen how, over large spans of time, processes resulting from matter and energy obeying the laws of physics eventually led to the evolution of intelligent, conscious beings. This chapter is about the incredible paradox that this situation entails and some of its implications.

An age-old problem in philosophy is the question of free will—essentially, whether human beings can *really* act freely in an apparently deterministic world of cause and effect where the past dictates the future. As with all philosophical debates, the arguments and conclusions hinge crucially on what one actually means by the terms in question. Often, this problem is framed in terms of choice, and the answer is meant to depend on whether a person "could have" carried out a different action than the one performed. This vague terminology opens the door to endless hours of philosophical ruminations and explorations of various scenarios. But if by free will we mean something more fundamental that we feel instinctively to be true— that, as individuals, we are the ultimate sources of our thoughts, desires and actions—then the conclusion that refuses to go away, like an unwanted guest one has to accommodate, is that free will is a subjectively experienced, though highly effective, illusion. Period.

Strangely, perhaps, something so profoundly important about our existence is rarely addressed directly outside the academic sphere, and even then often only timidly. Renowned philosophers intimately familiar with the literature on free will, neuroscientists studying the mechanisms associated with human consciousness and thought, and physicists penetrating the mysteries of deep reality try to persuade us, though often with muted enthusiasm, that we have at least some form of free will. It seems that many scientists and philosophers feel guilty about confronting the truth and revealing it too loudly, perhaps unsure about how their readers will react or concerned about expressing ideas that are too at odds with conventional wisdom. What should be obvious is pushed farther back into the future, in anticipation perhaps of new scientific findings or reflections that might shine further light on the issue and offer a convenient way out. It is almost as if they feel a responsibility to reassure, telling how fantastic scientific truth, technology and human resolve are, without helping their readers to come to terms with some of the deepest truths themselves. For example, towards the end of *Freedom Evolves*, a book that comprehensively explores the issue of free will and determinism, Daniel Dennett, one of the world's foremost and most respected thinkers about human consciousness and other major philosophical themes, optimistically argues that human freedom is an objective phenomenon. Reality is a little darker than many philosophers will readily admit. Including the concrete reality of millions of people suffering because we cling too tightly to the notion of free will, failing to show compassion to those to whom the laws of the universe have dealt bad cards, and neglecting to recognize the large-scale consequences of our collective, supposedly free behavior.

The free will issue has never quietly disappeared because, whether we like it or not, it concerns an essential, fundamental truth that cannot be discreetly swept under the rug. However unintuitive it may be and unlikely to be widely grasped and accepted, determinism and all its implications are where the search for the truth ultimately leads. And it needs to be confronted honestly, because it matters more than most people realize: it is central to our understanding of who we really are and where we are headed. In fact, it should really be seen as part of a larger issue, which is how deeply we are prepared to understand the human condition and admit the contradictions between how we generally perceive things—our most intuitive sense of what it is like to be a responsible, autonomous human being—and how things really are in a broader, objective sense. This is one of our biggest taboos.

Reflecting on determinism is far from being an intellectual diversion that contributes nothing practical to the search for solutions. You cannot address the big questions about what matters and what we should do about it if you ignore the fundamentals of how the world works and humans' place within the whole framework. Without accepting the implications of determinism, philosophical reflections and even editorial commentaries on politics and world events are fatally incomplete, as they fail to face an essential—perhaps *the* essential—aspect of the human condition. Until you grapple with the free will issue and understand human minds as integral parts of a system, you can never really grasp the essence of our existence and our predicament as a species in a fully meaningful way. Failing to more fully acknowledge the deterministic chain of causation *itself* has downstream consequences. I believe we desperately need to use this knowledge, gleaned from observing the system "from the outside", in order to have a positive effect on the workings on the inside. Dismissing the free will issue as irrelevant is actually mistaken and dangerous if it hinders us from adopting a perspective we might need in order to take more ambitious steps towards averting an unfortunate fate.

Now, I need to admit that I am using the concept of a deterministic world a little loosely. At its most basic level, at the subatomic scale where quantum physics dominates, the world is random, and the probability functions of subatomic particles, rather than causal determinism, best describe how things work. This randomness can even potentially have gigantic effects at the macroscopic level. Just to evoke one unlikely but entirely plausible scenario, imagine a deranged dictator who decides she will launch a nuclear strike if and only if an experiment that depends on a random, quantum event—such as the timing of the radioactive decay of an atom—yields one particular outcome. The existence of human brains can thus allow a minor quantum hiccup to have phenomenally significant consequences. This implies that even an omniscient being would not be able to predict the future. Even putting aside quantum randomness, chaos theory—which deals with the ability of very small changes in starting conditions to have huge macroscopic effects at later time points—means that, for all practical purposes, the future is unknowable in any degree of detail.

But what matters is not so much whether the state of the world at any point in the future is, in theory, entirely and precisely determined by its state in the past or present. What is far more relevant to the free will issue is the fact that we are an inherent part of a physical world with all its associated properties and trends, a giant network of interacting particles. The molecules bumping around in our bodies and everywhere else in the world follow the laws of physics. Everything that happens on a larger scale is determined by all these particles and molecules interacting.

Furthermore, much of the quantum randomness that occurs at the subatomic level still averages out at more macroscopic scales. As time moves forward, one thing still leads to another in a consistent and often predictable way as matter and energy collide—even if we cannot foresee all the consequences. The processes going on in our brains are no exception. Our thoughts and behaviors depend on everything else. Our whole functioning is like clockwork, like cogs in a giant machine generating thoughts, feelings and emotions, even though the meaning associated with these thoughts is absolutely real.

These facts should be entirely uncontroversial for anyone who accepts a rational, scientific understanding of the world, and yet consistently accepting all the implications is extremely difficult. Really, *really* understanding what determinism means and what it says about the human condition can produce a profound, even frightening epiphany, as if one is staring into the face of God. Even some who defend the truth at all costs probably don't realize just how difficult this particular truth is to make sense of. From our vantage point as complex, sophisticated, cocktail-sipping beings, we lose sight of the fact that the underlying physical world is still there, going about its business according to the same laws as ever, and that the happenings at that scale are still translated into events at a macroscopic level, including human thought and interaction. This means that everything is, in some sense, destined, even if this destiny properly resides in randomness and statistical probabilities, and that whatever we want or end up doing was determined by the rigid laws of particle physics and the higher-level patterns they exhibit with greater degrees of complexity. Our thoughts and actions really are the consequences of fate. And can we change fate? Not from an *outside* perspective.

The concept of determinism exists in a kind of "yin and yang" relationship of apparent opposites with that of consciousness. When you consider how counterintuitive (to conscious beings like ourselves) the phenomenon of consciousness itself actually is—that physical matter organized in a certain way yields subjective experience—, it is, perhaps, no more surprising that this consciousness ends up thinking of itself as being in charge, at the center of it all and dictating everything else. This point is rather subtle but so fundamentally important. If you think about it, its true significance can pop into focus in an "aha" kind of moment. There is an analogy here to how, if you stare long enough at a picture containing repeat patterns known as a stereogram, a 3-D image suddenly appears.[24] Seeing the hidden 3-D image requires you to relax the focus of your eyes on the 2-D picture, and in a similar way, understanding the significance of our identity with the physical world requires us to relax our intuitive but constrained perspective.

If it is impossible to fully fathom how matter produces consciousness, it is also difficult, in the reverse sense, to grasp that conscious creatures are still wholly physical ones. As conscious beings, we live under the continuous illusion that the decisions that determine our actions and shape our lives and immediate environment ultimately originate in our minds, when in fact, our thoughts, desires and actions are just part and parcel of the whole system and chain of events.

Does an animal have free will? We hardly expect an animal to behave independently of the physical universe, for there to be some aspect of its brain that operates according to non-physical laws. There is nothing about animal behavior that cannot theoretically be explained in terms of various levels of causes. But aside from the heavy use of abstract thought and the development of complex societies and culture, which add a whole new dimension of calculation to his behavior, a human being is not really that different from a bonobo or chimpanzee, our closest animal relatives. Yet as soon as we ask the question about free will with respect to ourselves in the first person, it suddenly becomes very difficult to be objective.

Our nature as physically determined beings—which, in the end, we cannot possibly be anything else but—is becoming less of a theoretical abstraction as the details at various levels of analysis are gradually being worked out, filling in the moat that separates our recalcitrant view of ourselves as unique, autonomous creatures from our view of the rest of the universe. At one level, for example, genetics is increasingly revealing to us details of the physiological basis of our behavior. Given that our genetic makeup has been solidly shown to contribute to a very large extent to our character, in a not-too-distant future it will be possible to make fairly good predictions about

---

24 See www.eyetricks.com/3dstereo.htm for some examples.

individuals' behavioral tendencies based on a simple analysis of their relevant genes. Of course, this raises a host of fundamental, extremely important and difficult practical questions regarding privacy, civil liberties and legal responsibility. But once the moat is filled in, maintaining a drawbridge is to live in denial.

As just one example of the paradox of invoking free will, it has been demonstrated that people with low serotonin levels in their brain are much more likely to behave aggressively. In fact, much of our decision-making will, as science progresses, ultimately be linked to molecular neurobiology and such variables as, for example, how tightly a particular neurotransmitter binds to its receptor.

Tendency does not mean certainty—there are so many different factors acting at different levels that determine our thoughts, emotions and behaviors, from strong synaptic connections created by momentous life experiences to random molecular noise. But when you add up all these different factors, there isn't anything else left. The combination of all the factors determines how the person actually behaves. So, for example, you might find that very low serotonin + x other brain chemical levels + y other genetic factors + z environmental factors all add up to near certainty of committing violent crime (with further chance events serving as the final trigger). The sense of freedom is entirely subjectively felt, if at all—and it is unlikely that a person with all these factors weighing against him would feel very free to act peacefully, despite attempts to constrain his impulses.

The roles of other, non-genetic factors in people's behavior are also continuously being revealed by psychologists, sociologists and economists, and the number of potential examples is endless. There are the broad determinants, including the usual suspects such as parental upbringing, education, encouragement and success as a child, relative wealth, social class, peer pressure, etc. And there are all the innumerable happenings and encounters in our daily lives, some of them insignificant in the long term, others life-changing. Everything that happens to us affects our behavior in some way. Scientific studies can help evaluate the average relative weight of different kinds of factors in different situations.

One anecdotal example I find mildly amusing of how one organism can directly affect the behavior of another is the evidence that infection with the toxoplasma parasite makes mice more likely to loiter in the presence of cat odor—an adaptation that makes the parasite more likely to end up in its preferred host, the cat. There is some evidence that toxoplasma infection may also make humans more likely to take risks.[25] Of course, an affected human would ascribe his risk-seeking behavior to something else—undoubtedly some intrinsic urge.

Indeed, numerous psychology experiments have revealed that humans are notoriously bad at knowing the underlying reasons for their decisions and actions, often inventing explanations that make sense to them after the fact. And neurological research has shown that humans are only consciously aware of decisions they make fractions of a second or even longer after the decision has already been made within the brain, as measurable by typical electrical signals.[26] Science, by digging away at the truth about things—at least at a mechanistic level—is continually pulling away the curtain that hides the "operator" behind the scenes, to use a reference from the classic American film "The Wizard of Oz".

So our sense of freedom is entirely an internally felt phenomenon. Viewed objectively, our thoughts, our emotions, our desires and our actions are all the result of our state-of-being at any instant—the momentary architecture of our brain—and the environment we encounter, and these in turn determine our future state-of-being. Any thinking process that results in conclusions, decisions and actions is always initiated by a previous set of causes—like billiard balls colliding, to use a frequent but useful metaphor. Even the positions we hold, arguments we make and actions we defend ultimately stem from a network of causes existing at various levels, rather than from some unassailable, absolute truth. From a broad, big-picture perspective, it also means that the universe is to blame for everything that happens.

The relevance to our everyday lives of understanding free will as an illusion depends on the circumstances. If a person who, as a result of a combination of intrinsically strong character, an encouraging environment and favorable circumstances, knows what he wants—for example, to become a highly paid investment banker—and ends up succeeding, most people would not think to deprive him of his pride and sense of personal accom-

---

25 Peter Aldhous, "The joy of parasites," *New Scientist* (20 June 2007).

26 Classic experiments showing a brief delay were published in the early 1980s by research psychologist Benjamin Libet. More recent experiments have shown an even longer delay of several seconds between the moment the brain displays activity indicating it is about to solve a problem and the moment the subject is consciously aware of it.

plishment by reducing his fate to the consequence of various specific determining factors, even if strictly speaking this is the case. If the aid of others played a role—perhaps a friend or uncle who pulled some strings—some jealous detractors might be tempted to make some snide comments, whereas the self-made man or woman tends invariably to be universally admired. But the question of free will would probably not appear relevant to most observers.

However, there are times when the future seems so open-ended and we don't know which future to choose. We may find ourselves unable to make a decision because, on reflection, we realize we don't actually know what we really want, or we may have a strong sense of what we want but not know the best way of achieving it. Our subjective feeling of autonomy can even come to a standstill. For someone who finds themselves in the clutches of depression or simply unhappy with how their life is going, and with no idea what to do next, the free will issue no longer seems so obscure. When a person's thought patterns don't result in the right behavior to achieve their goals, or where they cannot even manage to make a decision, blaming them for not picking themselves up and getting on with things is mostly an instinctive expression of frustration. People who find themselves in a rut need an event, often an external stimulus, to change their way of thinking or provide them with a new opportunity, and they may find themselves waiting to be hit by the right billiard ball—in the form of a useful or motivating discussion with a friend or stranger, an inspiring book, the determined roll of a die[27], a life-changing experience, or maybe even a few random molecular collisions in the brain that push a neurological process beyond the tipping point—to get on track. While there is no denying that the very act of blaming someone can sometimes be very useful in serving as this stimulus, this does not make free will any more of an objective reality.

We are all subject to greater or lesser degrees to "cognitive traps" where the focus of our thoughts is constrained by our mental processes and various external influences. In the absence of useful information, including knowledge about *which* information is most useful as well as a successful decision-making strategy, our freedom to get what we want is often illusory. In practice, all of our daily decisions are contributed to by a complicated web of interactions. We acknowledge the influence of others in our decisions, but there is a large space full of other, less visible factors which

---

27 The theme of a classic novel from the early 1970s, *The Dice Man* by Luke Rhinehart.

we prefer to leave untouched and to which we attribute our freedom. It is convenient but, objectively, not very truthful to reduce the sum of all these interactions and various factors to the exercising of our free will.

The ethereality of free will relates to that of identity, explored in the next chapter. The concept of identity can be seen as an attempt to impose a certain coherence and stability on a bundle of often competing desires or tendencies, the strongest of which people most closely associate with a person's "true" character. A range of factors determine which ones will dominate at any one time, as well as the outcome. The degree to which the things we consider important in our lives can shift when we change environments illustrates both how mutable our identities are and how readily our "free will" blows with the wind.

Our need as individuals to avoid the instability of cognitive dissonance, and our need as a society to maintain the notion of personal responsibility, are barriers to fully acknowledging determinism and drawing the appropriate lessons from it. There is a very fine, though critical, line between using this understanding to forgive the past and using it to excuse the future.

Dealing With It

What do we do with this deep truth? The supposedly liberating effect of thought and reflection can cause a sudden petrification of our sense of freedom as we more fully understand our own nature and grasp the bigger system it is part of. It can hardly be denied that observing the human condition detachedly through the lens of a scientist, regarding human beings as automatons and seeing free will dissolve like a mirage in the desert, may seem like the ultimate in dehumanization. If one is feeling existentially moody, it is like peering into a dark abyss and staring at the apparent dismal truth that life has no purpose because we are all just marionettes controlled by the laws of the universe, our subjective experience and sense of identity eternal hijack victims of physical reality.

Being conscious and simultaneously aware that one's thoughts are being determined by the current makeup of one's brain and immediate stimuli also has an inherent absurdity about it—in essence, trying to compress subjective experience and objective understanding into the same instant. It would be impossible to live continuously aware that the thought one is having at any moment is determined, for example, by *those* previous thoughts and *this* visual stimulus and *that* memory and *this* overall thought pattern and so on.

One could try doing the experiment for a brief period before suffering an existential headache from the rapid oscillations in perspective. One might well even go mad.[28]

Fortunately for us, the emergence of any strong tendency to harp endlessly on the lack of free will would be suicidal and would have been weeded out by evolution, and an illusion of having free will is the default state to which one's view of the world generally reverts in the absence of a conscious effort.[29] In everyday life, just as nagging thoughts about your overdue tax return are unlikely to unduly distract your attention from a new amorous interest (and if they do, you should invest in a good accountant), the fact that your thoughts and actions are entirely determined by your brain state and experience will not normally interfere with your ability to go about life as if you were an entirely autonomous being (and if they do, you should do less thinking and reading about philosophy and get out more).

Even without obsessing about it to the point of madness, reflecting on what it means for our own thoughts to be influenced by everything around us could make us just slightly more complacent, causing some people, even highly intelligent ones, to give themselves up just a little more frequently to their most primitive desires through the self-fulfilling and therefore technically "correct" reasoning that they had no choice. Of course, it does little good for achieving what one wants to relent submissively to the exterior world and wait catatonically for things to happen. If one falls into that trap, one can reasonably be said to have had the bad luck of being unduly influenced—perhaps by reading the wrong book. Doing so is logically equivalent to jumping off a tall building and claiming that this was the "will of the universe", and although this may be a correct explanation from a big-picture perspective, it just as surely reflects a disturbed psychological state.

But suppose we gingerly make that critical step in accepting that free will is an illusion, and draw all the other conclusions that follow. Well, figuratively speaking, there might be a pause, even a deafening silence, with just the distant, low frequency rumblings of the universe in the background. And then, little by little, the music starts to play again, the volume starts to pick up, and we say, "So what?" We proceed to go outside and walk in the sunshine, eat the most sublime culinary creations, drink the most complex

---

28 As suggested by Thomas Metzinger in his essay "The Forbidden Fruit Intuition" in *What Is Your Dangerous Idea?*

29 Chris Frith, "Determining free will," *New Scientist* (11 August 2007).

wines, fall in love, explore, travel, meet people, connect with them, talk, share, enjoy life in all its richness. Life remains what it always was. And we are armed with knowledge—even if we still sometimes long for the bliss of lost innocence...

Dealing as effectively as possible with the world's immense problems requires us to make that critical step as we face the essential truths about existence and about what ultimately matters, and question the assumptions on which so much of public policy is based. It means confronting aspects of reality that seem instinctively to be "dehumanizing" because they tell us things about ourselves that do not fit with our notions about what it means to be human and that we do not want to hear. Seeing the big picture and recognizing the degree to which we are all slaves to our human nature so that we can take appropriate practical measures can, in fact, also be seen as the opposite of dehumanization if it permits us to act less like animals towards each other. Understanding how the brain operates in all its mechanistic detail and knowing that it is part of a larger physical system called the universe is simply another layer of truth and need not detract from the kaleidoscope of deep meaning and emotions that emerge from this complexity. But our emotions should not handicap us in the search for pragmatic ways of reducing suffering.

As I alluded to early on, we need to accept that multiple explanations for phenomena can co-exist, each reflecting a different approach or level of understanding of the world, or relevant to a different subset of reality. Each explanation may be useful, and different ways of viewing the world can therefore each have validity, provided they do not lead to conflicting conclusions. While we can focus on some aspects or interpretations of reality more than others, we must be prepared to acknowledge the validity and insights of other compatible perspectives.

Now, there have recently been some controlled, small-scale psychological laboratory experiments showing that when people believe, or are led to believe through exposure to written statements, that free will is an illusion, they are more likely to cheat, less likely to be generous and more likely to act aggressively.[30] Although it is always unclear how much can be extrapolated

---

30 The following article references and discusses two such studies, one by Kathleen Vohs and Jonathan Schooler and one by Roy Baumeister: Jesse Bering, "Scientists say free will probably doesn't exist, but urge: 'Don't stop believing!'" *Scientific American Mind* (6 April 2010), www.scientificamerican.com/blog/post. cfm?id=scientists-say-free-will-probably-d-2010-04-06.

from such experiments to the real world, they do suggest that, by itself, the belief that we do not have free will can actually erode social or ethical behavior. Does this mean we should actually be economical with the truth about existence, rather than face up to reality?

I don't think we should take the implications of such studies lightly. Spreading the isolated meme that we have no free will may further a certain basic truth about existence, but taken *alone* it is likely neither to be properly understood nor to contribute to a better world. The truth needs to be handled carefully. The information on which people's attention is focused always has consequences, sometimes dramatic ones. But this does not mean that we should strive to cover up the most essential truths. Rather, we must be prepared to put these truths into a larger context that provides a paradigm in which to understand them and make effective, positive use of them.

It is not surprising that people are reluctant to take a detached view of the world that reveals how interrelated everything is and seems to remove a sense of control. There is a paradoxical need for self-deception. Even if, for a proper understanding of the human condition, we need to come to terms with free will being an illusion, we still need to assume this illusion for ourselves most of the time in order to *feel* free, entering an inspired state-of-mind where we believe we can achieve anything we want. We need to live *as if* free will exists, *as if* we are the origins rather than the conduits of our streams of consciousness, as an essential strategy to survive, motivate ourselves and live in a society that demands responsibility. The feeling of being in control is an extremely important state-of-mind for achieving self-realization. The illusion of free will thus has something of a self-fulfilling aspect to it. Being happy and successful in living your dreams requires you to view yourself as a source of desires and actions. We still need to relent to our instincts and claim free will for ourselves, even if we are intellectually aware that it is an illusion.

People often mistakenly think that if free will is an illusion, then their actions have no consequence: "If everything is determined, then it doesn't matter what I do." This is completely false: what we do always has consequences—potentially huge ones! Determinism pointedly does NOT mean that you cannot control events through your behavior and thereby influence the future, does NOT mean you cannot achieve what you want, and does NOT mean that you should not take responsibility for your actions. In fact, the very opposite can be argued. From *within* this physically determined system, we can still embrace the vision of a better future, acting as agents of change, and allowing ourselves to be persuaded by other agents who are also inside the system. So at least the greatest fear related to free will can be laid to rest. Nothing any scientist or writer says need indelibly change the everyday sense of what it's like to be alive, and this applies equally to the subject of determinism and free will.

A big-picture perspective on existence, including regarding free will as an illusion, need not be adopted as our primary, default way of looking at the world on a daily basis, and need not smother our instinctive pleasures with a pervasive fear of dehumanization. A deeper understanding of the processes we are part of is not by any means a substitute for, nor should it detract from, subjectively experienced beauty, meaning and human dignity. On the contrary, it needs to be seen as a tool or a catalyst for *achieving* these. Equations by no means capture the essence of meaning any more than understanding nerve impulses explains how anything actually feels. Just as a map is useful for providing orientation from time to time, the broad, objective view from outside the box can serve as a compass as we try to solve the world's most urgent problems. To use an expression attributed to philosopher Alfred Korzybski and popularized by the founders of NLP (neurolinguistic programming)[31], the map is not the territory. It is simply a guide.

Being regularly aware, in a non-obsessive way, that one's own thoughts are determined can be useful as a means of exteriorizing the sources of one's disappointments, drawing the appropriate lessons in order to be more effective in the future and, very importantly, putting oneself in situations that one knows will stimulate the thoughts and ideas that one wants. This can be as simple and practical as, say, putting Post-its with motivational reminders in places where we are likely to see them in order to influence our future thoughts and actions. In fact, much of the principle of NLP can be seen as putting in place a structure in one's mental processes that facilitates the generation of positive thoughts at the right moment—placing an easily triggered "billiard ball" in the right position. Analyzing how one's brain works allows one to be more effective in manipulating it.

One cannot, however, invoke determinism in order to write off one's own past behavior and demand understanding from others, even if the

---

31 NLP is an approach to psychotherapy that provides insights into how individuals can take better control of their own psychological functioning.

behavior was not cynically premeditated with this argument in mind. Although correct at one level, this argument would never be accepted by others, as people are expected by one another to act as if they have free will, and a system where the rule of law as well as past commitments are not respected would quickly collapse.

But recognizing that the world is essentially, on a large scale and for the most part, deterministic, that things happen as they happen and that people are how they are for x number of reasons, provides the individual with a critically important viewpoint from which to understand human nature. Regularly viewing others' behavior as a virtually inevitable or highly likely consequence of a combination of various contributing factors can be helpful in dealing with negative events and behaviors, allowing us to act less emotionally and more rationally and tolerantly with people whose behavior troubles us, both in the private and professional spheres.

This perspective does present its own challenges. Acting detached at all times is hardly a useful social skill, not only because one would be perceived as bland, uninteresting or weird, but also because the complete suspension of any negative emotional reactions to others' behavior could be perceived as acceptance. In dealing with others, one needs to play the game. An obsessively deterministic outlook would inevitably lead to cynicism regarding the consequences of one's actions and words on others, as one assumes the simultaneous roles of actor and observer. One might have trouble avoiding the feeling of manipulating others, even though at some level this is what we (subconsciously) do in practice in our everyday relations, regardless of our good intentions. But the perspective has to exist as part of our understanding, even as we allow ourselves to revert to our intuitive perspective in our daily interactions.

If a slightly detached, deterministic outlook is sometimes relevant on a personal scale, it is all the more so at the levels of domestic and international politics and in the context of global activism. We sometimes carry the notion of responsibility to extremes, preferring to imprison repentant human beings for decades rather than implement practical measures that will reduce the likelihood of the crimes ever being committed. Demanding responsibility does not prevent or absolve us from helping to shape a system where the call for responsibility is not futile or inherently cynical. It isn't enough to simply demand it—we have to create the conditions where we can reasonably expect it from people. And for those who are unable to act responsibly, a deterministic understanding of their behavior can often reveal compassion to be an appropriate response.

On the world's political stage, leaders' emotionally influenced reactions to what they perceive as ill-will on the part of their rivals can lead to irrational courses of behavior that threaten the well-being of huge numbers of our planet's inhabitants. And among organizations trying laudably to reduce human suffering and change the dangerous course that our planet is on, there is often a lack of practical detachment to reflect on the most effective strategies that take into account human nature, even though venting anger about human rights abuses and greedy corporate profit-making may be natural and sometimes effective in promoting change.

To summarize, it remains a huge paradox, and certainly one of the most fundamental ones concerning human existence, that an essential truth about our relationship to the rest of the universe and how we operate within it needs selectively to be both ignored and embraced. Surrendering ourselves to the illusion of free will is absolutely crucial for our own happiness as individuals, maintaining a sense of control, assuming responsibility as active agents of change and being effective in getting things done. But regarding the rest of the world with a strong dose of deterministic thinking and detachment, and understanding the human situation objectively, is critical to free ourselves from unproductive and, ultimately, dangerously distracting negative emotional reactions and empty moralism. This perspective on the rest of the world, which includes viewing it as a self-contained system in which everything is connected, with a certain unknown probability of terrible outcomes if left alone, can also spur us as individuals to take on *greater* responsibility to tinker with the system in ways that will improve the odds. Knowing that this deterministic—at some level—universe causes extreme suffering, if I can do something about it, then why shouldn't I, rather than passively observe the system's worst consequences and potential self-destruction? We cannot change the past, only the future. And although the past was determined by a previous chain of events, we can still decide to take responsibility for the future if we desire, regarding ourselves as critical nodes in a flow of causation on which a worthwhile future for humanity depends.

SCALING UP: THE BIGGER PICTURE

The molecules bumping around in our brains and in the world around us, interacting according to the laws of physics, translate not just into individuals' thoughts and actions but, ultimately, into the collective behaviors of large groups of people. We are part of a continuous system of atoms, molecules, people and populations in which everything is connected, and from the randomness and chaos, order of a sometimes predictable nature can emerge. In this section, let's explore this idea, both for the change of perspective it can induce when reflected upon, and for any pragmatic use we can make of it.

The collective properties of a large number of molecules in a system, for example, a canister full of gas, can be described by simple equations, such as those relating pressure, volume and temperature. In a similar way, the chaotic and essentially random behaviors of large numbers of distinct individuals following similar sets of rules also settle into relatively simple, large-scale patterns that can sometimes be described mathematically, although at this level of complexity, the immediate principles that come into play are further removed from the rock solid laws of physics. Complex systems, such as organisms or societies, have properties that can be better understood at a higher level than by adding up the individual properties and movements of the countless components. This concept was explored in depth by Philip Ball in his award-winning book *Critical Mass*.

Concrete, visual examples of this phenomenon include the awe-inspiring patterns displayed by large numbers of birds flying in a flock or fish swimming in a school, videos of which can be found on YouTube. If we just looked at the flight pattern of one individual bird we would not be able to guess that it was flying within the boundaries of a large, curved, wispy mass that was continuously shrinking and expanding. Neither would that bird or any other bird in the flock likely be aware of these larger-scale patterns of movement. The whole system can be seen as a computer program evolved over hundreds of millions of years, running simultaneously in each bird's brain, that dictates how to move in response to birds and other objects in the immediate vicinity, essentially applying just a few basic guiding principles.[32] The same idea applies to other kinds of populations, such as ant colonies. The aggregated behavior of individual ants, without any single ant

---

32 See, for example, Len Fisher's book *The Perfect Swarm*.

in charge and without any orientation session instructing them on what they are building, results in the construction of complex but well-defined, macroscopic structures.

These kinds of trends are commonplace in human society, such as in the predictable behavior of crowds, and often display a regularity that may at first defy understanding. Even though powerful individuals can disrupt or modify the system, the system is far more complex than any individual brain, making illusory any firm belief that we can guarantee long-term control over it, even of a benevolent kind. From a purely intellectual perspective, it can be humbling and even destabilizing to perceive ourselves as part of a larger system obeying its own rules, regardless of our individual illusions of free will and power. But there are also pragmatic consequences of understanding the larger system we are part of. When large-scale trends are found to be leading to an unwanted outcome, we can try to determine the leverage points through which these trends can be diverted or halted. Since we cannot currently do much to change the brain's hardware, we need to try to manipulate the conditions in which it operates in order to improve the chances of a favorable outcome.

If you put similar groups of people through the same experiences, you can generally expect to get similar outcomes. Although people differ genetically from each other and thus have different characters, large groups of people brought up in similar cultural settings will, on average, tend to exhibit the same behaviors. This is the kind of detached perspective we need on human nature in order to improve the future, even when our human instinct is to attribute blame.

Without a sufficiently big-picture perspective, well-meaning individuals and organizations can devote huge amounts of energy to trying to solve problems, including alleviating misery in the world, and yet their efforts are unlikely to be optimally effective. The reasons can range from a simple lack of awareness of the latest research on the most effective specific strategies to achieve a particular result, to ignorance of what is happening on a large scale—the kind of trends that, when revealed as straight lines plotted out on appropriate graphs, or when presented in more sophisticated, dynamic bubble charts, immediately capture one's attention with their stark simplicity.[33] When these kinds of oversights result in an unsuccessful market-

---

33 As an example, see physicist Sean Gourley's TED conference talk on the mathematics of war at www.ted.com/talks/sean_gourley_on_the_mathematics_of_war.

ing strategy for a product sold by a large multinational, some shareholders may be disappointed and a few managers may find themselves re-working their CV's. But when the well-being of many of the planet's inhabitants is at stake, we need to step outside of our emotional selves, coolly analyze what is happening on a large scale, and devise appropriate strategies based on an understanding of the underlying determinants.

So, how well do we actually understand the world? Intellectually, of course, we can feel we have a pretty good intuitive grasp of how things work, and we can spot and plot regularities in piles of past data, but the crux of the matter is whether we can construct models that provide us with useful information about the future. As essayist and former trader Nassim Nicholas Taleb states in his important, iconoclastic book *The Black Swan,* "Prediction, not narration, is the real test of our understanding of the world," and he argues forcefully that our actual ability to predict is extremely poor, due in large part to a lack of information, as well as to the mistaken belief that we actually know more than we do. Even crystal clear past trends may be poor predictors of the future, as there may be other important factors, however rare, hidden or unforeseeable, that can yet have a dramatic impact. Taleb writes, "We have trouble knowing the parameters of whichever model we assume runs the world." This does not mean that there is no web of causation, that things happen independently of one another, but simply that we do not know nearly enough about all the virtually infinite factors at play to always make meaningful predictions about specific future events.

However, we do know that there are simple underlying factors driving human behavior, and there are certain resulting trends that are likely to persist, even if they do not allow us to predict future events with certainty. In particular:

- People are fundamentally driven by self-interest and the quest for status
- Altruism and empathy are weak forces
- Clusters of genetically and culturally related people tend to seek the interests of their clan above those of others
- Self-interested political leaders regularly exploit populations' nationalistic feelings as a means of maintaining power

html, or any of global health researcher and statistics guru Hans Rosling's dynamic presentations of social and economic trends at TED conferences, such as www.ted.com/talks/hans_rosling_at_state.html.

- Wars have continually occurred throughout human history
- Complexity is increasing at an accelerating rate
- Technological advances are irreversible

How these factors will play out in terms of future events is uncertain, but it is likely to be explosive, as discussed in the chapter "Where We Are Headed". Preventing dire consequences requires some ability to anticipate potential future scenarios and implement large-scale efforts to avert them. We desperately need better models of societal trends. The challenge is to distinguish between what we know and what we don't, giving appropriate weight to both persistent trends and unpredictability.

Our instinctive faith in free will and individualism may, however, perversely be blinding too many of us to the large-scale trajectory of our species. We may well each be as free as a bird, but one that is flying in a large flock. We are uniquely human within, but viewed from the outside, we may be carrying out the universe's destiny through a modern incarnation of atavistic Darwinian urges, embracing the cult of the individual, unfettered markets and competition, optimistic about the uses of powerful new technologies, with an overly naïve faith in an unwritten principle that good will ultimately win. The most important causes of the trends taking place on our planet—the drivers of human behavior that evolved over millions of years—are simple to understand, and yet it is critical to take them more seriously into account if we want to have any hope of salvaging a better future. The exponential increase in complexity taking place on our planet at this moment is a resulting large-scale trend of the utmost significance.

Our situation can be roughly understood by imagining a science fiction scenario. A few identical robots are scattered across a planet, each consisting of a computer and high-precision mechanical devices that allow them to maneuver objects. Each is programmed to build new copies of itself at a rapid rate, maximize its chances of survival, use raw materials as sources of energy and building supplies, and follow a strategy of competition and cooperation with other robots, the balance of which depends on the supply of resources and the similarity of the robot to other robots. The building process is imperfect and causes changes to occur in each new robot. Tribes of competitive robots end up multiplying and expanding throughout the planet, developing tools that allow them to manipulate their environment and carry out complex calculations. Robots continually destroy each other on a small scale and, every now and then, tribes wipe out large numbers of other robots. The tools at their disposal become ever more sophisticated and potentially more destructive, and the intelligence at their disposal continually increases. Where does this all lead?

To add an additional layer of interest that changes nothing about the robots' actual behavior or the final physical outcome, we throw in a magical property we call consciousness that gives the robots sensations and emotions, allows them to experience their internal calculations as thought, and bestows on them the illusion of ultimate control. Welcome to planet Earth.

Of course, the above scenario is a simplification. It excludes the complex genetic component that more properly explains the sophistication of our survival and reproduction strategy—played out in the passing on of shared genes—and the balance between competition and cooperation. And by ignoring the relevance of mental states, it excludes the possibility that the robots' overall priorities could shift over time to giving highest priority to enhancing subjective experience and to devising cooperative strategies to achieving this. But the scenario embodies the key feature of agents set loose in the world with a simple underlying goal. Individuals' urges to satisfy their own needs, in the widest sense of the term, translate into large-scale trends at the level of the species, including the persistence of intense suffering and, increasingly, the emergence of existential threats.

It is for this reason, for example, that there is justifiable nervousness in the West about the growing economic and political power of a large, developing country like China, whose government is not unduly perturbed even by the suffering of some of its own citizens who stray too far from the mean, with what can seem like an unstoppable momentum propelled explicitly by national self-interest—no different than the urges that spurred the growth of numerous empires throughout history. Countries' spreading influence and attempts at cultural homogenization are comparable to the growth of a plant limited only by the constraints of its habitat and competition with other plants within the same ecological niche.

If everything is determined by powerful, hidden forces, and if the billionfold amplification of individual human nature to our species' population on a planetary scale leads to seemingly inevitable large-scale trends, how then can we really change the world? Well, a starting point is to want to. If enough smart, creative people want to shift the course of the world, it could potentially happen, by figuring out the most effective strategies that can lead to long-term stability. In that case, a better future will prove to have been in some sense determined, even if through what might be an improbable chain of events. Perhaps paradoxically, as suggested in the last section, the truth about determinism can allow us to understand with greater clarity the urgency of making a difference. It forces us to be pragmatic in favoring humanitarian values, and it can help promote a compassionate view of others by revealing their suffering as a potentially treatable symptom of the universe.

7. The Illusion of Distinct Individual Identity

Where does the end of me
Become the start of you?
—Tears for Fears, English pop duo, "Change"

As chaotic, uncertain and overwhelming the world around us often seems, if there is one thing we should at least be able to be sure of, it is that I am I and you are you. What can possibly be less subject to doubt? Yet once we permit ourselves to break a further taboo in thinking deeply about who we really are and probe the concept of identity, we discover that it is far more fragile and elusive than we might ever have suspected. And we gain further, dramatic insight into the absurd roles we find ourselves playing.

We instinctively attribute a unity to our own identity and to that of others: each of us a solid, indivisible entity that experiences a continuum of conscious moments in the first person and manifests them through behavior. The notion of each of us having a distinct, continuous, stable identity—a "self"—is absolutely essential for providing sense and coherence to our lives. But it is an illusion.[34] What each of us calls "I" is, in fact, a pattern—a pattern of thoughts, of ways of responding to the world, of multiple strivings, fears and emotions, recurring within what appears as one physical

---

34 Viewing the self as a construct or illusion is an element of so-called "post-structuralist" thinking. For an interesting article about multiple selves, see Paul Bloom, "First Person Plural," *The Atlantic* (November 2008), www.theatlantic.com/magazine/archive/2008/11/first-person-plural/7055.

being and continuously evolving. The relative stability of our memories and hardwired character traits provides us and the people with whom we interact with much of the sense of our having a stable identity over time. And the continuity in people's physical appearance provides a reliable cue to the stability of the mental processes generated within. But once we start to think about identity more carefully and shed our preconceptions, we are forced to come to terms with the illusion and its strange implications for who we are and how we relate to each other.

Most of the cells and molecules in our body are constantly being replaced over time. What does maintain a certain stability throughout our lives is the neural structures in our brains and the patterns of activity that determine our personalities and memories. And the information carried by our genes—which make a major contribution to our personality traits—remains essentially unchanged. The fact that we act as stable repositories of genetic information can be seen as a principal explanation for why we have been programmed through evolutionary processes to regard ourselves and others as having continuous identities. As far as evolution is concerned, you are a reflection of the genes that lie within.

The illusion of our having distinct, continuous individual identities can also be understood, at another level, as reflecting an innate need for stable reference points in a changing world. Although seeing our attitudes and behaviors as tendencies that can be influenced by situations is often a better reflection of reality than the more rigid connotations we tend to use, our instinct to generalize and categorize reflects a more effective survival strategy. Our view of the world is skewed towards the perception of discreetness and stability of traits. This is reflected in language. For example, we often use the verb "love" as if it were a continuous, stable state, even though in practice, there are instants even in a close relationship where one's emotional state can be much better described by rather different terminology.

When our environment is stable, the illusion of a stable, continuous identity is more easily maintained. But if our work or lifestyle has us regularly switching between very different environments and ways of experiencing and thinking about the world, our sense of identity and who we are can seem to fluctuate widely. And as our thought patterns evolve, a result of specific life experiences, new memories, reflections and physiological changes, we may bear little resemblance to our younger selves. It is partly in this way that our own identities vary over time. As an example of how we can disown elements of our past identity, an artificial intelligence research-er I mention later on wrote on his website, "You should regard anything from 2001 or earlier as having been written by a different person who also happens to be named 'Eliezer Yudkowsky'. I do not share his opinions."[35]

That a continuous, stable identity is an illusion is particularly relevant to how we relate to past suffering we may have experienced. We can only remember it to the extent that our memory is capable of registering and re-evoking what could potentially have been an extreme experience. When the memory is faint, it is almost as if it happened to a different person. This is why when someone lives to recall a horrible event or episode in their life, the person who actually experienced it is, from this perspective, no longer entirely there.

The notion that our identities are distinct and continuous over time underpins our criminal justice system, and it can explain why we absolve children of responsibility for their parents' crimes while holding people punishable for crimes they committed when they were younger. While this practice may seem entirely intuitive, if you think about it more detachedly it appears more arbitrary. People's behavior is influenced by and sometimes closely resembles that of their parents, while on the other hand, people ma-ture, and their thoughts and behaviors may bear little similarity to those of their younger selves. I am by no means suggesting that we ought to punish people for others' crimes. But society reinforces our instinctive notions of identity by focusing more—and, often, too much—on punishing individu-als than on targeting dangerous ideas that can spread among them.

We are nonetheless capable of recognizing a change in attitude and implicitly acknowledging a change in identity, to the extent that we talk about someone being "a different (or new) person", without recognizing the degree to which the statement can be viewed as literally true. The expecta-tion that a convict found guilty of the worst offense express remorse for his crime as a condition for a more lenient sentence can be interpreted as a de-sire to see a clear distinction between the identities of the original murderer and of the person later appearing before the judge.

The distinctness of our own identity from that of other people is also fuzzier than it seems. Especially in individualistic Western societies, the concept of each person being separate from the rest of the world is deeply rooted. Indeed, the perspective of each of us being a self-maximizer is a

---

35 http://yudkowsky.net

dominant theme in this book, as it remains one of the most powerful and insightful ways of understanding human nature and what is happening to us as a species. Subjective experience is always associated with an individual brain in its own unique, momentary environment, and in that respect remains the indivisible common denominator of the human condition. But that we each act autonomously, trying to improve our status and, we implicitly believe, our subjectively experienced feeling of happiness and sense of meaning does not detract from the fact that we are all very similar. From a big-picture perspective, we are all just variations on a theme, imperfect copies of each other, each striving to satisfy his or her needs. It is important to reflect on this aspect of identity in order to better understand our relationship to each other.

To further illustrate this point, let's carry out a thought experiment.[36] Imagine you discovered you had a long lost identical twin who, let's assume, was brought up under absolutely identical conditions and therefore shared identical memories with you. Let's say, then, that it was your exact duplicate. And imagine further you found yourself sitting opposite that person in a bare white room in which your experience was identical to theirs. With identical brain states and identical environments, you would each be looking at the other and simultaneously be thinking identical thoughts—perhaps, "How bizarre, he (or she) looks just like me. I wonder what he's thinking." But you wouldn't know what your double was actually thinking or experiencing until you started to talk, when you would find yourselves simultaneously uttering the identical words and realize that you were profoundly "connected" in your thinking.

Alan Turing, a highly influential 20th century mathematician and computer scientist, devised a classic test for human intelligence in a machine. In this test, one uses conversations to try to distinguish between a real person and a machine, both of which are hidden from view. According to his proposal, if one cannot distinguish between the two through dialogue, the machine can be considered intelligent. Somewhat analogously, it is through talking and other forms of communication that two people can discover a convergence in their thoughts and mental states, which implies a blurred separation between their identities. In theory, if the thoughts and mental states are indistinguishable, the concept of separate identities becomes

---

36 Thought experiments do not have to be practical or physically possible to carry out in order to provide deep insight into an idea and its implications.

rather meaningless, other than to reflect the fact that the mental states are being generated simultaneously in two physical locations. In between identicalness and separateness lies a whole spectrum of similarity which can be regarded as partial identity and represents an implicit connection between people and even animals.

The idea of us being imperfect copies of each other with overlapping identities and yet in competition with each other is subtle but important enough to consider further. Identical twins started off as a single fertilized egg and thus are as near as possible to being copies of each other, like two versions of the same person who have taken unique environmental trajectories. Typically, they grow up as extremely close friends. And yet, they may find themselves competing healthily with one another. A friend once told me a true anecdote about a friend of his who was looking forward with anticipation to the visit of a young woman he hoped to charm. Imprudently, he allowed his identical twin to pick her up at the station. Upon her arrival, his twin took advantage of their similar appearance to usurp his identity and reap the honors; obliged him to sleep in the bathtub; and, to add further insult to injury, poked his head in to ask if he had any condoms. Empathy is sometimes hard won, even towards those we identify with most strongly, who function very much like we do and share similar emotions. In that respect, we can paradoxically be competing with "ourselves". Each brain is programmed to maximize the satisfaction of its own needs, even though the subjective mental states generated by different brains, which represent the heart of identity, can largely overlap.

However, along with a sense of control and self-realization, there are few things that make people happier than to feel a bond of commonality with other human beings. We long to be respected and appreciated by others and, the rarest of all, to be understood. There is a great, inherent beauty when two or more people experience similar thoughts or emotions and feel that this is happening. This sense of shared subjectivity breaks down barriers between people, relaxing the boundaries between their identities, and it creates trust. A major disruption in our lives, such as the death of someone we love or a major catastrophe, can shatter our feelings of stability and control and immediately cause our sense of meaning to collapse down to our connections with other people.

The perception of stability and continuity in other peoples' identities gives us the confidence to feel a strong, unbroken connection with another person. Yet a loosening of our own sense of distinct identity can also free us up to better understand other people and connect more deeply with them, and also to care more about other conscious beings in general. Empathy with others is not just a psychological phenomenon but also the visceral perception of a deep, metaphysical truth.

Viewing identity as having less strictly defined boundaries helps us to gain insight into the relationship between the individual and the larger entity he or she is part of, and provides another angle from which to understand altruism. As opposed to cooperation, which is essentially rational and based on self-interest, altruism arises from an instinctive urge to help. As described earlier, it is strongest between people who are genetically closest. The family and the tribe, which can extend to a large political identity with a common language and culture, are perhaps subconsciously perceived as partial extensions of one's own identity, and can also be the object of one's own basic instincts for self-preservation. Efforts to loosely extend the notion of tribe to the whole species and, with a healthy dose of optimism, to other conscious creatures, can help to break down the barriers to altruism.[37]

Some of the conflict in values between different cultures relates to the differing relative importance of the individual and the group. In more individualistic cultures, there is greater emphasis on personal self-realization and on the individual having a great variety of experiences. But in cultures where an individual's sense of identity, well-being and meaning is more intricately tied to a larger entity, the good of the whole can be difficult to separate from that of its members. And in a very real way, people in less individualistic cultures assume less of a unique identity—reflected in a more homogeneous, less diverse range of experiences, memories and thoughts. At the extreme, people can act and be regarded like the tentacles of a single organism, shed if necessary to ensure the long-term survival of the whole— specifically, the community with which they share their genes and culture. In practice, this is what happens when soldiers' lives are sacrificed to defend the nation. Having them feel part of a larger entity is a very critical motivating factor for them to assume this risk. But this notion is also exploited in some countries where individuals are imprisoned, tortured or executed for "disturbing the public order" by daring to express opinions that differ from those officially imposed on the group.

---

37 This is a theme of economist and activist Jeremy Rifkin's book *The Empathic Civilization: The Race to Global Consciousness in a World in Crisis.*

This broader conception of identity also implies a very close similarity between making short-term sacrifices for longer-term gain, i.e. delayed gratification, and making sacrifices for other people. Delayed gratification implicitly means attributing some comparable degree of value to your future identity as to your present identity, while altruism means according some degree of value to others' identity. In both cases, you are sacrificing something in the present for the benefit of "someone else". From a detached, external perspective, the importance of subjectively experienced happiness should be independent of the sliver of space-time in which it occurs, i.e. whether it is you in the present, you in the future or someone else in the present or future. But of course, in practice we generally give highest priority to our present selves, while we are usually willing to make reasonable sacrifices in the present in favor of larger future gains, as this behavior has tended to be more successful in passing on one's genes.

In the end, understanding ourselves as repositories of genetic information trumps any other interpretation of identity in explaining our actual instinctive behavior, even if we consciously decide to attribute the greatest importance to subjective experience. The drivers of our behavior thus conflict with much of what matters upon broader reflection, and may take on an air of irrationality. For example, we aim for the survival of our near-future identities and, ideally, of our longer-term future identities, advocating indefinite life extension if possible, even if it no longer concerns the same exact person from the perspective of memories, character and physical appearance. Although defying death is the most natural urge, and not feeling it breathing down one's neck allows one to live with a certain tranquility, aiming for our own immortality is fundamentally not that different from aiming for the immortality of another human being.

"Why am I me and not someone else?"—i.e., why are the thoughts I am having happening *here* and not in someone else's brain—is a deeply existential question whose resolution illustrates, again, how different things are than our instinctive sense of identity makes it seem. Our very strong, evolutionarily determined tendency to identify ourselves with our physical body skews us away from recognizing that what we are experiencing at any moment could be experienced by anyone with a very similar brain architecture (and thus also having very similar memories of past experiences) and occupying the same physical location. At a given moment, I—my identity—, am *these* local sensory inputs impacting on *this* neural structure embodying specific memories and character traits. Again, I am ultimately just a pattern of information processing.[38] As discussed above regarding identical twins, the more similar the pattern to others, the greater the overlap in identity. The identical pattern generated by another brain could be seen as representing a momentarily equivalent manifestation of identity. Evolution has managed to hide from us a profound, essential truth about existence by making us favor our own bodies to an extent that we are blinded to the universality of subjective experience and our common identity.

Have you ever asked yourself why you are alive now and not some time in the past, for example, ten thousand years ago? This is another of those existential puzzles that you might once have tossed about in your head for a while before turning to a more gratifying activity. But the answer, which lies in the whole notion of identity as a pattern, is actually exceedingly mind-opening when you grasp it, unintuitive as it is. Although this might be your first guess, it is not that there are simply many more people around today, hence a higher probability of *you* existing. And it is not that you needed your specific mother and father and the specific egg and sperm that gave rise to you in order to exist at all—an extremely improbable thing to have happened. We think of ourselves as unique and our own existence as rare and miraculous. On a cosmic scale it may well be. But as we have been discussing, identity is not a black and white phenomenon, in spite of the entirely contrary way in which we are conditioned by our brains to perceive ourselves and everybody else. We share our identities to different extents with people alive today, with people who were alive in the past—from Aristotle to Audrey Hepburn—, and with people who will be alive in the future. In fact, there is even a partial overlap in identity with other kinds of conscious creatures. If it had been another sperm with another combination of genes fertilizing the same egg, someone with a similar but not identical identity would have taken your place. It wouldn't be you exactly, but it wouldn't entirely *not* be you, either. Our language, including such basic words as "I" and "you", reflects our instincts and how the world appears to us, not a deeper reality and the various shades of grey that it contains.

This entire perspective on identity may be highly counterintuitive at first, diametrically at odds with our overriding, instinctive sense of each

---

38 Cognitive and computer scientist Douglas Hofstadter offers a deep, mathematically tinged reflection on the meaning of "I", identity and consciousness in his book *I Am a Strange Loop*.

person as a distinct, self-contained entity with its own unique trajectory. But understanding identity in this way is the logical consequence of thinking about it, and also the only means of reconciling our subjective sense of uniqueness with a detached, objective understanding of everything else. And it becomes more evident when we allow certain aspects of reality to slip into our awareness.

Incidentally, this perspective also holds a key to understanding another existential mystery, namely, how it is, not only that the Earth has all the right parameters to support life, despite the extremely low odds of all the physical conditions (temperature, presence of water, chemical properties, etc.) being just right, but also that the physical constants of the universe—components of the laws of physics—are tuned just right within a very narrow tolerance range for life to have become possible—the so-called "Goldilocks Effect".[39] Although a very human answer is to say that someone must have created it so that the conditions were optimal, a simpler, entirely different answer is that we wouldn't be here otherwise. Any conscious, intelligent being that comes into existence is likely to ask such questions, regarding their own individual existence as a miracle and their identity as unique. But again, this is a subjectively felt illusion. If blades of grass had consciousness, the capacity for thought and the self-awareness that we do, each one would also be marveling at its own existence and asking the same questions—on Earth, and on any other planets in the universe where grass evolved. (This scenario recalls an old "The Far Side" cartoon by Gary Larson in which, in an Antarctic setting jam-packed with penguins, one of them in the middle is singing, "I gotta be me, oh I just gotta be me...") In fact, this reflection leaves wide open the possibility—perhaps even implies—that many other universes exist (or have existed) with very different physical constants, in most of which life failed to form. And in this particular one, we happen to have appeared. This unintuitive way of thinking about the world really does stretch the mind, and yet once you "get it", it all suddenly makes sense.

Still, the overlap in our identities with others by no means alters the fact that individual subjective experience remains the core locus of meaning and beauty. Any attempts by authorities to subjugate basic personal freedoms by appealing to the well-being of the amorphous whole give higher prior-

---

39 This term comes from the fairytale "Goldilocks and the Three Bears", in which the somewhat fastidious blonde-haired protagonist chooses porridge that is just the right temperature and a bed that has just the right degree of hardness.

ity to a concept—whether for misguided or malevolent intentions—than to real, flesh-and-blood, feeling human beings. Attributing importance to the whole as a *source* of meaning and security does not lessen the importance of individual consciousness. The popularized term "collective consciousness" is just a concept for explaining how many individual consciousnesses in a society can absorb the same ideas. Nothing can supersede the primacy of what goes on in individuals' minds.

If it is difficult to recognize that free will is an illusion and our thought patterns are the outcome of an intricate web of interactions, it is perhaps even more of a challenge to grasp the fuzziness of identity. Our identity is one of the things we value most highly, and putting the traditional notion into question collides with our instinctive sense of who we are. Viewing ourselves as patterns of mental states can seem literally dehumanizing if we find ourselves losing the thread that ties us to our past and future, and stopping to care as much about the things that matter most to us, even if from a purely metaphysical perspective this view is correct.[40] We still need to protect our sense of identity from disintegration in order for our lives to retain meaning and coherence in present moments. Philosophical ruminations should not be used to minimize the things we intrinsically care most deeply about.

But these reflections are of far more than just intellectual interest. Lying at the juncture of reflections about subjective experience and determinism, they are integral to a fuller understanding of the big picture. They offer deep insight into the ironies of the human condition and the relevance of others' suffering. In the right doses, they can also provide greater balance in how we find meaning in our own lives, and allow us more easily to shed aspects of our behavior that detract from our happiness. Because identity is ultimately best explained as a pattern, its relevance to life, consciousness and human existence may yet prove to be crucial in the near future as accelerating technology forces us to confront reality in ways that are difficult to predict, but which many thinkers are anticipating in potential scenarios, as discussed further on in the chapter "Where We Are Headed".

The identity illusion encapsulates our whole dilemma as a species: that the universe has bequeathed to us an innate urge to compete with variations

---

40 See, for example, an essay by philosopher Galen Strawson entitled "Why I have no future" that appeared in *TPM: The Philosophers' Magazine*, Issue 38 (October 12, 2009), http://www.philosophypress.co.uk/?p=726.

of ourselves—an urge that made us more efficient as we developed, with pain thrown in as a catalyst—rather than always cooperate in our collective interest. Every time one member of our species kills another, it is not just an extended form of fratricide, but in a metaphysical sense, a kind of suicide. Finding ways of effectively conveying the commonality in our identities— that we are, at our core, very similar, though with varying neurological dispositions and exposed to sometimes very different environments—may play an essential role in building empathy and reducing the tensions that lead to conflict. I see few things more important than encouraging people to step outside the boundaries of their own subjectively experienced, primary identities and explore others, seeking to respect and preserve beauty wherever it exists.

8. WHAT MATTERS?

To continue in our explorations, and in full awareness of the seeming naïveté of the exercise, let's now turn to that fundamental question that I referred to in the introduction: what matters? Virtually all of us have grappled with this question, and for all but the most solidly pragmatic and least philosophical of us, the question inevitably recurs as we go through life, experience bliss and pain, the passing of time, the kindness and cruelty of our fellow humans, the monotony of routine and the shock of unanticipated change, and reflect on our existence in this universe.

The question "what matters?" may seem as definitively unanswerable as "why am I here?" But how you answer the question reflects or determines your views on everything else and how you approach the other big questions. How people with influence implicitly answer it has huge ramifications for suffering on our planet and for the long-term well-being of its inhabitants. Without a clear, well-thought-out determination of what matters, it is impossible to adequately justify policies and courses of action as being any more than instinctive reactions to external events, or tactics to achieve specific, often self-serving goals, rather than part of a broader, coherent philosophy. As a question worth reflecting on, "what matters?" actually matters a lot.

Clearly, many things matter to individuals in their private lives, including close relationships with family and friends, good health, career, lifestyle, wealth, reputation, achievements, intellectual discovery, artistic expression, travel, adventure, gastronomy, community service, charity, religious affiliation, membership in organizations, hobbies, triumph over adversaries, sports, national pride, self-realization, sexual conquests, sensual and sensory pleasures, hedonism, spirituality, meditation, etc. But what matters in the broadest sense? And how do we find out? Is it what our parents told us as we were growing up? Does it lie in the wisdom of our teachers or professors? Our friends? Our religious or spiritual leaders? What journalists, news editors and radio and TV commentators devote their attention to? Politicians' speeches? The latest self-help bestseller? We easily absorb the values of everyone around us instead of thinking independently about the basis for them.

In the sense of the *very* big picture, nothing really seems to matter (unfortunately). At least not in the sense of the universe having a "purpose"—it just *is*, as far as we can tell. Its behavior is found to follow certain principles, and we can posit that there may be complexity elsewhere in the universe with characteristics strange beyond our imagination, but that is about as far as we can probably go in deciphering any larger meaning, at least with the knowledge we currently have. As hypothesized earlier, maybe there is consciousness existing at a higher level. Some computer scientists and physicists toy with some wild ideas, such as that our whole universe is actually a simulation on someone's very powerful computer. Maybe it is, and maybe there really is therefore a larger meaning. Maybe God is a junk-food-eating techie in a basement in another dimension, scoring points every time one of us registers a kill or, more likely, simply oblivious. Or maybe our universe is an infinitesimally small part of a larger entity with its own dynamics, with no beginning and no end. But even physicists and cosmologists have no obvious way of finding out for sure. For all practical purposes, our lives are dictated by the properties of a universe that are embodied in the laws of physics, regardless of how these came about, and nothing matters in a larger sense than that.

For some people that is inherently troubling, as we are by nature inclined to think of things coming about for a reason. But that is a trick that our minds play on us: we look for meaning and connections everywhere. That the universe may not have a larger meaning does not prevent our own lives from being full of purpose and meaning. Meaning is something that individuals and groups of individuals create and discover for themselves. We can understand how and why things happen without relating everything to a larger intent.

But still... Is there any way in which we can determine what matters in the largest sense possible, somewhere between the intense meaning of one's own subjective experience and the apparent meaninglessness of the universe? Will what matters always simply remain whatever we as individuals grew up to care about, under our various influences? Is there any larger sense in which things matter, at the scale of humanity, or does it all boil down to the exercising of the principle "might makes right"? Are there any universal reference points or values to guide our behavior, and if so, how do we find out what they are?

We have to accept that there is no way of reasoning about what matters without bootstrapping the process with some starting assumptions. But in contrast to mathematics, which is fully rooted in axioms that are universally recognized to be objectively valid, even though they cannot be rigorously proved (for example: $a + b = b + a$), judgments and assertions about meaning and values are also rooted in subjectivity. This fact is the arch nemesis of any attempt to build a solid system of ethics.

Simply stating that something matters will never give it objective validity. It just means that it is important to you, and to any larger group of people you identify with who care about the same things. The assertion can be a useful way of influencing others and making certain things matter to more people, but this still does not give it objective validity. This is a truth that we need to come to terms with so that our arguments in favor of a better world are as transparent as possible and our corresponding actions logically defensible. By voiding ourselves of opaque presuppositions, we can concentrate on just the core, essential truths and emotions that remain, and use those as a basis for our reasoning and actions.

I started writing this book with one primary purpose in mind: to explore how our preconceptions about the world interfere with the relief of suffering. I think that the overwhelming majority of people would agree in principle that suffering is, almost by definition, the biggest problem there is in the world, at the core of most of the big global issues we face. And it matters a lot to many people. Again, that fact in itself does not mean that it matters in an objective sense. I can only argue, from my own subjective point-of-view, that if anything at all matters in a more universal sense than just getting what I want, then it must somehow be related to others' well-being and, in particular, to the relief of others' suffering. We'll address suffering shortly, in the next chapter. But let's first reflect a little more on the central importance of subjective experience.

THE PRIMACY OF SUBJECTIVE EXPERIENCE

Ultimately, subjective experience—a conscious being's thoughts, emotions, perceptions and desires—must be at the heart of what matters. This is where meaning exists. Nothing else in this immensely vast universe that we are part of matters in and of itself. Everything in the physical world that matters relates to beings' subjective experience—how it makes them feel—, regardless of any illusion we may have that things matter in some sort of objective sense. Without subjective experience, nothing matters—by definition. There has to be someone or something *to whom* things matter. Analogously to Descartes's famously existential observation "I think, therefore I am", the all-importance of subjective experience is a self-evident truth that deserves axiomatic status. And it is the only reasonable point of departure in reflecting on what matters.

Acknowledging that subjective experience is the basis for all that matters by no means implies that we should minimize the existence and importance of the objective reality around us, the planet we live on and everything we do to shape our environment. But it means remembering why it all matters, in the end—something we easily lose track of, getting caught up in things rather than what they do for us internally, for our sense of meaning. I do not mean this here in the egoistic sense that the world only matters for what it does "for me", but more generally, that meaning always collapses down to individuals' subjective experience.

Consider, for example, the diversity of plant life on our planet. Many of us, recognizing the tremendous complexity and beauty that plants represent, as well as the functional role many of them play in specific ecosystems, value this diversity and support efforts to preserve it, including protecting plant species from extinction. Some individuals even feel a spiritual connectedness with plants, which are our very distant cousins (an additional reason to remember to water them more often). But as far as we know, plants do not have subjective experience, and therefore even the rarest and most beautiful of plants can only matter to things that do, not to themselves. (Of course, if plants really could feel pain, we would find ourselves faced with a deep existential dilemma on how to live compassionately.) If we seek to preserve diversity, it's because this is something we ourselves treasure.

While what matters always relates directly to people's subjective experience, to any individual, it is their *own* subjective experience that matters most. Here lies the root of most of our problems and of much of the suffering in the world. Our challenge—that of people who care about suffering—is to find ways of overcoming this obstacle, in part by finding ways of making *others'* subjective experience matter more, such as by exposing to people the commonality in our identities and giving them pleasure and meaning in feeling empathy.

The values and laws of Western democracies implicitly respect subjective experience in their utilitarian notions of general well-being. However, there are countless examples where, due to actual intent, residual laws and customs, or social phenomena, priority is placed elsewhere. Objects and concepts are attributed importance for their own sake without considering the consequences for anyone's subjective experience in more than the vaguest and thoughtless of ways.

Knowing that we are agents operating according to a sophisticated, high-level program running in each of our brains that tries to provide each of us with status and the ability to reproduce, we need to fully embrace scientific reflection and discovery to find ways of improving the parameters in which the program operates and enhance the quality of subjective experience. If we do not manage to place others' subjective experience at the center of what matters on a large enough scale, we will really then prove to be the equivalent of heartless robots, the vehicles and ultimately tragic victims of a dizzying increase in complexity occurring in the world.

Humanism is only in a narrow sense about extending certain legal rights to members of the same scientifically defined species, or about defending the underdogs in power struggles, or about ensuring human welfare. Implicitly and more broadly, it is about trying to place subjective experience smack at the center of what matters to a society. Unfortunately, humanism in many of its current institutionalized forms doesn't always retain this purity of purpose, losing much of its essence as it is diluted in the mechanics of international politics and bureaucracy, becoming just another cause among others, rather than the heart of what matters.

Subjective experience, wherever it exists, needs to be revealed as a critically important aspect of the truth, as significant as the truth about observable, objective reality. From this starting point, we can look in greater detail at what matters to people and reflect on its full significance. To the extent that it is relevant—and this concerns, at the very least, the avoidance of suffering—we also need to extend these reflections to any other entities with subjective experience. These detailed explorations are the subject of the next three chapters.

9. Avoiding the Abyss

Human Suffering

Finding happiness is a daily occurrence or the quest of a lifetime, depending on one's psychological makeup, personal circumstances, drives and desires. But virtually no one wants to suffer. To any unfortunate individual who is suffering intensely, this is what really matters, more than anything else. People have a higher tolerance for pain that they have control over, or that stems from situations they have voluntarily entered, but pain that is inflicted on them, due for example to disease or others' cruelty, can be unbearable.

For most of our history, humans have faced a constant struggle for survival, often living in harsh, competitive environments. Bloody conflicts and epidemics have been staple themes. Generation after generation, individuals have had to cope with the uncertainties of the world around them and the persistent threats of force and cruelty as they tried to eke out an existence. In less developed parts of the planet where disease and violence rule, people's lives are, today, still dominated by these same basic anxieties. Life has never been easy for the vast majority of humanity. The existence of each one of us, including those now living easy, comfortable lives within secure borders, is dependent on huge amounts of past suffering having occurred. This fact alone puts our current attempts to reduce suffering in perspective.[41]

Why does it actually matter so much to relieve other people's suffering? This is perhaps the fundamental question of ethics, and one of the central themes of this book. For someone who is naturally empathetic and acutely aware of what is going on in the world, the question is absurd. But simply saying that it is wrong not to do something about it is to beg the question: "why?" One would like—one might desperately want—to be able to provide an absolutely airtight, fully persuasive argument in favor of doing whatever is possible to eliminate at least the worst kinds of preventable suffering. The problem is, there isn't any such argument. A high-flying businessman living it up in the world's metropolises can perfectly well savor life while remaining immune to the world's suffering, and also impervious to any supposedly logical argument why he should care. If he is rationally self-interested, which, as mentioned earlier, economists assume—not always justifiably—people to be, and also constitutively cold-hearted, he may find that there is nothing in it for him in caring. End of argument. You may fume and deplore the callousness, but the power of reason will have brought you to a dead end.

In a universe where nothing "matters" and things just happen, the importance of relieving others' suffering cannot be proven. Unlike the self-evident importance of subjective experience to those having it, it is not even axiomatic. But it is as close as one can ever get in ethics, in a deep, intuitive way that most people would, in principle, fortunately agree with.

An ethical principle known as negative utilitarianism—a term coined by philosopher Karl Popper—explicitly places the emphasis of ethics on the minimization of suffering. This is not because promoting happiness does not matter. But the average level of happiness within a population says nothing about how happiness and suffering are distributed. Despite our tendency to think of positive and negative mental states as belonging on the same scale of hedonism, there is no reason to think that suffering and happiness, in the right proportions, can simply balance each other out. This is surely true for the individual: how many people would volunteer to be brutally tortured now in order to gain something for themselves in the future, how-

---

41   For an authoritative account of some of the recent atrocities humans have committed and an incisive analysis of the various factors that played a role, see Jonathan Glover, *Humanity: A Moral History of the 20th Century*.

ever substantial? Or would agree to go on living if this meant excruciating torture in a few years' time? This fundamental asymmetry between suffering and happiness is all the more relevant when it concerns different people, where one person suffering for another's indirect benefit cannot even anticipate future happiness as a personal reward. As succinctly distilled by philosopher David Pearce in *The Hedonistic Imperative*, a book-length web-based manifesto, "no amount of happiness or fun enjoyed by some organisms can notionally justify the indescribable horrors of Auschwitz." The principle of negative utilitarianism is an inevitable consequence of empathy, of an awareness of the real significance of others' subjective mental states. As a general principle, and avoiding absolutist interpretations of it that consider *any* amount of suffering bad[42], I believe that it is the essential, fundamental and ultimately most meaningful ethical stance from which to approach the issues we are faced with as a global society.

Negative utilitarianism implies that we "should" be prepared to take measures to relieve suffering, at least of the extreme kind, even if there is some cost. This principle is likely to be less popular among some who have been fortunate and talented enough to end up on the positive side of the happiness scale, as well as with extreme libertarians, as it seems to imply a need for the sacrifice of wealth and personal happiness. Fortunately, happiness and well-being need not be a zero-sum game, and this fact can be exploited by those seeking to relieve suffering, for example, by granting intangible yet real benefits such as recognition and respect to those who engage in altruism.

But let's continue and probe further the significance of relieving suffering and some of the psychological obstacles that exist. Try to consider the greatest pain, physical or emotional, that you have ever experienced. Can you remember its intensity and what it really felt like at the time? Have you ever been truly aware of what it means for someone else to undergo excruciating agony? Read or watched accounts of the worst forms of torture? Of life imprisonment in a tiny, dark, filthy jail cell? Of the pain caused by some of the worst untreatable diseases? Of the barbarities caused by soldiers? Of gang rapes? Imagine that it was a person close to you who had gone through any of these terrible experiences.

---

42 See www.utilitarianism.com/pinprick-argument.html for a discussion by David Pearce of the absurd consequences of absolutist interpretations, even if the alternative is an intellectually less "pure" ethical system.

Most of us have had moments of great happiness. Few of us have had the misfortune to be tortured. But because the closest access we can usually have to other people's subjective states requires us to have undergone similar experiences, for most of us, the word "torture", while firmly evil in its connotation, evokes images of the actual practices rather than the experience they induce in the victim.

If we were to look for examples of the worst atrocities committed by humans against other humans, the choice would be soberingly and depressingly vast. Some of the so-called "medical" experiments performed by the Nazis, including the infamous "Angel of Death" Josef Mengele, on concentration camp inmates are among the best documented. Victims, previously plucked from their homes where many of them had been living lifestyles familiar to many of us, were used as living guinea pigs and routinely forced to undergo surgical experiments without anesthetic, subjected to extreme conditions to measure their bodies' responses, exposed to diseases and toxic chemicals, and various other horrors, in a climate of absolute terror. And reading about the varied torture devices and techniques used during the Spanish Inquisition and at other times throughout history, including under recent and current totalitarian regimes, it is difficult to accept that human beings built just like us are capable of such vicious sadism. Yet without being exposed to such a situation oneself, one probably cannot fully imagine just what any of these countless torture victims were actually forced to endure, and why it is so crucially important that such acts not be allowed to happen.

The narrative that humanity has been passing on for generations, that conflict, war and pain are an inevitable part of life—sometimes related with almost fond nostalgia in reminiscences of historical battles or, more recently, of ordinary people's valiant struggles against dictatorships, depicted almost romantically in grainy black-and-white footage from Latin America in the 1970s and accompanied by melancholic Spanish music—is the tale told by the robust or fortunate ones who escaped serious harm, and by the next generations. The wartime rape victim with a vacant gaze has not a hint of romanticized detachment in her voice, nor does the soldier who has seen his buddies blown to bits by a roadside bomb. The glorification of war is not exercised by those who suffered or fell victim.

In a way, it is simply too difficult to come to terms emotionally with both the amount and the degree of suffering taking place on our planet. Our problem is not simply an inability to experience empathy, but the cognitive dissonance between our desire to enjoy life and an awareness of how intense others' suffering is. The tendency to block out the rest of the world once the television is turned off, to act as if the suffering out there exists only vaguely or in some abstract way that is not connected to our immediate lives, is a kind of solipsism and yet understandable. We would be paralyzed by inaction if we felt empathy every time we encountered suffering.

But we are also confronted with another manifestation of the phenomenon I call compression, where the values at the extreme ends of a scale are not properly appreciated or understood for their true significance. For example, the scale for measuring the strength of earthquakes is logarithmic, which means that an earthquake with a magnitude of 9.0, such as the one that ravaged parts of Japan in March 2011, actually has 10 times the amplitude of one that measures 8.0 and 1,000 times the amplitude of one that measures 6.0. Humans have trouble intuitively grasping how values can climb so quickly as you go up such a scale. The problem is all the greater when it relates to the subjective experience of pain, for which we usually just have language to guide us. Because most people have never had to endure excruciating suffering, they don't grasp its full significance.

Suffering is not divisible into discreet units: many people suffering a little is not equivalent to a few people suffering a lot. One person suffering intensely, such as at the hands of a torturer, is qualitatively different and, logically, incomparably worse than a million people suffering from a mild hangover. This may seem an obvious fact, yet there are examples to the contrary, such as a proposed multipliable unit of pain termed the "dukkha". The priorities we set also do not always reflect this fact, perhaps because one million people with headaches have greater political and economic power than one torture victim. But if we grasped its significance more viscerally, our highest priority would be to ensure that no one experience preventable suffering beyond a certain degree. Some things should never, ever be allowed to happen. A truly compassionate system of ethics would insist that this is the one thing that really matters above all else.

Those trying to relate what they endured under sadistic totalitarian regimes do their best, stringing words together in the hope that these will give others a glimpse. The books that relate these horrors take for granted that their depravity will be perceived as such by the reader. Some things are assumed to be so obvious that they are left unstated. But we often just don't get it. And our senses become dulled by repeated exposure to the media, the acts themselves becoming banalized. The statements of some politicians, even in democracies, that play down the horror of torture or attempt to nuance it are hardly a supportive contribution.

Additionally, those who were tortured or treated with abominable cruelty and lived to tell about it tend not to stand out physically, and they are often able to describe their experience with calm and lucidity. It's easy to think that while the experience must have been terrible, all's well that ends well—as if the person's return to freedom and a physically pain-free existence somewhat mitigates the significance of the pain they had to endure at the time.

Survivors of torture or other terrible suffering are like first-hand observers, trying to communicate vivid memories that continue to haunt them. As mentioned earlier in the chapter on identity, the actual victims somehow reside in the past, and the intensity of the subjective experience can be next to impossible for the survivors themselves to adequately relate.

Every instant counts. It's just that the past is no longer under our control. Reconciliation and firmly moving forward towards a brighter future require that guilt and regret not have a crippling hold on the present. But the past happened, and it mattered then as much as the present does now. Our challenge is to prevent such pasts from belonging to the future, and for that, we need to keep the intense memory of those pasts alive.

French-Colombian politician Ingrid Betancourt, held hostage for over 6 years in the jungles of Colombia, said regarding a play she initially planned to create, "Those who will see what I experienced will understand that we must be careful never to fall into this abyss."[43] There are limits to the usefulness of language to faithfully evoke a sense of what a victim endured, information delivered as words often being insufficient to trigger the extreme ends of the emotional scale. That is why Betancourt, soon after her release, turned her thoughts to other effective media, such as performance art, that could more fully communicate the nightmare she lived through (although she eventually did write a memoir in book form, *Even Silence Has an End*).

Surely the atrocities going on right now, hidden from view in foreign countries, matter as much as similarly great suffering caused by Nazi death camp doctors. If we knowingly allow people to suffer and die when we could

---

43 "Betancourt plans play on ordeal," BBC (6 July 2008), http://news.bbc.co.uk/2/hi/7492144.stm.

do something about it with relatively little sacrifice on our part, we bear an uncomfortable similarity in our behavior to passive populations that, in the past, closed their eyes to genocide occurring practically in their backyard. And we expose as hypocritical any grand claims to morality. In the face of continuing terror and the emergence of new threats we cannot control, we easily become prey to the phenomenon of learned helplessness[44] and shut ourselves off from reality. But by absorbing ourselves in the microenvironments of our own lives and shunning information that we find unpleasant and that might make us feel compelled to act, we are nonetheless "guilty" of inaction. Finding ways of breaking down these barriers is therefore our ultimate challenge.

At this point in our reasoning, we are, of course, no longer describing objectively how people actually tend to act under certain circumstances, but allowing subjectively felt compassion to take over and drive the argument. And it must. If the avoidance of suffering is not regarded as a fundamental priority, then we are putting the satisfaction of our own desires above higher principles, essentially doing what we can get away with. For anyone with a shred of idealistic passion, pure self-interest cannot be tolerated as the sole determinant of how a society or the world is allowed to operate, as it implies that might indeed makes right, and what cannot defend itself— whether minority populations, inhabitants of small countries, human rights activists or non-human creatures we use for our pleasure—may be made or allowed to suffer, potentially excruciatingly, without consequence.

ANIMAL SUFFERING

In a world in which human beings are still tortured, massacred, and left to die of disease and malnutrition, some would claim that it is a serious confusion in our priorities to focus too much attention on the welfare and suffering of other conscious beings. I used to receive anti-vivisection tracts in my mailbox, and I found it irritating how, to advance their cause, the authors spuriously denied the objective contributions of animal experimentation to very real medical advances that have prevented the suffering and deaths of countless human beings. Even today, if I am to be honest, were it my own child who was suffering from a terrible genetic disease for which

---

44 Learned helplessness is a psychological term that describes how humans and animals, having learned that they are unable to avoid a painful situation, fail to adapt their behaviors when the situation changes, falsely believing they are still impotent to exert control.

animal experimentation could help develop a treatment, I dare say I would still downplay the significance of the well-being of a few mice.

The problem is, suffering is still suffering. Pain and extreme distress that occur on the other side of the species barrier can be equivalent to what we ourselves are capable of feeling. Yet the conscious experience of animals is often largely ignored as a relevant item of consideration when we decide on our priorities. While an anthropomorphic view of animals that was once fashionable among scientists studying animal behavior was criticized during much of the 20th century both for the arrogance of using ourselves as a model for how animals think and feel, as well as for a lack of objectivity—a trend that has since reversed with recent scientific insights into the emotional world of various animal species—, it is arguably more arrogant to deny that other creatures have a similar capacity to suffer.

We don't know exactly how other living creatures experience suffering—we have enough trouble empathizing with the suffering of our fellow humans. But the assertion that they don't feel pain in the same way that we do, expressed even by many scientists eager to carry out their experiments, is simply untenable. For a wide range of animals, the contrary is likely to be true. Simply disregard the feathers, fur or scales and the inability to compose music and conduct abstract thought, and focus on the ancient, evolutionarily useful functions that we share with other animals—which undoubtedly include pain perception and distress. Indeed, aside from the many published studies demonstrating the cognitive capabilities of animals very different from us, numerous other studies suggest that even much simpler creatures are able to feel pain. Furthermore, while humans can develop rational coping mechanisms to deal with their own suffering, most animals are probably far more helpless when faced with distress they cannot avoid. With subjective experience so difficult to infer and document and yet as real as anything else in the universe, we take a stand that is both cavalier and intellectually dishonest in minimizing its significance in creatures other than ourselves.

The subjective experience of suffering by any creature, regardless of its phylogenetic[45] classification—whether it is a cow, a fish, a rodent or a crustacean—, must be as inherently worthy of avoidance as a similar quality and intensity of suffering in humans. To suggest otherwise would mean that,

---

45 The term "phylogenetic" refers to the evolutionary relationship between organisms.

in fact, it is not others' subjective experience itself that really matters, but how it makes us feel as observers, and that whatever we don't worry about doesn't actually matter. And there, we are back to the egoism of pure self-interest. If torture is considered so horrible an experience to endure that it is banned by international treaty in even extreme wartime situations, why should the imposition of any similar experience on any creature other than humans be any more justifiable? If one agrees that intense human suffering should be avoided for its own sake, then logic and consistency imply that other creatures' intense suffering must matter as well. And yet, the intensity of concern and discussion about "mainstream" sources of suffering like torture and massacres committed against humans drops off dramatically when the focus shifts to cruelty to animals.

Not all animals display suffering with the grimace or high-pitched yelp or cry we would recognize. The cues may be different or imperceptible to humans but the suffering equally present and equally intense. For example, an article describing the discomfort of whales exposed to U.S. Navy sonar exercises mentioned various analogies, such as "having a highway built next to your house, having a jet land next door, or standing next to a rocket blasting off."[46] And frequently, in articles about the harm done to animals such as whales, references to environmental concerns and biological diversity often eclipse concerns about the actual subjective experience of the animals in question and the core issue of suffering.

The fact that pain and suffering are integral elements of nature does not make them any less relevant an issue. There is currently no conceivable way of preventing the pain that is naturally inflicted on animals by other non-human animals (although David Pearce, one of the most compassionate and idealistic philosophers reflecting on these issues, advocates the future bio-engineering of nature as a way out). But it is nothing less than terribly cruel to be a knowing perpetrator oneself, and tragically callous to play the role of a deaf, dumb and blind accomplice. If one is logically consistent, then accepting the above reasoning requires adapting one's behavior accordingly. But since the conclusions require sacrifices that many people do not want to make, the issue is sheepishly skirted. Suffering is so seemingly ethereal and intangible that it is convenient to pretend it doesn't exist. Even as adults,

---

46 Nick Anthis, "Supreme Court to Address Navy Sonar Exercises", *ScienceBlogs* (24 June 2008), http://scienceblogs.com/scientificactivist/2008/06/supreme_court_sonar.php#more.

we act in a way that is reminiscent of children who think that when they close their eyes no one can see them. We shift our attention away and—poof!—that reality vanishes.

Let me provide a concrete example from personal experience. I grew up an omnivore, and I very much liked foie gras once I discovered it as an adult. Animal rights activists often disparage it as diseased liver, but from a purely sensory point of view, I shared the common perception of it as a culinary delight. Although I had many times heard the claim that force-feeding is cruel, I didn't initially believe that simply putting excess food in a duck or goose's stomach was in itself such a bad thing, and I was sure I had seen footage of seemingly happy, free range geese on a foie gras production farm, waddling over to the farmer to be fed.

Then I discovered the reality. The majority of foie gras production is performed industrially in a setting that, were these humans and not birds, would be called a torture chamber. The birds spend their lives in narrow cages where they can scarcely move, and at regular intervals they are grabbed by the neck and long metal pipes are shoved roughly down their throats. Videos are visible on YouTube (type "foie gras cruelty") that are simply shocking for the callousness displayed towards birds' visible suffering, both from physical pain and general distress. While it is convenient for the pursuit of one's own pleasures to ignore this evidence, maintain that the birds do not suffer or insist that their suffering is irrelevant—and many people, even aware of the evidence, will affirm, "but it tastes so good"—, for someone otherwise capable of empathy, this stand reflects an unwillingness to think rationally and independently and to apply one's principles consistently. The consequences of many people holding this position are horrific.

But industrial foie gras production is just one notorious example. The pitiful conditions under which so-called farm animals are raised industrially by the *billions* and eventually slaughtered for food are meant by the meat industry to be kept out of the public eye, but they have been well documented and the cruelty exposed. The skinning *alive* of furry animals in some countries, including China, is another documented phenomenon, videos of which are too appalling to watch. There are many others. Even when farm animals are well treated during their lives, slaughter is usually carried out in a violent manner and anticipated by the animal during its last moments[47]—a far cry from the way pets suffering from terminal illnesses are gently euthanized.

The issue of animal suffering is distinct from the question of whether animals ought to be killed altogether, and it is important that we not confuse the two, even if they are sometimes closely related. The very idea that humans take the lives of animals, though itself a valid topic of often heated debate, has to be the secondary concern. The fact that the animal kingdom from which we evolved is a constitutively brutal network, and that throughout our history, right up to the present day, we have been killing other animals for food, clothing and other purposes, are by no means a sufficient rationalization for continuing the practice. We are not bound to perpetually kill just because we have always done so. But realistically, as a species, we are (still) very far from transforming ourselves into pacifist vegans with a generalized moral view that taking the life of any conscious creature is wrong. When carried out under the most humane conditions—admittedly a rarity—, an animal life can, in theory, be wiped out in an instant with no warning or physical pain and thus no suffering and little consequence, other than for any human or animal survivors emotionally attached to that individual being. While it is cruel to cause conscious beings to dread having their life extinguished by others, most animals' reduced understanding of their situation puts them on a rather different level than humans. Ethicist, humanist and animal rights activist Peter Singer has argued strongly against "speciesism"[48]—discrimination against non-human species—, but such a case is most convincing when it concerns respecting animals' equivalent subjective experience, rather than evoking any intrinsic right they have to die of old age or predation.

The adoption of veganism out of principle—the refusal to kill or exploit other sentient beings—is at least as much a reflection of how *we feel about ourselves*, about our relationship to the rest of the world, and about life. It represents a refusal to ultimately betray the implicit trust felt by a domestic animal towards its caretaker, regardless of whether it ever becomes aware that this trust will be betrayed. Conceptually, the vegan movement also helps keep our moral compass pointed in the right direction by pressing us

---

47 James McWilliams, "Eating (Synthetic) Animals," *The Atlantic* (June 2010), www.theatlantic.com/food/archive/2010/06/eating-synthetic-animals/58930.

48 See his influential book *Animal Liberation*.

to become less permissive about killing animals rather than more permissive about killing humans.

Obviously, these are not minor considerations, and they bring us back to fundamental questions about our own humanity, the limits of compassion, and even the extent of our "right" to assert our existence and take pleasure in it. There are no clear, absolute answers to these questions, regardless of activists' insistence on the contrary. But reducing cruelty to animals—a practical consequence of veganism—is more directly about how *they feel* and is thus the principal ethical concern.

Of course, in reality, the way most animals are slaughtered makes the distinction between suffering and killing a moot one and can blur the line between us and them to the point of insignificance. Shunning the niceties of trying to make such a distinction and taking a strong, principled stance about any use of animals is clearly the most compassionate attitude, although for advocacy efforts, it is important that the core issue of reducing suffering not be diluted.

The extent of suffering inflicted by humans on animals is unfathomable.[49] Because it is so widespread and commonplace, it is all the more difficult to come to terms with how bad it really is, as this would force us to acknowledge that we have been making a terrible mistake all along, and that our belief in ourselves as good people reflects a devastating, though often unintentional, hypocrisy. The use of animals as objects is so entrenched in human cultural practices around the world that to step aside and see things objectively requires almost a Copernican paradigm shift. We cannot change the past. But we can change the future.

NON-BIOLOGICAL SUFFERING

Compared to the very real suffering of millions and millions of flesh and blood humans and animals, it may really appear a needless distraction to evoke the suffering of other entities. We think of consciousness as unique to the animal kingdom, and the idea that technology could create new forms of consciousness might seem to belong to the world of science fiction. But this concern is neither fanciful nor irrelevant. There is endless attention paid to artificial intelligence—essentially, the ability of machines to manipulate and create information—but comparatively little regarding any subjective experience associated with this intelligence. As discussed earlier in the sec-

49 For further insight, see www.meat.org.

tion on consciousness, we still don't know what kind of wiring it takes to produce subjective experience, such as pain. But as computers and intelligent networks become ever more complex, it is not inconceivable that one day—and we cannot be absolutely sure that this has not already happened—they really will become conscious in some way.

Sooner than we think, we may be creating conscious inorganic beings with locked-in syndrome—having some form of subjective experience which they are unable to communicate to others. Perhaps a computer would only be so for brief moments at a time as it carries out calculations, like a drugged human continually drifting into and out of consciousness, without any change in outward appearance and without anyone ever knowing. If it doesn't feel pain or boredom, perhaps it won't matter so much. But the technological evolution of new beings that have the capacity to suffer should not be ignored as we learn more about the physical correlates of human consciousness. Again, we may never know with absolute certainty if they are conscious, since consciousness cannot be directly observed, only inferred from observations that might correlate with it. But there could be "someone" there inside—perhaps not even a thinking mind, but a center of pure pain perception—, and what we consider as mechanical tools might turn out to be suffering beasts of burden.

Except for some of the religiously devout, most of us do not fear eternal damnation, the prospect of a human being suffering forever and ever. However miserable one's existence, death at least brings an end to suffering, and this thought may, perversely, also make it more bearable. Endless suffering may seem like an abstract concept, but if you are unable to imagine being kept in a tiny cell and subjected to gruesome torture day after day, then, more mundanely, think back to the worst hangover you have ever had—a splitting headache and nausea which you desperately wished would stop—and imagine that it continued forever. We joke about hangovers because they are the short-lived price paid for hedonistic excesses, but the grin would rapidly disappear if a hangover never ended.

Something like it could happen. Counterintuitive as it may sound, it is entirely within the sphere of plausibility to create an artificial conscious being that would suffer the most intense distress for what felt like eternity. Even if it was not our intention, by creating electronic circuits with an architecture similar to humans' neural circuits, we might inadvertently or indifferently cause tremendous, subjectively experienced chronic pain of which we were entirely oblivious. And because the subjective experience of time might actually be greatly expanded in proportion to the number of calculations performed per second, during even a very short passage of time these electronic beings might suffer terrible pain for what subjectively felt to them like an extremely long duration. What could possibly be more horrible? A computer that feels and one that doesn't would probably differ only in the specific wiring of their circuitry and their code. These differences might, of course, be enormous, but they might also be bridged very easily.

Imagine we discovered, through the careful scientific mapping of our own neural hardware, using high resolution brain imaging and other approaches, and extrapolations from it, that some types of computers were almost undoubtedly conscious and experienced pain. Would we stop using them? Indeed, a recent scientific paper found "striking similarities" in the organization of human brains, the nervous system of the nematode worm, and computer chips, further supporting the possibility that computers could experience pain.[50]

The last reflection is part of a broader question of supreme importance: is there any point on the scale of suffering that would, if we were aware of conscious beings subjected to it, cause us to drop whatever we were doing and come to their rescue? The evidence from our current behavior is not encouraging. It is likely that the reality of extreme suffering will only ever have a vague meaning to most of us, like the perception of the color blue to a blind person, or bats' perception of sonar to a human[51]. The phenomenon of compression may prevent us from perceiving the full significance of further increments in the scale beyond our usual range of perception. Intellectually, we have enough information about pain to draw appropriate conclusions about what should never be permitted to happen. The deeper problem may be that self-interest and the avoidance of cognitive dissonance may once again cause us to ignore what the facts tell us.

In the chapter "Where We Are Headed", I discuss the predicted overtaking of biological intelligence by non-biological intelligence in a few decades. Although the focus of a visionary book I refer to that makes this

---

50 See "Chips, worms and gray matter: More similar than you think," *e! Science News* (22 April 2010), http://esciencenews.com/articles/2010/04/22/chips.worms.and. gray.matter.more.similar.you.think.

51 Philosopher Thomas Nagel's classic paper "What is it like to be a bat?" addresses the inaccessibility of other creatures' subjective experience. Available at http:// organizations.utep.edu/Portals/1475/nagel_bat.pdf.

prediction is on intelligence and, somewhat more implicitly, on consciousness, directly associated with these developments is the likelihood of non-
biological suffering. The implications of these developments seem not yet to
have been thoroughly explored, but the possibilities are potentially terrifying. The wrong kind of electronic intelligence in a position of power could
intentionally cause the worst kind of suffering imaginable. Preventing this
from ever happening sounds like the kind of challenge worthy of a futuristic
Hollywood action film, but we are already on the edge of the future.

SUFFERING BEYOND OUR REACH

If the universe is as complex, vast or strange as many physicists believe,
there may be a lot more suffering going on than meets the eye. A cruel joke
the universe may be playing on us is that the amount of suffering we are
confronted with may be the tiniest fraction of what's out there. Renowned
cosmologist Carl Sagan apparently raised the whimsical but thought-pro-
voking suggestion that the atoms in our universe could contain an infinite
series of smaller universes within themselves, and that our universe might
be a minuscule component of an infinite series of larger universes, which
would also imply that an infinite amount of suffering is occurring. Less hy-
pothetically, gazing out at the evening sky and at a minuscule fraction of
the stars that our known universe contains, one can imagine that there may
be huge amounts of unknowable suffering going on and being perpetrated
in the cosmos on any number of life-bearing planets where conscious creatures commit horribly cruel acts upon each other. And the theory of multiple parallel universes would just amplify everything by orders of magnitude.

These contemplations make our own lives and reflections appear very
small and insignificant indeed. Attempts to relieve the suffering of humans
living in distant parts of our own planet, placed into a broader context, may
really appear part of an infinitely Sisyphean task. A metaphorical image
comes to mind, inspired by a scene from Soviet director Andrei Tarkovsky's
classic film "Stalker", of two despondent characters in a gloomy, industrial wasteland, standing thigh-deep in a huge cesspool of toxic, radioactive
sludge, each armed with just a bucket and with the task of cleaning it all up.
Where do you start? When do you stop? And why bother altogether if there
is no end in sight?

Of course, it is also possible that we really may be alone in a unique universe, with life actually being the rarest of flukes. One might have expected,

as Martin Rees has written, that at least one intelligent civilization would have built self-replicators that spread throughout our galaxy and made contact with us. Then again, intelligent life may always be a very short-lived phenomenon, wherever it arises. We just do not know.

Even keeping our sights fixed on our own planet, the situation is rather grim.[52] There is a huge amount of unavoidable suffering occurring among humans and throughout the animal kingdom, much of it terribly intense, for which even our best efforts would be impotent. In fact, our very existence, even that of the most compassionate pacifists, might inevitably cause suffering of unknown intensity among countless insects and other small invertebrates we tread on unknowingly as we go about our daily lives.

If you were entirely consistent in applying the principle that we must prevent all extreme suffering that we can, you might reach the conclusion that, as intelligent human beings, we have a duty to destroy the Earth so that no more such suffering takes place, in the way that we kill an injured animal in order to put it out of its misery, or that we allow euthanasia on an adult who wishes to be spared continued suffering from an incurable disease. Essentially, pulling the plug on the planet in an act of collective empathy.

I am the first to admit that that scenario sounds absolutely mad. Because this frightening conclusion is another seeming consequence of rigorously applying negative utilitarianism, some philosophers have concluded that this ethical principle itself is wrong and dismissed it altogether. Their argument is not entirely baseless. But if you aim for logical consistency and, presumably, you don't want to destroy the Earth, must you then conclude that all the otherwise unavoidable, intense suffering that occurs is "tolerable"? This may be the ultimate paradox haunting the humanist, struggling for compassion but striving for existence.

But the more subtle and, perhaps, "reasonable" answer is that, however bad some suffering is, we can aim to do our best to reduce the preventable kind, but categorically refuse to intentionally destroy the planet and eliminate ourselves and everything we care about in the process, even if it demands putting up with all the residual suffering that occurs. There is no logical requirement to treat negative utilitarianism as a simplistic dogma and extend it to its most absolute limit, where it requires the destruction

---

52 See www.utilitarian-essays.com for essays on wild animal suffering and attempts to reduce suffering in general.

of life. Value systems are grounded partly in emotions, and even a compassionate humanist or humanitarian activist can have a deep desire to see life continue. To clarify this position and distinguish it from absolutist variations, we could call the principle "negative utilitarianism *plus*". We'll come back to these reflections soon.

10. Satisfaction

Happiness

Obviously, people want to be happy and not just free of suffering. This fact matters not only for its own sake and for the pursuit of any utopian world made up entirely of blissful inhabitants, but also because people's quest for happiness often comes at the expense of others' suffering. Pragmatic approaches to relieving suffering therefore require determining and creating conditions that meet people's desire for happiness in a way that is not overly detrimental to others and, ideally, leveraging their pursuit of happiness in a way that actually helps relieve others' suffering.

Happiness is more difficult to define than less positive emotions like sadness, boredom, or anxiety. It is something of a blanket term used to refer to a spectrum of emotional states that can range from the void of deep meditation to the ecstatic heights of major achievement. The term is also used to try to reflect the average of many momentary emotional states over a period of time, or the general level of contentedness with one's life. For this reason, self-reporting about happiness is inevitably imprecise, as is the general use of the term in the media and even in many academic articles.[53] Studies involving large enough numbers of people can, however, still make

---

53 In this excellent TED talk, Nobel laureate Daniel Kahneman explains the significant difference between happiness as we experience it and happiness as our memories perceive it: www.ted.com/talks/daniel_kahneman_the_riddle_of_experience_vs_memory.html.

comparisons and draw meaningful conclusions based on average reported happiness levels, provided one is clear about what is being measured.

Regardless of the actual quality and nature of happiness, it can be understood at a basic level as the satisfaction that comes from having one's physical and emotional needs fulfilled, and also the confidence in being able to continue to fulfill these needs. It is therefore a combination of living in and appreciating the present moment, something of a Buddhist concept, and feeling in control of one's own future, more of a libertarian notion.

The present moment can yield happiness in sublime ways, such as through close connections to others, or by entering the state of "flow" described by psychologist Mihaly Csikszentmihalyi, where one is fully absorbed in an activity in which one feels self-realized. More banally, simply having one's brain constantly occupied—a state of being that seems increasingly common as our lives become ever more absorbed by the latest technologies and the range of products that use them—may also be enough to produce a subjective experience of happiness, although this is a fairly meaningless way of existing that, in the long run, may lead to a sense of emptiness.

Because the actual fulfillment of one's needs depends to a large extent on self-confidence, on the feeling of being capable of aligning one's future, including in the very short term, with one's desires, the illusion of free will can be critical for achieving happiness, both for the subjective sense of control over one's destiny that it permits and for actually achieving what one wants. As discussed earlier, this is perhaps the main reason that thinking about the big picture and how our thoughts and actions are dependent on everything else can be so frightening to people, as it seems to remove their subjective sense of control over their lives.

There is, of course, no definitive pathway to happiness. Each person's individual character, life experience and opportunities define their interests and the lifestyle they gravitate towards. People with relatively uneventful lives tend to derive a contented form of happiness from the comfort of routine and personal relationships, while those living in more hectic environments may live a perpetual adventure involving a quest for excitement, significance and recognition.

Although most of us would not want to live in a society that defines how we should be happy, there are various contributing factors that progressive societies take for granted as being universal, such as a healthcare system that meets people's needs, a sense of physical security, a minimum income or level of well-being, recreational opportunities, an efficient infrastructure and basic personal freedoms. Some degree of stability is an essential element in people's lives, with familiar situations and environments providing a sense of comfort, predictable risks and the ability to anticipate future pleasures.

The psychologist Abraham Maslow devised a well-known hierarchical system, often represented as a pyramid, depicting people's needs in order of priority, starting from the most basic material needs such as water and food, through to a sense of belonging, up to the highest level needs for self-actualization. The more of one's needs that are taken care of, the greater the degree of happiness one is likely to experience, as the subjective experience of happiness is integrally related to such factors as physical and emotional comfort, a sense of meaning, diversity of experience and status. The emotional comfort and sense of meaning that can be conferred by marriage and religion can explain why studies find these two factors correlating so strongly with happiness.[54] People's sense of belonging to a larger group is often an important part of their identity and source of meaning. Another key message from Maslow's hierarchical system is that we tend constantly to be striving for more, and even those occupying the highest level in the hierarchy are continuously searching for self-actualization and meaning.

It is an observed facet of human nature that, within a given community or society, people with more tend to be happier than those with less. Conventional wisdom holds that it is simply a matter of absolute wealth: the more you have, the happier you are. But since the 1970s, conventional wisdom has been turned upside down with evidence that the determining factor is actually *relative* wealth. Happiness levels were found to correlate poorly with income in international comparisons among either rich countries or poor countries, and tend not to increase within countries over time, despite rises in income—a phenomenon known as the Easterlin paradox after its discoverer, economist Richard Easterlin.[55] Happiness clearly depends on absolute wealth if your basic needs are not assured, and poverty is one of the greatest causes of unhappiness. But beyond the level of

---

54 The Pew Research Center has carried out numerous studies over the years tracking happiness trends and their determinants. See http://pewresearch.org.

55 See Carol Graham's article "The Economics of Happiness" in *The New Palgrave Dictionary of Economics*, also available at www3.brookings.edu/views/papers/graham/2005graham_dict.pdf.

basic needs, it seems that far more important is how you perceive what you have in relation to your neighbors and everyone else—and, implicitly, how you think they perceive you. A photo accompanying an article I once came across on this topic showed a shantytown juxtaposed next to an affluent housing development from which it was separated by a fence, powerfully capturing the essence of relative wealth. Being at the bottom rung of society, especially with little perspective on how to become upwardly mobile, is a match for even sophisticated positive thinking techniques.

A recent study in the United States probed more deeply into the effect of money on happiness, dissecting happiness into two components.[56] It found that "emotional well-being"—the quality of momentary experiences of emotion such as joy and anger—actually plateaus at a certain income level (about $75,000). Beyond that point, money does not actually seem to buy more of these positive emotions. However, "life evaluation"—how satisfied people feel *about* their life—continues to increase steadily with income, provided that income data are plotted on a log, rather than linear, scale. This last, seemingly minor detail illustrates how critical it is to plot data appropriately in order to discern relationships. The log scale is needed here because an extra $1,000 of income is clearly more significant to someone making $20,000 a year than to someone making $200,000 a year. It is the *percentage* increase that matters.

In fact, when international comparisons of life satisfaction are also plotted on this kind of graph, part of the Easterlin paradox itself no longer seems to hold: there is a clear and steady increase in life satisfaction as one moves from the poorest to the richest countries.[57] But this does not mean that relative wealth is unimportant. As economist Angus Deaton, the study's author, suggests, citizens of rich and poor countries likely compare their life situation with global reference points. Life satisfaction still seems to depend on how well you feel you are doing in life compared to others. And the fact remains that happiness levels in the United States and other countries have

---

56 Daniel Kahneman and Angus Deaton, "High income improves evaluation of life but not emotional well-being," *PNAS* (6 September 2010). Available at www.princeton.edu/-deaton/downloads/deaton_kahneman_high_income_improves_evaluation_August2010.pdf.

57 Angus Deaton, "Income, Health, and Well-Being Around the World: Evidence From the Gallup World Poll," *Journal of Economic Perspectives*, Volume 22, Number 2 (Spring 2008). Available at www.gallup.com/se/File/127634/AngusDeaton_Whitepaper.pdf.

not increased over the decades, despite a steady increase in income.[58] The world may be getting steadily wealthier, but it is not at all clear that it is becoming happier.

Considering that competition and the striving for status are behaviors so deeply hardwired into our brains, it should hardly come as a surprise to find that people are happier when they have more than others. While studies can try to determine more precisely the relationship between wealth and happiness, it would be very strange if they yielded results totally at odds with what we know about basic human nature.

Neither should it be a surprise to find only a limited correlation between absolute wealth and happiness. The absolute wealth or income of our cave-dwelling and hunter-gatherer ancestors, and of remote rural tribes today, would be minor compared to today's developed societies, if standardized to a present-day currency. Yet who would honestly claim that a tribesperson living a primitive existence within a tight, supportive society would rate themselves less happy than would a stressed, if well-paid, urbanite working long hours for a slave-driving corporate boss?

We are increasingly good at using new technologies not only to occupy ourselves but to tinker with our brains' and our bodies' existing pleasure centers to trigger the high ends of our hedonic scale at will. Bungee and BASE jumping provide intense but controlled, pleasurable adrenaline rushes without the inconvenience of having to go to battle. Synthetic chemicals can yield uniquely euphoric mental states. Electronic music can be crafted in a way that precisely triggers specific emotional states or moods. And a device popularized in the TV series "Sex and the City" has (apparently) given pleasure to countless women in a way that Mother Nature herself never dreamed possible. But some of the strongest, most fundamental determinants of happiness—those that affect how people feel about their lives—have not changed over the millennia.

There is another, less obvious though related point. This is that what people want is not, itself, necessarily what makes them happy. The trick that evolution has played on us in order to keep us competitive is to design brains for which happiness is attained in part by pursuing a carrot dangling always just a little out of reach. We get a taste often enough to provide

---

58 Alok Jha, "Happiness doesn't increase with growing wealth of nations, finds study," guardian.co.uk (13 December 2010), www.guardian.co.uk/science/2010/dec/13/happiness-growing-wealth-nations-study.

pleasure, but never enough to stop us in our tracks. The constitutive desire to innovate and a fascination with newness ensured that humans were constantly creating and discovering diverse solutions that might lead to competitive advantages, but it is often the newness itself that gives pleasure, not the solution. How many people are in a constant state of striving, hoping for some future circumstances they think will provide them with greater, sustained happiness without allowing themselves to find it in the present?

Indeed, for most of those who blindly trust their instincts and the conventions of society, there will never be a point at which they will have enough. Classical economics defines value in terms of what people actually want and studies, in part, how to improve efficiencies in achieving it. Since the drive for status makes people value "more", economic efficiency accelerates its attainment. The world's dynamics are largely a consequence of 7 billion people trying to gain or maintain status by achieving relative affluence compared to their neighbors—and their fellow global citizens. And those who invest time and energy in accumulating wealth have a vested interest in preserving a societal worldview that values it. But happiness is usually left out of the equation. Economics and psychology have to concede that they are often not only using a different language but talking about very different things, even though the first discipline often seems to want to subsume the second. Even *The Economist*, traditionally a voice of economic liberalism, has admitted that capitalism can make a society rich, but you shouldn't ask it to make you happy as well.[59] Economists essentially seek to lubricate a process that stems directly from human nature. And because society is the product of Darwinian beings competing for status, broader, big-picture reflections about what matters conflict with the dominating mantra, even though deep down many people sense that there is a hidden truth.

The paradox is that with everyone implicitly aiming for higher status, we all find ourselves struggling simply to catch up with one another, often working long hours out of a sense of compulsion, without getting any happier—a process that has been termed a hedonic treadmill. Of course, many people are fortunate to be paid for doing something they love. And many others with more mundane work would anyways be at a loss on how to occupy their time in a way that they found satisfying, even if they had more of it. But if we could all agree to spend more time doing things we

---

59 "Happiness (and how to measure it)," *The Economist* (19 December 2006), www.economist.com/node/8450035?story_id=8450035.

are passionate about and less time financing consumption, we might be able to find a way out of this endless rat race. The glaring obstacle is—once again—the fact that some will always be striving for more, drawing everyone else into the game. The same phenomenon also occurs globally between rival nations—with dramatic consequences such as the ever-present threat of deadly conflict and the erosion of our planet's biosphere. The desire for more in a competitive world is like a constitutive addiction, for some as pleasurable as a caffeine fix regularly satisfied by an exotic roast, but for many, as destructive as a heroin dependence.

The cleft between economics and psychology thus mirrors the tension within an individual between their innate urge to compete and their desire to be happy—a deep existential challenge. We easily lose perspective and get caught up in struggles to the point where we lose sight of the purpose of the game we're playing. Is life a challenging game to be enjoyed, a deadly serious game that we cannot lose, or a balance between the two? While we learn the rules of the game and how to play it, we don't always seem to be clear about its goals. We concentrate on mini-goals that we think are very important and forget to have fun playing. In *The Book: On the Taboo Against Knowing Who You Are*, philosopher Alan Watts put his finger on one of the unfortunate aspects of our existence: we always seem to need a winner and a loser.

The insidious pressure to conform and compete that we internalize, reinforcing our native urges, means that, today, despite an earning power that, if they chose to do so, would already allow much of the developed world's population to spend long periods of time travelling in other, less expensive parts of the world—exploring, taking in the sights and smells, meeting people from different cultures, listening to beautiful, inspiring music, having many experiences and feeling wonderfully free—, there is a lingering tendency to perceive all this enjoyment of life as a distraction and not actually the point of it all. Ironically, then, we find ourselves in the 21st century still in the clutches of a system that steers us towards devoting most of our lives to remaining competitive rather than experiencing beauty. It is almost as if we feel an eternal debt to the toils of past generations to keep up the sustained work ethic, regardless of where it leads us now. We resemble Wile E. Coyote in the old Road Runner cartoons, who continues running even after he's gone off the edge of the cliff. The unfettered free market system espoused for decades by industrialists and entrepreneurs, deeply rooted in a philosophy of individualism and probably the most efficient system for creating economic value through the harnessing of human creativity, also locks many of us into a life routine in which we have little free time available to appreciate much of the beauty and diversity of the planet we inhabit for so short a time. We create value and benefit from the material comforts it affords us, but we are simultaneously conducted into a path of conformity as parts of a larger machine. How individualistic is that?

The recent field of happiness economics, in which the legendary economist Daniel Kahneman, co-author of one of the papers cited above, has played a pivotal role, tries to bridge the disciplines of economics and psychology by attributing value to happiness. By determining what makes people happy, governments can try to adjust their priorities away from mere economic measures such as GDP. Elucidating the economic and other determinants of happiness is a difficult exercise, with so many variables involved, many of them inter-related, and different studies sometimes yielding contradictory results. It has not been conclusively shown to what degree income disparities cause unhappiness, and it is unclear how much reducing inequalities would automatically lead to greater happiness among a society's poorest.

But these questions matter deeply. A priority in our increasingly globalized world has been, to a large extent, on continuous, significant economic growth—with the not unreasonable justification that increased wealth tends to benefit all of society—, rather than increased happiness for the world's inhabitants. But people generate wealth within an interconnected global society in which everyone's actions affect and are affected by everyone else, not always positively. To the extent that all this wealth generation can be used to make more people happier, we should find ways of doing so more effectively than concentrating it in increasingly large piles.

Yet while keeping inequality within bounds may be critical for assuring everyone a minimum level of well-being, only a highly controversial, major redistribution of wealth through taxes and other measures could dramatically reduce the status and associated happiness gradient within a society. Trying to radically compress status differences would run up against one of the most engrained human drives, depriving people of much of the incentive to innovate and of a visceral sense of freedom.

It is also likely that a hypothetical global elimination of struggle would lead to a loss of purpose and meaning. Hardship is by definition rarely a source of pleasure in itself, but facing lesser challenges can be stimulating, and successfully overcoming even painful obstacles can yield great satisfaction. Although few people other than former dictators would ever wish a return to totalitarianism, one BBC TV reporter astutely observed on the 20th anniversary of the fall of the Berlin Wall, "You can't experience the joy of freedom without having experienced the sadness of oppression." A utopia where the details had been so finely worked out that there were no challenges, and only minor differences of opinion fluctuating tightly around an average, would risk being sterile and uninteresting. A Norwegian film called "The Bothersome Man" depicts the exasperating predictability and grey dullness of a fictional society where everything is arranged for you, including job, home and girlfriend.

We need breathing space in which to exercise our freedom, room for disagreements, and the chance to take risks and even fail. In a world where there were no major uncertainties, no drama to be waged, no death or danger to defy, and even no tragedy, the challenge might be staving off boredom. In Western societies that have sufficient wealth to provide all their residents with a respectable standard of living, people find minor, sometimes absurdly trivial concerns with which to occupy themselves (as many foreign residents of Switzerland would agree). The need for challenges also explains much of the universal appeal of competitive sports. Maybe a certain degree of competition is needed, and a certain probability of falling below the mean, in order to make life interesting. Any attempts to promote stable solutions to large-scale problems need to consider that the complete elimination of obstacles is not a viable solution, and we need a certain degree of grittiness, without it having to depend on extreme polarization. This is one of the key reasons why happiness requires a degree of free market libertarianism—so long as we keep it something of a game, be good sports and treat the wounded.

MEANING

While fleeting emotional states can give a sensation of happiness, meaning goes to the heart of existence, providing happiness with structure, color and texture, and contributing to overall life satisfaction. A sense of life having richness and continuity, and that things *matter*, rather than just fulfilling one's basic needs or inducing momentary pleasures. It comes from a diversity of connections of thoughts, ideas, impressions and sensations. The complexity often needs to be savored at face value without being scrutinized for underlying explanations that would dispel the mystery and beauty. But—and this is what makes us such extraordinary beings, at least as much as our ability to solve problems and manipulate the environment— meaning also comes from our self-awareness and self-inquiry, our ability to think about the wonder and absurdity of existence, to ask why we are here. We can communicate these explorations by expressing ourselves through art, literature, music, drama, cinema and dance, and capture others' sense of meaning by exposing ourselves to these media.

New meaning is created from new internal states-of-mind. For example, the melancholy wailing of a violin—the kind associated with the eastern European cultural tradition and that typically accompanies black-and-white historical documentaries—can add a layer of intense drama to experiences that would not otherwise provoke as strong emotions, making life feel extremely important and meaningful. It is itself a source of meaning that did not exist before the violin was invented.

The richness of meaning grows with the complexity of the elements that contribute to it, and this is why diversity is so fundamentally important to our lives. It adds an entire dimension to happiness beyond any sustained state of bliss that could be achieved, for example, by administering someone with a controlled, continuous dosage of an opiate or related drug for the rest of their life.

The process by which we evolved doesn't say anything at all about what life ought to or can mean to people, and today we have the capability to tweak our environment and squeeze as much meaning as we can out of life, within the limits of the brain architecture we happen to be stuck with. Even when meaning does not quite seem to coincide with happiness, it can sometimes substitute for it, the darker moments adding textural relief and interest to our lives. Many people could hardly imagine living a life devoid of sadness and melancholy, and would not choose it even if they had the option.

The culture we live in provides a kind of scaffold on which a sense of meaning grows, embellishing our lives. The products of one person's imagination can spread to occupy a place in the collective consciousness of an entire culture and beyond, through popular novels and movies or works of art, fictional characters taking on an almost mythical status and becoming larger than life. But because the thoughts that occupy our minds are so strongly influenced by our environment, and because there are a limited number of ideas and perspectives we actually have the time and opportunity to consider, our culture can also shield us from knowledge about the rest of the world and how others derive meaning.

Routine, the pressure of society and the power of large corporations are factors that compress much of humanity's experience into a narrow band of homogeneity. If the variety of cultures, sub-cultures, moods and states-of-mind in the world can be likened to a sprawling candy store the size of a large supermarket, most people fill their shopping baskets with the contents of just one shelf. Our innate tendency to conform blinds us to the polychromatic range of experience that is possible. The diversity of cultures in the world is valuable not just for its own sake but for the many ways it shows that people can organize their lifestyles and achieve happiness. In wealthier societies, where individuals have greater resources and are exposed to a broader range of experiences, stimuli and influences, the potential variety of mental states that people enter is conceivably larger than in countries where the average person spends most of their time laboring to feed their family.

Wealth and technology are a double-edged sword. On the one hand, they dramatically expand the potential richness of experience available to people who seek it out. On the other hand, technology can become a focus in itself that occupies people's brains and time with banality. While basic human needs are essentially immutable, what life feels like is changing for many. New forms of communication alter not only the means by which we communicate with others, but also the quality and content of this communication. We easily get drawn into new technology interfaces that for many people become a reference for communication and define how we use much of our leisure time. Facebook, for example, can be invaluable as a means of expanding our web of connections with other people, keeping abreast of events, staying in closer contact with those we care about, and even changing the world. But it is also a uniform space that has succeeded in occupying an important slice of attention in the daily routine of tens of millions of people as they post and comment on the most prosaic, meaningless details of their everyday lives according to a limited number of pre-determined formats.

Meaning is the beautiful side of the universe, the tremendous richness with which moments can be felt which can never be adequately described with words. This goes to the core of what matters to people. As suggested earlier, understanding how the world works at the most fundamental level may not bring you any closer to understanding the unique quality of subjectively experienced meaning. Even the most rational beings have a romantic side that allows them to derive this pleasure. Science itself is in a sense tasteless and odorless, its rewards intellectual. Ecstasy in life often comes from plunging in drunkenly, acting like a player rather than an observer, suspending knowledge and cynicism and surrendering oneself to perceptions, sensations and fantasy. Our overriding challenge is to determine how we can diminish the evil side of the universe as it manifests itself on this planet—the excessive need for domination to the point where it causes suffering and prevents others from having happy, meaningful lives.

TRUTH AND DELUSION

The truth is so universally extolled, and its pursuit so closely associated with "virtue", that we easily overlook its relevance as a means to an end: the achievement of happiness and meaning. In many cases, the truth about reality allows us to shape the world to our own benefit, and the suppression of the truth is often used for self-serving purposes, manipulating the information that others have at their disposal. But the same, valid truth can also be a source of deep meaning for some while a source of bitter unhappiness for others. What matters is not just the accessibility of the truth, but which truths our attention is focused on and how these are exploited.

We all need some degree of delusion to protect ourselves from unpleasant information. What we believe about ourselves and our level of self-esteem are often more important to our happiness than the actual truth about how we objectively measure up to other people. And we need fantasy to make our lives richer and more fascinating. Every culture creates its own myths as a source of meaning. From an evolutionary perspective, seeking the absolute truth about everything has not necessarily been the best survival strategy under all circumstances. There is a great deal of wisdom in the old saying that ignorance is bliss. And ignorance is often like virginity: once lost it cannot be regained.

Blindly seeking the truth about everything would lead us down many dark alleys containing unpleasant surprises. For example, would we really want to know what everyone else we come into contact with thinks of us, and what our interactions with them imply about our mutually perceived relative status? Would we want to be constantly aware of the best underlying explanations for our friends', colleagues' and acquaintances' behaviors in terms of self-interest? Would we care to know every detail about our partner's past? Would we necessarily want to know if we had a fatal genetic disease that we could do nothing about? Would we want social scientists to determine how well various behavioral and psychological traits correlated with our ethnic group or culture, and for these findings to be splashed across newspaper pages, especially if there were unflattering aspects, and knowing how readily people generalize? Would we want to discover just how much less original our thoughts are than we would like to think, and how many others have expressed nearly identical ideas in books or films we have not yet happened upon?

Too many truths about subjects we are interested in is not always useful, either. For example, research has shown that having too much information can actually reduce the effectiveness of people's decisions, obscuring the relative importance and relevance of the information and making it difficult to prioritize.[60] As discussed at the beginning of this book, the huge amounts of information we have to filter through today are one of our biggest obstacles to thinking about and evaluating what matters and how to achieve it.

There is, of course, another, more sinister way in which too much truth can really be dangerous. Given the human propensity to dominate and for people and countries in positions of power to take full advantage of opportunities to seize resources and gain influence, information that can help them in these endeavors is likely to be exploited. With the exponential increases in technological know-how and computing power, information that can provide one party with a decisive strategic advantage can have sudden and dramatic implications. The Hiroshima and Nagasaki bombs are one pertinent example from the mid-20th century. Higher-tech 21st century equivalents could be unrecognizably different.

The scientific pursuit of the truth—the attempt to understand how the world works at the level of the hard, objective reality of matter and energy, and to push back the limits of the doable—is itself pursued in large part for the subjective experience of satisfaction that it yields. As humorously captured in many of Gary Larson's classic "The Far Side" cartoons, scientists can derive an almost childlike glee from discovering the nature of reality and the underlying laws of the universe while keeping company with their peers. The truth matters to the people who seek it, and to any others

---

60   See Barry Schwartz's *The Paradox of Choice.*

who acknowledge its value. But this search is sometimes carried out with an enthusiasm that can eclipse concerns about others' subjective experience, present or future, including how both experimentation and the use of technology might generate suffering. Open-mindedness towards the truth includes recognizing that subjective reality exists and is at the center of what matters. There is a fundamental flaw in the argument that if something cannot be measured then its existence is in some way irrelevant. A glaring example of this is the approach some scientists take to consciousness, in which the relevant parameters are more often intelligence and measurable outputs than subjective states. Those who ignore others' subjective experience make science a cold ideology.

Scientists' respect for the truth and the high standards that are expected of them by their peers confer on them enormous value to society in a world where the truth is so often bent to meet self-interest. But there are other things that are—legitimately—more important to people, like happiness, and the truth can sometimes be a threat to it. The truth can be used to further both self-interested and compassionate agendas, or be denied or ignored for the same reasons. Sun Microsystems co-founder Bill Joy, in a thoughtful and influential article in Wired magazine about where technology is taking us, wrote, "The truth that science seeks can certainly be considered a dangerous substitute for God if it is likely to lead to our extinction."[61]

Science as an approach or discipline can offer an understanding of how things *are*, but it cannot tell us definitively what we *should* do, or what matters. Science can help us get from A to B most effectively, but something else has to tell us what B ought to be. And that something else, one of the main subjects of this book, really matters. As I will argue further, the need for firmly entrenched humanitarian values among those with access to powerful information is therefore becoming ever more critical, and as long as this cannot be sustainably ensured, we incur potentially enormous risks to our collective well-being. As an illustration, the release of huge numbers of diplomatic cables by WikiLeaks elicited widely differing reactions, depending in large part on people's confidence in their government to act according to humanitarian principles. The search for the truth is only useful to people when it serves their interests, however broadly defined. Pursuing the truth

---

61 Bill Joy, "Why the future doesn't need us," *Wired* (April 2000), www.wired.com/wired/archive/8.04/joy_pr.html.

about reality therefore requires protecting people from its consequences. The truth matters profoundly. But as a guiding principle, it is not enough.

The question is how the truth is used. Who has access to it and how much influence do they have? How does the truth affect their thinking and behavior, and how does it interact with other truths? Most relevantly, how does the desire to understand how the world works interact with the desire to act in a way that reduces suffering? To what extent does one need to suppress certain knowledge from one's active daily awareness in order to be more effective in reaching one's goals?

Even in writing a book like this one, there is a certain paradox in wanting to contribute both to an understanding of the big picture and to the relief of suffering. Not only is not all understanding useful, some may be counter-productive, particularly if it results in diminished hope or even apathy. Continually and persistently asking "why?", even about the negative value of suffering, ultimately leads to a recognition of the absurdity of it all and the impossibility of leading a blissful yet purely compassionate existence. The net effect of this understanding still needs to be a sense that the beauty and meaning available to be experienced not only make life worth living but are worth fighting for on behalf of others.

Although science cannot tell us which truths to value most, philosophical reflections on subjective experience and identity can guide us. Only when others' subjective experience is universally regarded as an essential truth to explore and to value can we more broadly seek the truth with equanimity. Without this truth, there is no basis for compassion.

SPIRITUALITY AND RELIGION

Viewed externally, the narratives of many religions can be interpreted as an institutionalized form of self-deception—the acceptance by populations of unverifiable or irrational explanations for how the world works. But religion can also be understood as a natural response to the search for broader meaning in a strange universe. Although some concepts associated with religions, such as the existence of a soul existing distinctly from one's body, or an entity that actively listens to and registers one's prayers, are constructs that make life seem safer and give people a source of hope—even though they are at odds with what reason and observation suggest—, so are many of the various other filters and perspectives we apply to reality to maintain a sense of coherence and meaning in our lives, such as the idea that our identities are distinct and continuous, that people are the ultimate causes of their actions, or that our instinctive notions of good and bad are true in an absolute sense. So even people who dismiss religion as mythical nonsense have their own instinctive ways of dealing that bend reality.

As touched upon earlier in the section on consciousness, the deep nature and origin of matter, energy, the universe and consciousness remain a mystery. We may have different personal explanations for these phenomena, but we can respect those who hold explanations we do not agree with. Even the greatest scientists are unable to provide entirely satisfying answers to these fundamental questions. There may always remain something mysterious about the existence and intensity of subjectively experienced emotions and feelings, pain, happiness, love and meaning. The fact that meaning and emotions actually come into existence at all in this vast universe of quarks, leptons and bosons[62] somehow implies "something". The distinction between many religious and non-religious people, equally awed by the outcome, is simply whether they label this something with a name or can understand it as a long series of equations. A fundamental cleavage only occurs with those who expect this something to bend the laws of physics in answer to their prayers, or whose fear of purposelessness or, alternatively, punishment leads them to ignore massive empirical evidence about how the world actually functions and the processes that have been at work over billions of years.

A dose of mysticism in one's life, not as a definitive means of explanation but as an individualistic means of living, need not even be incompatible with reason. While rationalists reject dogmatic monotheistic fundamentalism as a means of understanding the world, many see appeal in mystical perspectives such as Buddhism, with its gentler, more tolerant approach to life. Spirituality, including of a religious nature, can be a source of intense states-of-mind, something which makes life worth living for many people. I suspect that some of those who mock religion probably have only a limited grasp of the potential range of subjective experiences that humans can achieve. By extolling reason to the point of trying to banish religious-like spirituality, some rationalists minimize the fundamental importance of diverse and intense subjective experience and, as addressed in the last section, overlook the fact that the acquisition of truth is itself often appreciated for the subjective sense of satisfaction it provides.

---

62 Quarks, leptons and bosons are three kinds of subatomic particles.

At the risk of descending into caricature, a warm-hearted, generous, deeply religious person with close family bonds for whom life is rich, satisfying and full of meaning, confronted with a slightly grating scientist who claims that God does not exist and life has no greater meaning, can fairly ask, "which of us is living right?" Nobody should be told how they ought to live, to the extent that their actions are compatible with the well-being of others, and nobody should have someone else's meaning imposed on their own life. The role that religion plays in many people's private lives is too intricately associated with their own sense of meaning to realistically expect them to abandon it. In absolute terms, religion can make life matter more. As Helen Phillips wrote in *New Scientist*, "Even the most logical and articulate argument against religion will never eradicate this evolutionary sense of meaning."[63]

The ubiquity of religion among humans of the most diverse cultures living at the widest reaches of the globe indicates that it is a fundamentally human activity, as is, for example, art in all its forms. The emergence of religion can be seen, analogously to the imprinting of a mother figure on freshly hatched baby geese, as the manifestation of a father figure on freshly emerged conscious, intelligent beings, for example, through such awe-inspiring phenomena as lightning storms and volcanic eruptions. Religion's likely contribution to quality-of-life among its practitioners over the millennia, providing meaning to evolved brains otherwise capable of grasping the absurdity of existence but without the means to handle it, probably conferred it with survival value. Even today, some studies have shown that religious Americans tend to live longer, although teasing out cause and effect makes the interpretation of these studies difficult. Religious belief can be profound, yielding a state-of-mind that provides an all-encompassing sense of comfort and purpose that others may fail to understand. For all its shortcomings, religion can help to ensure an attachment to others and shield people from an alienating view of a world that they wouldn't know how to deal with. Religious beliefs and religious identity are intertwined, and even if an individual attributes greater importance to the identity aspect, they may not feel comfortable explicitly denying the underlying foundations.

While many rationalists who are keenly aware of the risks we now face as a species have the capacity to take things in stride, not everyone

---

63 Helen Phillips, "The origins of faith," *New Scientist* (1 September 2007). (Available online as "What good is God?")

is equipped with this detached, self-confident resignation to being alone in a meaningless universe. While the truth should be sought out and not covered up, on an individual level, people should be respected for doing what they can to make themselves happy, including engaging in religious practices if they choose. It is naïve to expect the truth about existence to be itself a source of endless wonder and satisfaction to everyone. For the average individual, knowing about string theory and the "Theory of Everything" does not in itself bring them closer to happiness. And it is delusional to expect large numbers of people to discard the comfort and stability they derive from their religious identification.

Once, early one evening in Switzerland—a fairly secular country where religion plays a discreet, private role in most people's lives—I found myself listening to the insistent ringing of church bells breaking the silence, and I had the thought that they were like a desperate, half moralizing, half pleading call from a long gone era. Yet one cannot realistically expect central religious authorities to examine the evidence, decide that it weighs against some of their teachings, and consequently pack their bags and throw a huge, final going-away bash, perhaps accompanied by a liquidation sale. In fact, the spread of Evangelism and the growing interest in less dogmatic forms of religious practice suggest that, even in the West, religion is hardly on its way out.

Furthermore, to continue the pragmatic line of argumentation, no matter how much one disagrees with religion either as a matter of principle or, when hijacked by fanatics, as a source of violence and suffering, attacking it is a potentially counter-productive and dangerous strategy. Many religious devotees, including Muslims, have their identities so firmly associated with their religion that they see any attack on their religion as a personal one.

There is, however, a major caveat to this whole discussion. An enlightened society, respectful of the individual and of humanitarian values, cannot impose religion on people as a means of explaining the world, and cannot use it as a justification for interfering with open-minded enquiry and denying the truth about physical reality. As discussed later, for educated, thinking people with compassion for others, religion is also not needed as a source of values, and indeed, there are more fundamental, universally applicable values that humanity should support that are still compatible with religious observance among those who choose it. This is a principle that even religious leaders need to respect.

The sense of comfort that faith can provide also bears the potential for complacency due to misguided confidence that "someone else" will look after things. The fact is that we have inherited a complex mess of a world that arose spontaneously over time. It is up to us to try to prove, in a display of collective assertion rather than passivity, that the laws of physics and mathematics, combined with some good luck, allow sustainable global humanism. Otherwise we can incorporate Murphy's Law into any grand unifying theory of how the world works.

The launch in 2009 of Project Reason, an initiative to spread scientific knowledge and secular values in society, by Sam Harris, author of *The End of Faith* and a firm opponent of religion for the violence it can spawn, and the critical review it drew from *Critical Mass* author Philip Ball in the pages of the scientific journal *Nature*[64], provide an example of how differently rationalists can view religion and its co-existence with science. In a more recent clash between two other prominent scientists cited elsewhere in these pages, Richard Dawkins none too amicably referred to Sir Martin Rees—who since won the lucrative 2011 Templeton Prize, which recognizes contributions to spirituality—as a "compliant quisling" for his accommodation of religion.[65] This seemingly endless debate illustrates how smart people can agree on factual details and disagree so strongly on the practical conclusions to be drawn, and also begs two principal questions. The first is whether religion can exist without promoting hatred or thwarting scientific understanding. And the second is, even if it does often have these highly negative consequences, what is the most practical solution in this very flawed world we inhabit?

As I argue in this book, a priority should be to try to vanquish hatred and suffering, and this is most likely to happen when conditions are created where reason and the search for truth are not perceived as a threat to people's physical well-being or way of life. By accepting religious moderates in a spirit of tolerance, though still demanding respect for rational enquiry and unfailing abidance by humanitarian values, support for extremists is more likely to be shrunk. I entirely understand why scientists and others who defend rational thinking become so frustrated when they hear power-

---

64 Philip Ball, "How Much Reason Do You Want?" *Nature* (14 May 2009), www.nature.com/news/2009/090514/full/news.2009.476.html.

65 Ian Sample, "Martin Rees wins controversial £1m Templeton prize," *The Guardian* (6 April 2011), www.guardian.co.uk/science/2011/apr/06/martin-rees-templeton-prize.

ful people saying things that all the evidence in the world and logical think- ing contradict. But the search for peaceful solutions means we simply do not have the luxury of taking absolutist stances and refusing to engage the other side constructively. This does not mean giving up our knowledge and understanding of external reality, nor does it mean relinquishing people's right to seek the truth. But it means recognizing that, overall, there are other, sometimes higher priorities than fighting for the truth all the time.

The focus in Eastern philosophies on inner subjective experience and connectedness between beings bears a very different message than the monotheistic religions with their emphasis on external actions and the ever-hovering threat of punishment. It also represents a fundamentally dif- ferent approach to life than the Western obsession with producing things and the evolutionary rut of competition as a raison d'être. Endless medi- tation will never lead to the medical breakthroughs that can cure a dying child, or the technology than can put thousands of songs in your pocket, nor expose you to the diversity of possible experiences that make life rich and exciting. For these, a culture of curiosity, problem-solving and achievement is needed. But Eastern spiritual traditions serve as a healthy reminder of the central significance of awareness—of oneself and of others—in a world where we are so easily caught up in and tossed about by a frenzy of external influences.

11. Preserving Life

How Much Does It All Really Matter?

> It started when we stopped dreaming
> When we stopped hoping anymore
> Look at the street, how it's empty
> We've already forgotten how to play
> —Aviv Geffen, Israeli singer/songwriter and peace
> activist, "Sof Haolam" ("End of the World")

Asking about the very value of life and existence may seem to be another meaningless exercise. And yet it is profoundly important, both for the change in perspective it can provoke when reflected upon and for its relationship to the big decisions we make that have an impact on others. Trying to provide an answer really requires determining the magnitude of the upper end of your scale of caring about things. In practice, it is reflected in the effort we are willing to make both to live life to its fullest and to preserve it for others.

As a child, pleasantly naïve and ignorant, the world seems vast, all-important and full of vague, limitless possibility. As we get older, increasingly understand how things work and focus on earning a living in a competitive world, we easily become jaded and forget what it all can mean. The phenomenon of compression causes a truncation in our emotional response—we lose the facility to experience the high end of the emotional scale.

But how much we care about things is not a detail—it is *everything*. It determines whether we embrace life for all it's worth or just survive, waiting for retirement and hoping to get through it unscathed. Whether we gain an independent enough outlook to be able to enjoy life on our own terms and resist the Darwinian trap of continuous competition. And it determines how much effort we are willing to make to protect our planet and its inhabitants.

At its most intense, life is wondrous and beautiful. A shiver from listening to certain music and feeling something sublime that you wouldn't know how to describe, but that you resonate with. An electric spark looking into a lover's eyes and feeling a powerful connection and mutual attraction. The magic in the air watching a sunset on the beach in the company of others. A transient whiff of burning shrubs that brings back memories of travels to hidden valleys in the mountains of Asia. A celebration reuniting family or close friends. The pride and satisfaction of accomplishing long sought after goals. An intangible mental state where you just feel extraordinarily good and full of inspiration. A feeling of deep happiness that makes you wish life would go on and on and on, forever.

But overall, has life come to be worth less to many of us in the developed world? Are we so obsessed with whatever the mainstream media throw at us that we lose track of the larger issues, of the thread of history and our link to it, and of what it means to be human? Have we internalized both the boredom and anguish of living in an increasingly globalized, converging world of excesses and hyper-competition? Are we quietly suffering from claustrophobia on a shrinking, wounded planet where there seems ever less mystery, ever less adventure to be had? Has the phenomenon of compression reduced our subjective sense of things mattering to the point where the fate of the world and the fate of one's stolen iPhone have a comparable value? Have we become blasé about the rewards of struggle and the purpose of it all? Does the bittersweet angst of an Ingmar Bergman film seem distant and otherworldly for its unfamiliar intensity, even as it lays bare certain truths about existence? Are we missing those wailing violins?

THE VALUE OF A LIFE

Let's break another taboo and ask: are all lives of equal worth? Your own, your family's, your friends', your acquaintances', your countrymen's, a stranger's? Or are some lives worth more than others? Are future lives worth as much as current lives? How about the life of someone who will be alive in 20 years? In 200 years? And if there are differences, can or should they be quantified for the purpose of allocating resources and setting priorities?

These are difficult questions, as they lead inexorably to disturbing contradictions between, on the one hand, the theoretical conviction most of us have, reinforced by the declarations of statesmen and international organizations, that all humans are created equal and have lives of equal value; and, on the other hand, the reality that most of us value the lives of our close family members more than those of other human beings, are more willing to reach for our wallets or otherwise help to rescue a few dozen fellow countrymen in dire straits abroad than a few million dying citizens of a developing country, and, in countless daily decisions and non-decisions, reveal that we value some people more than others. This is a psychological consequence of our genetically rooted instinct for self-preservation, which we extend to others we most closely identify with.

Indeed, how many people would even willingly sacrifice their own life for the survival of the species? This reflection leads to a somewhat bizarre conclusion, which is that, in practice, the average person probably attributes greater value to their own individual existence than to the existence of 7 billion other human beings. Mathematically, if your own individual life had a value to you of 1, the true value to you of the entire species might be described as having a fractional value of less than 1. This is an unavoidable consequence of human psychology as it has evolved, and we have to work with it. It does not mean that people will not devote their lives to helping others or make great sacrifices to relieve others' suffering, but under everyday circumstances, the average person is more concerned about surviving and being happy than about any grander notion.

Similarly, if you heard on the radio that a nuclear explosion had gone off in a large city where one of your closest relatives lived, it is likely that, despite a million innocent people dead or injured, foremost in your mind would be the possible loss of a single person you love. This is just human nature. Additionally, as artificial intelligence researcher Eliezer Yudkowsky wrote in an essay on how we assess risk, "Human emotions take place within an analog brain. The human brain cannot release enough neurotransmitters to feel emotion a thousand times as strong as the grief of one funeral."[66]

---

66 Eliezer Yudkowsky, "Cognitive biases potentially affecting judgment of global risks," in *Global Catastrophic Risks*, edited by Nick Bostrom and Milan Cirkovic

The very fact that the preservation of human lives is so important to so many people as a source of meaning for their *own* lives is a strong argument in its favor. But, as discussed earlier, the fact that something is important to many people is not a rock solid defense. For a while, not that long ago, the destruction of innocent life took on surprisingly great importance to many of the citizens of a large, highly cultured country in the middle of Europe.

The concept of all lives having equal value is admirable in theory but blatantly contradicted by reality, to the extent that value is defined with respect to someone doing the actual valuing. One can—indeed, *must*—stick to the idealistic notion of lives being equal as a driver of change, but as a description of what is actually valued in this world, it fails miserably. It is small comfort to a child dying of malaria in Africa and to her grieving mother that her life is officially deemed by some faraway international body to be of equal value to any other human life.

Even in a society with strongly anchored humanitarian values, there is still usually the need to incite some people to put their lives at potential risk, for the simple reason that in the absence of military deterrence, a country can be forced to submit to the will of another country that doesn't respect it and its citizens' integrity. This is just one of the more obvious ways that the life of an individual is risked or sacrificed to benefit the whole, which can be more cynically explained as the outsourcing of risk by those who can afford to pay for it.

The potential loss of an individual human life is of greatest significance to the person whose life is threatened and is struggling to survive, as well as to any others with whose lives his is intertwined. These can be close relatives or friends, or any of potentially huge numbers of anonymous individuals around the globe whose lives have in some way been touched by the person in question. The loss of an individual destroys the knowledge and wisdom he has accumulated and the force for positive change he might represent. But if there is no one else who is affected, the loss is essentially to himself, and once he is gone, he is no longer around to experience it. If he is not missed, the loss becomes in some way irrelevant. Even awaking in the morning is like the birth of a "new" person who has inherited your memories and character. If you don't wake up, it can't actually matter to

---

(Oxford: Oxford University Press, 2008). Available at http://singinst.org/upload/cognitive-biases.pdf.

you anymore—even though we all expect and very much *want* to wake up in the morning!

Addressing the very value of individual lives in this way may appear somehow "wrong" or misguided, especially if we already suspect that in the grand scheme of things our individual lives might have no greater meaning, and that any such deep philosophical reflection about the value of life risks thereby leading to a further, terrible devaluation of what we cherish most. But questioning our basic assumptions can allow us to shift our perspective in a subtle but significant way, and to acknowledge more clearly two fundamental aspects of life that make it so important to preserve: an individual's freedom to exist without fear of his or her life being taken away, and the meaning a person's life has for others. A perspective that starts from the primacy of subjective experience is ultimately more humanistic than one that regards lives abstractly as numbers to be maintained. No such reflection need cause us to care less about things that matter to us, especially if we are guided by compassion.

Even the hypothetical instantaneous, unanticipated deaths of human beings, in the absence of any mourning survivors, need hardly be something we would tolerate as a society, at the risk of having a cynical, dehumanized self-image reflected back to us. But then, the desire for a compassionate self-image should also lead us to view the destruction of other, non-human life with at least a hint of doubt as well. Furthermore, a value system that allows us to take away the life or consciousness of another animal, even with minimal awareness of what is about to happen to it and with minimal suffering when it does happen, implicitly justifies a more powerful intelligence doing the same to us. If we value the continuity of consciousness and life as a basic principle, then we might find ourselves at the very least confronted with the question of how consistently we apply it.

The Value of Humanity

Reflecting on the value not just of an individual life but of our species may seem absurd, cynical or heretical to an even greater degree, but given the current existential threats we face, it is a question that merits contemplation. Because for all the apparent self-evidence of the intrinsic importance of our species, our actions on the ground suggest otherwise.

I will make an assertion that at first glance seems banal but is potentially provocative: humanity has no intrinsic value without humans. Not in the trivial sense that humanity cannot physically exist without humans to constitute it, but in the more philosophical sense that it has no meaning without humans to contemplate it. Value is, after all, a concept directly linked to humans (or any other creatures that experience desires and meaning), and without humans, nothing has any value anymore, since someone needs to be there to ascribe it. As Danish scientist and poet Piet Hein noted in one of his poems known as Grooks[67], if the universe didn't exist, it wouldn't be missed.

Let's take an extreme situation. Extending the reflections of the previous section, imagine a catastrophe of unparalleled proportions that wiped out the human race in an instant. What would be the greatest tragedy, the immense loss of human lives, or the loss of humanity itself? If humans ceased to exist as a species, this would be a tragedy for us if we knew in advance it was going to happen. But once nobody is left to contemplate the situation and care, the question becomes irrelevant. (And many animals would probably be happier.) Whether our species exists in something like its present form for just another 50 years or for another 1,000 years matters only to the people alive at the time. Of course, it can still matter to people a lot, and it must if we are to have a chance of not killing ourselves off. But thinking about it in this way confronts us with the uncomfortable contradiction between our instinctive respect for the sanctity of life and the subjectivity of the meaning and values linked to our transient existence.

Saving the whole—a concept which, in its minimal form, could be represented by a few reproducing specimens—is distinct from saving the individual. But we often act as if the former can substitute for the latter, just as some environmentalists worry more about saving whale species from extinction than about the painful death by harpoon of individual whales. There is something almost obscene about according greater importance to the concept of the whole, of the collective mass, than to the thoughts, subjective experience and well-being of the individual living, breathing, thinking and often suffering creatures that make it up. Humanity is a concept to be appreciated, but once again, the essential unit of meaning is the conscious experience of individual human beings. A world where subjective experience and the avoidance of extreme suffering are valued, which is presumably the world most of us want to live in, requires us to regard preserving the integrity of each individual as the highest priority.

---

67 Many of these Grooks—short, pithy poems containing existential truths and wisdom that were published from 1940 to 1963—can be found on the Internet.

Of course, the longer our species survives, the more people will be able to come into existence, experience and enjoy life, and be thankful that their ancestors—including those of us living in the early 21st century—managed not to self-destruct. People who exist are usually glad of that fact. But should we care about the existence or lack thereof of any future human beings? Can we go so far as to feel a sense of *responsibility* for someone who never exists? In an essay written in 1914, Henry Salt, a vegetarian who argued on compassionate grounds against raising animals for consumption, called it a fallacy "the assumption that it is a *kindness* to bring a being into the world."[68] And couples are—rightfully—not made to feel guilty about deciding not to have a larger number of children and thereby depriving potential human beings of existence.

Concerns about the continued survival of the human species can be seen as the reflection of a deeply hardwired instinct for self-preservation. Indeed, one of the central themes of major religions is the furthering of the species— the Biblical command to multiply, and interdictions against birth control and homosexuality, however incompatible with the basic human freedoms that compassionate societies now take for granted.

But even if we take the view that the welfare of individual living, breathing human beings should have higher priority than humanity as a concept, and also putting aside the critical fact that the loss of humanity in a future major catastrophe, rather than by erosion through lack of reproduction, would involve the accidental and probably painful deaths of billions of people—as worthy of compassion as the billions of people inhabiting the planet right now—we can still desperately hope that humanity survives, just for its own sake. If we view life as beautiful and meaningful, it is natural to want more of it. And most people would consider the preservation of humanity to be a fundamentally important objective. From a human perspective, if anything on this Earth is worth preserving for eternity, it is humanity itself, several notches higher on the priority list than civilizational relics that are accorded UNESCO status and protection.

The survival of humanity is important for making us feel part of a continuum rather than the final phase of an ultimately failed experiment. Perhaps there really are infinite universes extending infinitely in time, each

---

68 Henry S. Salt, "Logic of the Larder," in *The Humanities of Diet* (Manchester: The Vegetarian Society, 1914). Available at www.animal-rights-library.com/texts-c/salt02.htm.

harboring life, making our own existence painfully irrelevant in the much grander scheme of things. But regardless of whether or not that is true, our continued survival as a species gives greater meaning to life on Earth in the present, providing us with a feeling of hope and making our own individual deaths appear less catastrophic.

There is also something inherently beautiful about preserving consciousness, as if it is a precious gift, accidentally given to us by an otherwise uncaring universe, that we need to handle with extreme care. Whether or not we view it as a "kindness", to use Henry Salt's terminology, allowing future human beings to come into existence and take pleasure in it—which is equivalent to preserving the phenomenon of consciousness, though with fresh brains unencumbered with old memories—is hardly a concept of neutral value to anyone who appreciates existence. Our self-destruction would, indeed, also make us seem rather clumsy as a species, a possibly rare vanguard of life existing 14 billion years after the universe's creation, armed with intelligence, wisdom and technology, and nonetheless subject to a major "oops" moment. In *The Meaning of the 21th Century*, James Martin wrote, "To run the risk of terminating *Homo sapiens* would be the most unspeakable evil." I don't agree with his use of the superlative, as I will make clear below. But what a shame if, just when things were "really" starting to get interesting after eons of relatively sluggish (though, overall, tremendous) developments, we blew it all on this planet in the blink of an eye because we couldn't figure out how to get it right. These alone are strong, though ultimately still subjective, reasons to fight for the survival of our species.

To those of us alive now, there is also an inevitable curiosity to see what the future will come up with and to what degree our planet will be transformed by technology over the next centuries. But with the astounding growth of technology, our desire for the preservation of the species begs another question: which aspects of our species is it that we actually most want to preserve? Are we truly dedicated to preserving the subjective experience of pleasure and meaning? Or are we more concerned with preserving intelligence and complexity? Because the longer we exist as a modern civilization without a cataclysmic event that eliminates us or strands a few scattered survivors in a post-modern Stone Age, the greater the degree of complexity that will emerge. And without a concerted effort around agreed upon goals, which I have argued must center on individuals' subjective experience, the evolution of complexity may in any case follow its own path and achieve its own endpoints. With the emergence of non-biological, human-like intelligence, we may soon be faced with a very different and much more immediate kind of threat to our survival that goes to the essence of what it means to be human and makes many of our traditional assumptions, including some made in the paragraphs above, obsolete. I discuss this threat in the chapter "Where We Are Headed".

Still, the objective of ensuring the survival of our species is of little direct benefit to an individual eking out a minimal existence, whose life should seemingly be accorded at least as much importance as that of any potential future inhabitant of planet Earth yet to issue her first cry. There are over a billion people right now living in misery, suffering from poverty and preventable diseases. There are thousands hidden from view who are being tortured by cynical regimes. If we can't muster up the courage and creativity to do something to improve these people's lives, why should we care about the welfare and even existence of humans who have not yet existed? Regardless of how profoundly significant our existence may in fact be for the universe, our first obligation is not towards the universe, but towards the quality of subjective experience.

The concern about preserving the future should not allow the relevance of human misery in the present to be downgraded. To the extent that steps to encourage reproduction are based on an atavistic, religiously anchored concern that the species procreate, they should in any case not be taken at the price of sickness, agony and death in the present. The future is a faraway place for people struggling to put food in their stomach and survive, let alone be happy, today. For most people, what matters is now. This does not, of course, by any means contradict the complementary and equally valid claim that it is wrong to live carelessly today at the expense of tomorrow's inhabitants, who may find themselves living on a transformed, waste dump of a planet.

What if the survival of our species required the curtailment of some of the basic individual freedoms we take for granted in Western democracies—for example, perhaps forcing couples to have children against their will? This would imply placing the future survival of the group above the well-being of the individual, conscious beings that make it up. If this is the path we needed to take, we could legitimately ask, "why?"

In our high-tech, globalized age with the loss of nuclear families, dramatically sunken fertility rates in Western countries, and the focus on careers and life objectives other than bringing new human beings onto this planet, some might well be concerned about our species eventually dying out. But with all the dangers facing us as a species, the danger of us disappearing for lack of procreative sex seems, in any case, to be one of the least likely. In European countries where the reproduction rate has fallen to historically low levels, significantly below those needed to maintain a stable population, there may well be fewer native Italians or French or Poles in the future. But the issues are more likely to be of national identity and culture, as well as of the brain-drain on struggling economies, as immigrants from poorer, overpopulated countries are brought in to fill unoccupied jobs, than a threat to the survival of the species as a whole. Even in a futuristic scenario where technology increasingly takes over human roles, where our lives are increasingly concerned with turning on our brain's pleasure centers rather than raising children, and where the number of humans on the planet starts to dwindle, those couples with the strongest genetically-rooted instinct to have children might end up re-populating the Earth.

With the current pace of change, it is impossible to predict what the future will look like. But if we are intelligent about ensuring the welfare of all individuals, the welfare of the species—in some form—is in any case likely to follow. For as long as there are couples who want to have children—and there are few urges more natural—society will strive, albeit probably clumsily, to ensure that the world their offspring grow up in is livable. And as long as there are old people, means will be found to incentivize the supply of younger ones to look after them. Humanity is far more likely to end via a giant cataclysm than through a lack of reproduction. Even with birth rates at half their present values, there would still be humans around for many more centuries.

We can always find ways to incite couples to procreate if we need to (though South Korea's idea of turning off the lights at work may not be one of the most effective[69], and we will have plenty of warning beforehand. Even in the unlikely case that there are just a few remaining wealthy hedonists left on the Earth, they may discover that having a few extra babies is not such a bad idea. And if they don't, well, it will turn out that the fate of an intelligent, technology-driven civilization, despite well-meaning efforts by some of its members, is indeed extinction through pleasure, as posited

---

69 John Sudworth, "South Koreans told to go home and make babies," BBC (20 January 2010), http://news.bbc.co.uk/2/hi/asia-pacific/8469532.stm.

by evolutionary psychologist Geoffrey Miller as an explanation for why we have been unable so far to detect other intelligent life out there in the universe.[70]

In a previous chapter, I touched on the idea that negative utilitarianism—an ethical principle based on the prevention of suffering—implies to some that the Earth itself ought to be destroyed, a suggestion that admittedly sounds outrageous. However, reading detailed accounts of some of the innumerable, unspeakable horrors that people have been made to experience at the hands of others, I don't actually think one would have to be mad at all to conclude that no amount of beauty and meaning justifies maintaining a world where things like that happen. In the final, dramatic scene of the film "The Fifth Element", Milla Jovovich's character Leeloo views a series of horrific pictures of war, including of Nazi death camps and the explosion of an atomic bomb, and, tears falling, momentarily loses faith in her mission of saving the planet. "What's the use of saving life when you see what you do with it?" she utters.

If you were in the hypothetical situation of having to decide whether the whole narrative of life should be started all over again, perhaps on a new planet, would you press the button, or add water to the vial, as the case may be? Knowing in particular that it would undoubtedly mean another Auschwitz, and countless other genocides and repetitions of past horrors, and millions of tortured creatures and humans dying on battlefields? And, for that matter, all the chance suffering arising from diseases and gruesome accidents? Victims of the cruelest torture still hope to come out of the experience alive, the innate will to survive sufficiently dominant, although many would undoubtedly take a cyanide pill were one available. But how many would agree to go through it again? Imagine that you yourself were to be transported into this new world and be among those experiencing one of these indescribable horrors—torture horrible beyond belief that you wouldn't wish on your worst enemy. Or that you knew that there was a small but not insignificant risk, say 1 in 1,000, of being slowly killed in an excruciatingly painful manner. And that some people—imperfect copies of you with an equivalent capacity to experience suffering—would, in any case, definitely be subjected to that fate.

---

70 Geoffrey Miller, "Runaway Consumerism Explains the Fermi Paradox," in *What Is Your Dangerous Idea?*

For these specific reasons, as much as I personally love life and the sub-lime beauty and exquisite variety of experience it makes possible, I'm quite sure I would not make the decision to re-start it all from scratch and allow our whole bloody history to repeat itself. And I would guess that most people, if forced to confront the very worst concrete consequences of such a decision, would reluctantly concur. We cannot feel guilty about depriv-ing hypothetical future lives of their existence, especially when they require more extreme suffering to occur. Implicitly, we should even be prepared to say that if we could take back all the worst suffering that has happened in the past, we would—that if we could make time go backwards and reverse our existence and all the pain that had to occur for us to come into being, we would do it, even if such a "commitment" requires no actual sacrifice, given the laws of physics as they are widely understood.

However, as we already exist, the question we face is a *very different one*: how can we preserve the future in a way that minimizes suffering? We can also turn the question around and ask, conversely, how can we minimize suffering in a way that preserves the future? Because we could never end the world in a way that was instantaneous, physically painless for everyone, unaccompanied by anxious anticipation and, not least of all, universally ac-cepted. Even most torture victims would not wish the whole world to end on their behalf. How then can we re-engineer existence to the best of our abilities, taking this imperfect, vulnerable thing called consciousness and creating the right circumstances for it to thrive happily? These consider-ations are part of a principle I referred to earlier as "negative utilitarianism *plus*".

The demise of our civilization would have additional potential conse-quences beyond the deaths of the planet's human inhabitants, as it would represent a lost opportunity to reduce preventable suffering that seems not to be widely considered. Today, after millennia of bloody conflicts and cru-elty, we have just entered an era of fairly stable national borders and a no-tion of universal human rights, however poorly respected it is in some parts. If we destroy ourselves, this pseudo-stable situation will be lost, and highly intelligent life will likely evolve anew out of the animal kingdom, leading to a repetition of the countless horrors humanity has already inflicted on its members, including wars and torture. If we are unable to preserve and improve on our current situation and serve as stewards of compassion, the whole mess will likely be repeated all over again.

I believe that we need to take seriously these kinds of reflections and use them as a basis for our decision-making. Even most scientists and philosophers do not seem prepared to dig down this deeply in their ethical thinking and put into question some of civilization's most strongly anchored and widespread beliefs. Philosophical enquiry is often constricted by an implicit need for arguments that are consistent with life being intrinsically worthwhile—a conclusion that we obviously want to arrive at but, if we are to be honest, is not foregone.[71] This is one of our greatest taboos. But ironically, it is also one that prevents us from drawing further conclusions that would force us to take more seriously the priority of working towards a kinder, gentler world. To gain a more complete perspective, we need to be prepared to touch the void.

For the reasons mentioned above, I believe that preventing intense suffering should have higher priority than preserving the species, though not in a mutually exclusive way. Focusing our energy on the former should as a consequence ensure the latter, and may, in practice, well be the *most effective means* to ensure our continuity, if carried out in a positive, non-destructive manner. And if the fate of our species nonetheless really were then to become extinction by pleasure, I'm not sure that this would necessarily be the worst of all possible scenarios.

Leeloo is finally encouraged to save the Earth from destruction, despite all the awful things done by humans to other humans, by a declaration of love from Bruce Willis's character, Dallas. Love and other strong emotional connections between people are perhaps the most intense sources of meaning there are. As our world is transformed by fate, perhaps love is the one element that gives us a reason to keep fighting to preserve it all by evoking the high end of the scale of meaning, and also the one reliable tool that can help us in the endeavor. But to be useful on a large scale, connections between people need to be broad and not just focused on a few others. Perhaps this is part of what is missing in mainstream society today. And, very possibly, this is a key to the vision we ought to be striving for globally.

---

71 Philosopher David Benatar represents a notable exception with his boldly argued book *Better Never to Have Been: The Harm of Coming into Existence*.

12. In Search of an Ethical Anchor

The Maddening Relativity of Values

In an attempt to grapple with vague but fundamental questions such as what matters and how much, and addressing the importance of relieving suffering and the value of life and of the species, we have found ourselves up against that seemingly ever-present, maddening wall of relativity. In moments of sublime intensity, life can matter terribly, but things only matter to individuals, not in any objective sense. Does this mean that there really is no basis for a core set of universal values? Can we not solidly anchor a system of ethical prescriptions in anything?

There are few notions more engrained in our psyche than that of right and wrong. The words "good" and "bad" are among the first that any child learns. The fact that the large majority of people have such a notion in a violent, competitive world is at least a source of some reassurance. There is strong empirical evidence for a universal, innate moral sense that provides guidance to individuals about how to act, through the hardwired instinct that certain behaviors are right or wrong.[72] The usual reaction of abhorrence at the idea of killing an innocent person who poses no threat to oneself or others is a reflection of such a sense.

---

72 See, for example, Mark Hauser's *Moral Minds: How Nature Designed Our Universal Sense of Right and Wrong.*

But while we may wish to believe that how we have learned to behave represents an objectively valid truth about what is right, it becomes evident, upon reflection, how much less straightforward our ideas about right and wrong are than we thought. Our consciences and the notions associated with them are rooted in deep Darwinian evolution and emerged through millions and millions of years of chance and natural selection. The result is a mixture of character and behavioral traits, skewed and reinforced by our specific cultural environments, that have been optimized to yield the most successful reproductive strategy for our genes—not specifically to relieve suffering or optimize overall happiness. The process of evolution has hindered us from perceiving the commonality in our identities with all other human beings and the objective equivalence of one person's happiness or pain with another's. Those who cared most about the well-being associated with their own bodies and their families' were most successful at reproducing.

It is the survivors of evolution who determine what it means to be human and what matters to people on average. Throughout the history of our ancestors, the pillager and plunderer—expressed less romantically, the large-scale murderer and rapist—tended to be effective at spreading his pillage-and-plunder genes. It is estimated that, today, about 0.5% of the world's male population is descended in its paternal lineage from Genghis Khan, one of the greatest takers of human life of all times. And in many parts of the world, people are still murdering on a large scale to get their individual points of view across. The Nazis were, in a perverse sense, primitively Darwinian in their thinking (though, fortunately, ultimately unsuccessful in practice), stripping a population of an evolved culture of tolerance and compassion to tap into atavistic human instincts.

So, it's one thing to observe how people actually behave and how their instincts guide them, quite another to then declare that this is what is "ethical". Basing ethics on our innate sense of right and wrong bears a similarity to economics and the improvement of market efficiencies, simply facilitating the translation of our natural instincts into practice.

The growth of technology, globalization and material wealth has tamed us, making cooperation more frequently beneficial and allowing the notion of common global values to spread. When resources are sufficient to satisfy most of our basic needs and our security is ensured, our raw, survivalist instincts are muted and altruistic behavior more readily flourishes. But our hardware has not changed in any substantial way, and the regular emergence of political leaders with an urge to dominate is as predictable as crocus flowers poking out of the earth in springtime.

If as a species we were constitutively and unreservedly nice to one another, focused on living life intensely and compassionately, life would surely be far more enjoyable for virtually all of us. With each of us constantly holding others' interests in mind as well as our own, tensions resulting from threats to people's survival or ambitions would be replaced by connections between individuals living in an aura of warmth and security. Jealousy as an emotion would not exist. For most, life really would be a utopia.

This scenario is not unimaginable. It would simply mean that our psychology would be skewed in a way that emphasized the most peaceful and generous aspects of our current emotional spectrum, and our overall functioning as a society would be quite different, if not wholly unrecognizable, from how it is today. A way of understanding why this is not the situation in most societies is that, even had it been the starting point, once, as a result of mutations and selective pressures, individuals emerged with a tendency not always to be unreservedly kind to one another and who put their own interests above those of others, they would over time have come to dominate the population, out-competing the indiscriminately altruistic types.

Relying on your innate moral sense—doing what you instinctively think is right—may point you in the "right" direction and make you a relatively good person by common standards. We tend to be kind to people whose pain we sense and whom we do not perceive as a threat. But instincts alone are dangerous, and relying on them and perceiving the world as good (our values) and bad (any conflicting values) places us squarely in the billion-year-old competition for survival among the entire range of life forms. They are all the more inadequate in a world where reducing suffering requires more than just spontaneous gestures that make us feel we are doing the right thing while extreme, preventable suffering continues to occur out of sight.

Our specific values are to a greater or lesser extent a reflection of our own cultural biases and upbringing, and they vary tremendously from one individual and culture to another. Asserting the superiority of one's own values or those of one's culture for their own sake, and defending them at all costs, in the absence of an underlying deep reflection about their universal applicability and respect for subjective experience, can lead to terrible conflicts. The battlefields and execution rooms of history were littered with the bodies of those whose existence posed a problem to others who were standing up strongly for their beliefs. Simply believing fervently in the values one grew up with does not give one the moral upper hand. Defending them blindly is better regarded as stubborn than courageous.

People are so often convinced that their values are self-evidently correct and judge other people's behavior accordingly. A glance at the polarized, angry comments that follow many online newspaper articles and YouTube videos provides ample proof. But disgust with others' values does not reflect any intrinsic, objective universality of one's own values. The definitions of "good" and "bad" behavior evolve over time in any society, reflecting the average actual behavior and evolving trends. It is easy to overlook the fact that there is nothing absolutely right or wrong about a culture's specific value system at any particular point in time. While values that deny other individuals' freedom and happiness are immediately suspect as vehicles of self-interest for some at the expense of others, other values can represent a specific society's attempts to preserve the average well-being of its members within the constraints of its own, possibly challenging, environment. This does not justify these values as being worth preserving—but it explains them.

As just one example of the evolution of values, the prohibition against adultery was engraved in the Ten Commandments, and many societies continue to impose severe punishments for this transgression against the traditional core institution of society, the family. In most Western societies, on the other hand, adultery is now no longer a crime, on the view that what consenting adults do with each other is their own business (although consensual cannibalism still poses a problem—fortunately a rare one—, as was seen in a case in Germany a few years ago). Marriage, as the result of an evolution in societal norms, is no longer the sacred institution it once was, to be preserved with the aid of draconian laws at the expense of personal freedom. On the other hand, the way that we continue to treat animals in even apparently sophisticated, highly developed societies says volumes about how good we are as a species at continuing to inflict atrocious suffering on related conscious creatures while shielding ourselves from the evidence. If preventing suffering is the core of a humanistic value system, our values still have a lot of evolving to do, to say the least. To anyone who maintains that Western society has somehow attained a pinnacle of enlightened moral goodness, our treatment of animals is in and of itself sufficient proof of the contrary.

Whenever we use the word "should" or "ought", we are really talking about what we ourselves think is right—what course of action we implicitly believe stems logically from our or our society's value system and the facts that are at our disposal. Such words can be rhetorically effective as a way of bringing people over to our point-of-view, including through shaming, but they are only meaningful with respect to an underlying belief system or emotional stance. 18th century philosopher David Hume's famous assertion that one cannot derive an "ought" statement from an "is" statement is as valid today as when he first expressed it, and it should serve as a constant reminder to people with otherwise admirable intentions that, however much we might wish otherwise, we cannot prove anything about how people ought to act in quite the same way that we can establish facts about objective reality, or even in the way that we can make solid inferences about the quality of others' subjective experience.

The word "responsibility", implying what one "ought" to do, is similarly a term that is actually loaded with subjectivity. We attribute responsibility as an excuse for locking up an intellectually challenged delinquent with a history of child abuse, but shirk it when it concerns saving people from deadly diseases in other parts of the world.

The paradox about ethics, as suggested earlier, is that the more you try to construct arguments about it and try to pin it down with precise prescriptions about the morally appropriate behavior in different scenarios, the more readily it escapes you, like a slippery fish. As a strict system of reasoning, it will always fail in the details, as there is no solid anchor on which to base it, and virtually any specific starting assumption can lead to paradoxical situations that undermine the validity of the whole argument. The apparent solidity of our Western system of values is under the constant threat of erosion by the cognitive dissonance of paying 100 dollars for a very good bottle of wine (or 10 thousand dollars for a very good wristwatch, or 10 billion dollars for a very good particle collider[73]) when that money could

---

73 This example, while intentionally provocative, is not meant to disparage the hugely significant research being performed at CERN (European Organization for Nuclear Research, near Geneva) at what just happens to represent a highly visible concentration of research funding in one place, nor any other research that aims to extend our knowledge of the world and the universe. But the wider philosophical reflections stand regarding the choices we make.

literally save the lives of human beings or change the course of severely underprivileged children's existence, and the ethical juggling act we perform in our minds to rationalize such decisions. Inevitably, rather than adapt our behaviors, we adapt our ethical standards in order to be able to sleep at night.

Even well-meaning concrete prescriptions like trying to save the greatest number of lives can lead compassionate people to psychologically untenable positions. For example, a classic scenario in the ethics literature is that of a trolley car on an immediate collision course with several people who are directly on its path, but which could at the last moment be diverted onto another track on which just one person is located. The decision to divert the trolley car would save lives but cause someone who would otherwise have remained alive to die as a direct result of the decision. From an objective point-of-view, the principle of saving a maximum number of lives would favor a diversion of the trolley car's trajectory, but many people would not decide to actively carry out this action.

Calculating the weight of lives and suffering in different situations—trying to attribute numerical values—quickly leads to absurdity. Does one try to save 1,000 people here or 1,100 people there? What if one of those 1,000 people is a close friend? What if one group includes more children, or more parents? What if, what if...? In practice, this is the eternal dilemma of anyone, whether a government minister or NGO (non-governmental organization) administrator, who has to prioritize limited funds and resources to relieve suffering and save lives, obliged to make decisions that have *intuitive psychological appeal*, rather than which can stand up to the ultimately illusory rigor of ethical thinking. As Stephen Anderson wrote in an article in *Philosophy Now*, "Ethical judgments remain continually vulnerable to that old question, 'Why?' We live, so to speak, suspended in mid air."[74]

An action that directly results in less suffering to another being, with no other consequences, is the easiest to justify psychologically, because it is essentially axiomatic, at least to anyone with compassion, that more suffering is bad, less suffering is good. But while reducing the overall number of people suffering also seems to make sense intellectually, we have greater psychological difficulty viewing one person's suffering as equivalent to an-

---

74 Stephen Anderson, "The Unbearable Lightness of Ethics," *Philosophy Now* (July/August 2007), 22-24, www.philosophynow.org/issue62/The_Unbearable_Lightness_of_Ethics.

other's, whatever a detached understanding of identity tells us. As soon as there are tradeoffs or exchanges of one person's well-being for another's, as there always are, the supposed objectivity of our decision-making quickly falls apart. We will always have greater empathy for some people than for others, whether because they are part of our clan or because we have developed even a momentary attachment to them.

People devote their free time or even their careers to causes and charities that aim to help radically different numbers of victims. Can we possibly consider devotion to ending the suffering of a very small number of people ethically "wrong", simply because greater impact in terms of numbers could be had elsewhere? What about charitable organizations that strive to have maximum impact, but limit themselves to their specific issue of interest: should they really shift the entire focus of their activities in order to reduce the maximum number of people suffering, regardless of the cause? Should we really avoid funding research on rare diseases for similar reasons, even if it means depriving their victims of hope? Should activist organizations really choose their issues solely on the basis of the number of victims? And how do purely self-interested organizations that decide—perhaps as part of a corporate social responsibility initiative—to do a little external good on the side fit into the whole equation?

The fact that strong emotions are ultimately what drive ethical behavior ensures that the basis of ethics will always be subjective. Our rational capacities allow us to draw conclusions from assumptions, but what ultimately drives our arguments and decisions is how we feel about things, including others' suffering. Negative utilitarianism—including the *"plus"* variant I proposed earlier—, the idea that our highest priority should be to focus on reducing suffering, is rooted in empathy and provides an essential basis for ethics, but while it can serve as a rough guiding principle, it cannot provide an objectively valid, absolute code of conduct that dictates all aspects of our lives, behaviors and decisions. Some situations seem so obvious as to require no reflection, others leave us deeply puzzled as to what to do, no matter how strongly we wish to end suffering. And even our capacity for compassion is still constrained by our own psychological needs. We can draw guidelines we feel comfortable with, but the notion of ethics as a solidly grounded discipline is a mirage whose existence we can argue about eternally from a distance. A moral argument is ultimately an attempt at persuasion, one that attempts to focus attention on and attribute importance to certain truths about subjective experience. As a strictly logical argument it will always fail.

The dizzying relativity of ethics is nowhere more apparent than in the waging of war and the impossible decisions made, involving the weighing of thousands of lives like kilograms of meat, and the varying degrees of personal responsibility felt for such decisions. In the best economic spirit, one can even attribute fractional life values to human beings on opposite sides of a conflict. However cynical they may appear, the fact that such calculations are made altogether is, perhaps, at least a sign that the value of lives and suffering has not dropped to a negligible level. But the search for absolute answers as to whether particular behaviors are justified, including such horrors as the bombing of targets with full awareness of the painful deaths of civilians that will ensue (not to mention the painful deaths of soldiers), will always be futile, as there are no solid ethical anchors, and even bountiful compassion has limits when the survival and freedom of oneself, one's family and one's tribe are threatened. But we continue endlessly running around in circles searching for absolute ethical answers that do not exist, because we cannot reconcile ourselves with the impossible, terrible conclusion that the universe leads even well-meaning human beings to cause others like themselves to perish in agony. For example, as at the end of World War II, by dropping powerful bombs that caused innocent people's faces to melt while they were still alive, the intense heat released through the harnessing of processes related to those that provide our planet with light and energy and permitted intelligent life to emerge in the first place.

THE UNRELIABLE ROLE OF RELIGION AS A SOURCE OF VALUES

The idea of values being relative is terrifying to many people, who insist that we need an absolute source, such as that provided by religion, in order not to slide down a slippery slope into a chasm of moral chaos. There is no denying that religions that preach compassion can potentially serve as a useful force for good. There are also many religious charities doing important work to relieve suffering. But the reliance on religion begs several questions. Firstly, which religious tradition can one rely on as a source of values, given the large number of religions competing for adherents, the various combinations of values they each hold, and the incompatibility of some of these values between religions? The religion you are born into, if any, is an accident of birth, and although it may have great meaning to you, this certainly does not imply it has meaning for all of humanity. Secondly, as expounded by Sam Harris in *The End of Faith*, huge amounts of suffering have been inflicted and innumerable wars and conflicts have been waged in the name of religion, with religious leaders often wielding great influence. Over the centuries, religions have hardly earned a "most favorable" rating on the humanitarian scale.

Most fundamentally, religious traditions themselves are essentially based on bootstrapping, through an assertion not even of values but of faith. God is usually seen as the ultimate arbiter and one to please, and goodwill towards others, while often an element of the faith, is never the absolute priority. The Old Testament, for example, is scarcely a model for tolerance among nations. Furthermore, many religions would have you believe that thinking objectively about the world can be dangerous, because it may lead you astray from the faith. In other words, the search for truth is discarded as part of the bargain. This is hardly the preferable approach to finding common ground for humanity.

Even if we do not look to religion as the ultimate source of ethical values, we can recognize the compatibility between a secular approach and some religious fundamentals. Religions tend officially to espouse, though sometimes with dismaying hypocrisy, the sanctity of life as one of the highest values. What could be more admirable and consistent with this principle than preserving liberty and respect for others, preventing suffering, and taking concrete, positive measures to ensure the survival of humanity? Furthermore, I believe we have a better chance of achieving peace and drastically reducing suffering if we are open to religious traditions, provided—and, again, this is a major caveat—religious leaders pledge to work together in promoting human rights and the reduction of suffering, and not try to position themselves as opponents of scientific enquiry and reason. Fortunately, most religions can be interpreted as being compatible with these values.

THE BATTLE FOR COMPASSION

In the previous chapters, reflecting on what matters to people, we considered the avoidance of suffering and the achievement of happiness and meaning, including such contributing factors as status, challenges, connections to others, diversity, spirituality, the hope for continuity, and sometimes truth. These are the things that individuals want for themselves and strive for in their self-interested pursuits, satisfying the impulses of a biological program that aimed for survival in often rougher but simpler times. The problem is that individuals' desires often collide and cause suffering. The challenge, for anyone who cares about others' suffering, is to find ways to reduce it.

But if ethics has no objectively valid, solid ground on which to stand, is it all really, in the end, still just a matter of "might makes right"? If values are ultimately relative and subjective, how do we ensure that humanitarian ones are respected in the future, and that attempts to dominate at the expense of others' suffering do not continually regain the upper hand?

The only certain conclusion is that we need to fight for them. As observed by the pioneering linguist and outspoken social activist Noam Chomsky, the trend towards more rights and more freedom is in competition with the trend towards more destruction, and who wins determines the fate of the species and is in the hands of people like "you".[75]

In the end, yes, it is a battle. But a battle waged not out of egoistic self-interest in disregard of others' well-being, but out of compassion. Out of compassion for other beings with whom we share part of our identity, whose suffering we have some sense of through introspection and empathy. Out of outrage at the atrocities humans inflict on humans and other creatures. Out of defiance of a universe that causes intense pain to emerge. Out of resolve to use our intelligence, creativity and knowledge about how the world works to try to have a positive impact, bucking the long trend of conflict and suffering in order to defend what matters.

There is a strong tendency in philosophy to pigeonhole philosophical views into distinct, mutually exclusive schools of thought, and the field of ethics is no exception. Philosophers still disagree about what ethics is about and the significance of "right" and "wrong". As I suggested at the beginning, these disputes are often fundamentally about word definitions. In some cases, apparently different views about the nature of ethics may also reflect philosophers' personal emotional stances. Someone who cares deeply about human suffering may have trouble admitting that values are subjective and relative. But it is not at all contradictory to espouse moral relativism—the position that judgments about "right" and "wrong" have no absolute validity—as an accurate *description* of the world, and yet to have a strongly compassionate perspective for which one is willing to fight. This perspective is based on empathy, on the knowledge and awareness of oth-

---

75 From an interview in the French film "Chomsky & Cie".

ers' subjective states, including suffering, and thus on a more complete truth than just what is objectively observable. By fighting to spread not only this knowledge and awareness but also a sense of responsibility to act upon it, one crosses an intellectual frontier from the detached, analytical culture of "is" into the empathetic, social activist culture of "ought". Noting the existence of this frontier is crucial as a reminder of the terrain we are standing on and the culture and language associated with it. A lot of energy seems to be wasted on verbal border disputes. But crossing this frontier need not be more than a formality, like flashing a passport as one walks across a border.

Making the recognition that someone else's suffering is comparable to one's own a universally respected agenda of the highest priority requires that people who care about it use all the knowledge and creative tools at their disposal to make it more of a reality. A persistent quest for the truth about how the world works, including the realization that everything is determined by a web of physical interactions, is only a good thing if it is accompanied by a knowledge of what others' suffering is like. As suggested earlier in the section "The Value of Humanity", the fact that even many scientists and philosophers express views at odds with the reasoning about ethics developed here, and in particular, on the fundamental importance of negative utilitarianism, further underlines the challenge of pressing for the primacy of compassion.

Ethics has no higher level significance than as an attempt to institutionalize compassion and provide limits to brutal human nature. This understanding of ethics is more relevant than ever to today's post-modern world of rapidly growing scientific knowledge and existential threats than the framing of ethics by classical philosophers and their idealistic, absolute notions of virtue.

The universe that contains our world is a closed system that will play out according to the laws of physics, and the degree of sustained compassion that emerges is ultimately a question of probability within the constraints of this chaotic system. Reflecting on our attempts to engineer compassion from within the system, we are forced to acknowledge the precariousness of it all and the delusion of believing that an objectively valid system of ethics exists. But we can at least have some confidence that the greater the degree to which a culture of compassion spreads, the greater the probability of reducing suffering over time. Theoretical arguments and reflections about ethics can still serve as a source of understanding and meaning, helping people to change their perspective and care more. Although these arguments always reflect subjective positions, they can be used to provide institutions with unambiguous prescriptions on how to act in specific situations. The essential criterion for making "ethical" decisions is that they be driven by compassion for others, with the additional caveat that they employ rational thinking so that objectives can actually be reached. Any ethical argument ultimately rings hollow unless it has downstream impact in reducing suffering, drawing on empathy, self-interest and reason as tools of persuasion, and unfortunately, in some cases, on the threat of force.

In the worst cases, new suffering is created to spare other suffering. As stated above, the suffering generated by any one brain can be viewed objectively as equivalent to the suffering generated by any other brain, and therefore reducing the absolute number of brains suffering might seem always to be justified. But the moment you take an action that causes suffering to take place that otherwise would not, you find yourself on very unstable ground. The use of physical coercion and violence for supposedly compassionate motives not only can lead to great psychological dilemmas but can undermine the empathy that serves as the driver of it all. As a practical means of leading to a world where less and less suffering occurs, we may sometimes feel obligated to navigate an ethical no-man's-land and play a dispassionate numbers game, but we should not be surprised when the victims and survivors of this strategy resist—using all means available. Creating suffering as a means of reducing suffering will always be a risky and distasteful exercise, to say the very least. Coming face to face with the reality of this newly created suffering can at least ensure that compassion continues to maintain a defining influence over the decisions made and raise the attractiveness of alternative strategies.

The overriding practical challenge is how to promote compassionate behavior in a way that is compatible with people's self-interest. When this is objectively clear, logical argumentation may suffice. But when the self-interest of compassionate behavior cannot be made obvious, ways need to be found to *make* it in people's self-interest, either by touching their emotional side, or by manipulating the environment, such as through economic or other incentives. And in the worst cases, compassion may indeed demand that force be used to prevent people from harming others.

What provides hope that these attempts might succeed in a sustainable way, if carried out intelligently, is the fact that global cooperation around universal values can be strongly argued to be in virtually everyone's self-interest, considering that the alternative may be the destruction of our planet. The other hopeful element is the nearly universal human capacity to respond emotionally when confronted with extreme suffering, causing us to feel in a deep, instinctive way that its avoidance is the most worthy objective.

One of countless possible reference points remains the Nazi Holocaust against the Jews[76], an event that, for many, represents the epitome of evil. The suffering that was incurred is so well documented that it can readily be referred to whenever efforts to promote compassion are downplayed as overly idealistic. Attempts, often clumsy, to compare less comprehensive or less ideological persecution and murder with the events in mid-20th century Europe under the Nazis have been criticized, sometimes rightly, for belittling the enormity of the Holocaust and the atrocities carried out during that period. There is in part a fear that by drawing an analogy between horrors committed on a much smaller scale and the Holocaust, the latter is rendered more banal and loses its symbolism as a benchmark for absolute wickedness. This concern was implied in the coining of Godwin's Law[77], which states that references to the Nazi period, however absurd, are increasingly likely to occur as an online discussion progresses.

While the scale and methodical character of the Nazi crimes stand virtually unparalleled in modern times, Joseph Stalin and Mao Zedong are still less widely known to have been responsible for the deaths of huge numbers of Soviet and Chinese citizens in the post-World War II period, and the suffering of the Nazis' victims is echoed in countless acts of mass cruelty that have continued to be carried out to this day, even beyond the well-known, large-scale atrocities in Cambodia, Rwanda, Bosnia, Darfur and the Congo. We cannot leave the Holocaust untouchable and beyond comparison, like an ominous symbol. Values regularly shift and new standards of behavior slowly become the norm without people taking notice. We need to stand vigilant and fight to keep reference points vivid in people's minds, continually evoking past atrocities. And critically, we must not shy away from

---

76 While the Jews were the Nazis' principal, most systematic target, groups such as the Romani (less commonly referred to today as Gypsies) and millions of other victims suffered similar fates.

77 Mike Godwin, "Meme, Counter-meme," *Wired* (October 1994), www.wired.com/wired/archive/2.10/godwin.if.html.

drawing comparisons when there is a real danger of the present drifting uncomfortably close to the past.

Left to its own devices, there is always the risk that raw human nature will lead to domination, destruction and suffering. The battle for compassion is therefore a continuous effort to drive conditions away from the "natural", spontaneous equilibrium towards a happier state and to put solid barriers and processes in place that can stave off the sometimes dramatic consequences of unfettered self-interest. At this critical point in history, it is more important than ever to promote and entrench a core set of universal humanitarian values based on compassion and the things that matter.

Universal Humanitarian Values

The search for an ethical code that can serve as a stable reference point for society is probably as old as humanity, and philosophers and teachers throughout the ages and from a wide variety of cultures and religious traditions have derived many prescriptions. These have tended to be very succinct. They are often variations on the themes of reciprocity, probably the most widespread ethical prescription, also known as the Golden Rule and expressed in one of its negative formulations as, "That which is hateful to you, do not do to your fellow"; universality, in particular, Immanuel Kant's categorical imperative, "Act only according to that maxim whereby you can at the same time will that it should become a universal law"; and utility, such as Jeremy Bentham's utilitarian notion of "the greatest good for the greatest number". Each has received its share of criticism, including the Golden Rule for its failure to consider people's differing desires, and utilitarianism for its failure to consider the asymmetry of suffering and happiness. But the overriding theme is compassion: a concern for others' subjective experience.

Universal values are ones that we can reasonably expect people to adhere to regardless of their religion or the country they live in. As was made clear during the Nuremberg War Crimes Trials and the rejection of many Germans' defense that they were simply following orders, we implicitly expect people to think independently and to reject any orders they receive from their governments to harm others. A broadly applicable set of values should serve as the underlying basis for how we conduct ourselves as a global society that respects all its members.

The more detail is added to a core ethical code, the less likely it is to have universal appeal as people disagree about the specifics. It therefore needs to be kept as broad and simple as possible. But it needs to be sufficiently precise to specify reasonable limits to people's behavior and make our drive for power and personal well-being compatible with a fundamental respect for others' subjective experience.

In trying to define a practical, essential set of core values, how much detail can one add beyond merely advocating compassion, the reduction of suffering and the preservation of the few essentials that matter most? In fact, not much. All the preceding discussions and arguments about subjective experience and what matters point to two essential humanitarian values of primordial importance for ensuring a minimum of happiness and preventing suffering. And I would argue that there are two additional ones that are also essential for giving our lives as much meaning as possible.

The first value, hardly a surprise, must surely be freedom. This value respects human nature and the need for self-realization. It encompasses the right to physical and emotional integrity, to security, to be free to think and speak openly, to live and experience life as one wishes, and to have the perception of control over one's mental states, so long as one's behavior does not seek to deprive others of the same freedom. And it includes the freedom to hope legitimately for a future worth working towards.

The sense of being human flourishes most when we can exercise our own individual capacities to the limit and ascribe maximum meaning to life. Freedom provides an outlet for creativity and self-expression. Although freedom from the rest of the universe is an illusion, the feeling of being fundamentally unthwarted in one's ambitions to achieve one's desires is an essential component of happiness. It depends on not perceiving or sensing other intelligences unduly controlling one's own behavior, or trying to compress the society we live in towards a dull, homogeneous average.

Freedom means providing people with the opportunity to develop and exercise self-confidence. It acknowledges the human urge to express, create and gain status, while implicitly placing limits where these directly infringe on others' such rights. As a value, freedom can thus be seen as both an individual right and an obligation towards others. The latter aspect is more fully developed in the second value.

The all-importance of reason as a means of understanding the world and deriving truths from other truths can be subsumed under freedom, as it derives from it. When you have freedom, the truth eventually comes out.

The second value is solidarity. This value is rooted in compassion, encompassing respect for others' subjective experience, and an awareness that we are all subject to the human condition and interdependent. It places a check on the first value of freedom and also demands taking active steps to help others attain a minimal level of well-being. It follows the principle of negative utilitarianism *plus* in giving highest priority to the prevention of avoidable suffering beyond a certain intolerable limit, to the extent that it is in our power to act without unbearable sacrifices. This applies to human suffering as well as to that of *any other* conscious beings, most notably animals.

Solidarity based on negative utilitarianism *plus* implies assuring, globally, the physical minimum for people's well-being, including clean water, food, nutrition, good health, lodging and clothing. It means not allowing people to fall off the edge, protecting them from marginalization and hopelessness, and taking measures to limit the degree of economic polarization occurring globally. It means not carrying out actions that are likely to put other people in harm's way, and not manipulating people into harming themselves. And it means not causing animals to suffer for our own enjoyment. The value of solidarity can be seen as an obligation, although it can only be sustainably promoted through positive means that appeal to people's capacity for empathy and pursuit of self-interest.

Freedom and solidarity are the two most important values there are, as they provide each individual with human dignity and a sense of control while respecting others' well-being as of essential importance. These values respect human nature for what it is, recognizing what people need to be happy and have meaningful lives, while placing limits on competition so that nobody is destroyed in the process. Ultimately, then, trying to preserve the beauty of consciousness while shielding it from the worst influences. There are two other, secondary values that are important for ensuring that our lives have meaning.

The third value is continuity. While I argued earlier that the survival of the human species, a concept, should not come at the expense of actual human welfare, the preservation of human intelligence and consciousness in a way that is compatible with the previous two values is important for our lives in the present to have meaning and a consequence of appreciating existence. It does not imply forcing people to procreate, but it means taking steps to ensure indefinite continuity into the future, including in any world where non-biological intelligence dominates (discussed in the next chapter), and to ensure the continued welfare and sustainability of our planet for as long as life depends on it. This value provides a general, long-term goal to continually strive towards, of fundamental existential importance, that carries with it urgent obligations regarding how we live today.

But just as empathy would preclude making a hypothetical decision to start the world all over again, preserving continuity requires that we strive to eradicate preventable suffering as part of the deal. It also implies that parts of the cultural traditions handed down to us may need to be re-evaluated for their compatibility with the other values.

The fourth and last value is diversity. As argued previously, diversity is a source of meaning and richness in our lives. It makes a wide range of subjective experiences possible and provides a context in which freedom is meaningful. It requires taking steps to prevent people of one culture seeking to stamp out other cultural traditions through domination and homogenization. It means preserving complexity and information, including that of evolved life. It is a value that has grown in urgency with globalization and advances in technology.

To summarize, we can say that freedom, in all its facets, provides the individual with a context in which to assume a sense of control, exist in a meaningful way and achieve happiness. Solidarity is a necessary accompaniment to raw freedom, placing limits on the harm that can be inflicted on others in the pursuit of self-interest and coming to the aid of those who suffer. And continuity and diversity provide a kind of existential insurance that it is all worthwhile, a basis for hope in the future. There is a certain pleasing balance in this core value system—I, you, eternity and complexity—, somehow analogous, perhaps, to the aesthetic symmetry scientists expect from the laws of physics.

These universal humanitarian values are simple and broad-ranging, incorporating what nearly all of us desire. They represent a potential set of fundamental, all-encompassing starting assumptions of the widest possible acceptability for any argument about how we ought to act, though with plenty of room to discuss the details—preferably in a civilized manner.

Driving a compassionate agenda demands that any position or course of action should be defendable according to these values, even at the risk that previously held ideas about specific issues no longer make as much sense. Of course, in the end, it is all a matter of where the limits are placed on freedom, and this can be endlessly debated and, unfortunately, lead to violent conflict. To deny people a certain degree of freedom is to deny them their ability to strive successfully for what they want, but to allow individuals to acquire unrestricted power is to limit others' freedom and well-being. A viable and compassionate balance between the two requires the setting of limits, and there will always be some variation between societies, and arguments within societies, regarding where the precise limits are placed. This is why compassion must be fought for in a way that is perceived as transparent and universally fair and applicable.

THE UNITED NATIONS UNIVERSAL DECLARATION OF HUMAN RIGHTS

The United Nations Universal Declaration of Human Rights (UDHR), adopted in 1948, may be the closest there is to a Holy Grail of humanitarianism. A document with significance for international law, it serves as a common reference point to strive for within the constraints of a multi-polar, international system of sovereign governments and fixed borders.

The UDHR is not so much a basic value system in the conceptual sense as a specification of the practical baseline requirements for what life should be like for every human being. It goes into detail about the specific rights all humans theoretically have. The freedom of the individual is the principal theme underlying the UDHR, along with the respect that each individual should be able to enjoy and the notion of a minimum standard of living.

The UDHR explicitly relates universal human rights to a variety of specific situations and the obligations of signatory states, in order to avoid ambiguity regarding its interpretation. As such, the UDHR is a document of great practical importance. It does not address the means to achieve these rights so much as it seeks to confer states with responsibility for their residents and limit their intrusiveness into people's lives. Unfortunately, United Nations bodies such as its Human Rights Council sometimes take skewed or self-serving positions that are in contradiction with the very principles of the UDHR. But this fact does not detract from the value of the document itself. If its signatories fully abided by both the spirit and letter of it, the world would be an unrecognizably better place. Universal adherence to the UDHR remains an essential goal to work towards.

A key weapon in the battle for compassion and the defense of universal values is the use of reason to unearth the underlying assumptions and values behind people's statements and behavior. In fact, it can be argued that the goal of *all* commentary and debate on politics and current affairs aimed at fostering a better world should be to pinpoint argumentation and policies that diverge from universal humanitarian values and their logical implications, and to unmask self-interest parading nonsense as the truth. Most arguments on behalf of an activity, political or otherwise, reflect inherent assumptions related to the protagonist's own beliefs and striving for well-being, however well hidden these assumptions are. The degree to which these assumptions are compatible with universal values is a key measure by which the arguments should be judged.

If an interlocutor is inherently uncompassionate and has no shame in admitting it, explicitly rejecting the relevance of universal values and the need to relieve suffering, reason will only get you so far in pushing a compassionate agenda. In those cases, one must use effective tools to impress upon people the relevance of others' suffering and generate empathy, appeal to self-interest as a means of persuasion, and potentially, in the most extreme cases, resort to force to protect others. But reason can compel impostors to reveal their true underlying motives and, ideally, lose support that they mustered through the use of lies. Invoking reason is a little like referring to the fine print at the bottom of a contract: if you break the rules, you can no longer claim to be playing the game legitimately. Of course, when someone points a gun barrel at you, explicitly communicating their own interpretation of how to make a point, it obviously does not help to whip out the rule book of reason. But as long as people are prepared to dialogue peacefully and achieve a meaningful determination of the best course of action, reason provides the ground rules for saying things that make sense. Even those with the wearying and even dangerous tendency to compensate for a lack of logical sense with a lot of noise cannot defy the rules indefinitely without being caught.

The probing character of the little word "why?" makes it an invaluable tool in this endeavor. People tend not to ask "why?" too insistently, satisfying themselves with an immediate cause in most situations. It provides them with the information they need to make sufficient sense of the world for their own purposes. It also prevents them from becoming an annoying bore, since most people just cannot be bothered to answer the question "why?" more than a few times in succession, after which the person you were having a stimulating conversation with is likely to dig in their heels and reply with a stubborn "just because" rather than provide further justification. The word "why?" makes people vulnerable, ultimately forcing them to come to terms with the big issues, namely, the meaning of life and the contradictions inherent in their own existence and lifestyle. By repeatedly and honestly answering "why?", people may well be forced to acknowledge deep-seated, hidden reasons for their behavior, or long-held beliefs, that may conflict with values they purportedly adhere to. But persistence is crucial.

The world is satiated with people saying we ought to do this and we ought to do that. Debates rage in newspapers, on TV and on the Internet about controversial issues concerning politics and society. And in the same way that a court of law is supposed to be a battleground for conflicting arguments, out of which the truth is supposed to emerge to the unbiased, objective jurors, conventional wisdom holds that an open, fully argued public debate will lead to an eventual shift in opinion towards the more reasonable views. But the only way to sift through all these prescriptions and assess which ones to follow is to ask "why?" and follow the logical arguments down to their source, determining the reasoning they implicitly rest on. Repeatedly asking "why?" may reveal flawed reasoning or contradictions with universal values and force a reconsideration of the appropriateness of a particular action.

Most debates do not dig that deeply—there is not enough room, time or attention span. As a result, many of the underlying assumptions never get questioned. Leave these assumptions untouched and you cannot hope to change the specific opinions. That leaves much of public debates akin to shouting matches between people who speak different languages.

Because expounding the whole line of reasoning behind every assertion would be tiring and use up a lot of energy, much is accepted on the strength of conventional wisdom. The average person cannot be expected to do all the thinking required to determine whether an assertion or explanation really makes sense. Relying on the word of scientific experts and other respected figures of authority is a common shortcut to get at the truth. But this only works when these authorities are fully transparent about their assumptions and rational in their argumentation.

Changing people's most fundamental assumptions and beliefs may indeed be very difficult or practically impossible, as these may be closely tied to their basic psychological makeup and sense of identity—in many cases, including in the United States, of which there is a strong religious component from which everything else flows. But by forcing open-minded people—those who are willing to address the question "why?", rather than simply asserting what they like and don't like—to explain their belief system, there is at least the possibility for an understanding of the basic reasons for diverging opinions. Even where a divergence of views boils down to blind faith versus a more rationalistic approach, common humanistic denominators can still be found, even between people with very different perspectives on the world.

Consistency plays a crucial role. In the heat of the 2008 United States presidential election campaign, comedian Jon Stewart, host of the popular satirical news program "The Daily Show" and a wiz at sniffing out hypocrisy, poked fun at various political commentators for, on separate occasions, making opposing arguments about similar issues, depending on the protagonists involved—for example, whether a candidate was more or less qualified for office based on the size of the town they were mayor of.[78] The audience found the video clips entertaining because, while the commentators were obviously trying to appear logical and credible, their arguments were clearly being adapted to the conclusions they wanted to draw on each occasion, even when it meant contradicting themselves.

Consistency means holding views that are compatible with one another, and also acting in a way that is logically compatible with these views. It is a prerequisite for proposing solutions and carrying out actions that are based on universal values, and that square with truths about life and how the universe seems to operate. And reason represents the backbone of consistency.

In practice, people are famously inconsistent in the things they say and do. They profess beliefs they do not really hold very strongly or have not thought about very carefully; hold positions that, if they thought things through logically, they would find contradict with more deeply held beliefs; say things they think others want or expect to hear but which are not consistent with how they act; and, in order to avoid cognitive dissonance with what their actions imply about their beliefs, as well as to try to persuade

---

78 www.thedailyshow.com/watch/wed-september-3-2008/ sarah-palin-gender-card

others, selectively pick arguments that support the conclusions they want to reach, rather than argue from basic principles.

Yet there are few things people dislike more than hypocrisy. A person who does not practice what they preach is regarded as manipulative, using words as mere instruments of personal gain. Ultimately, hypocrisy usually means that one is not being open about underlying, self-serving starting assumptions. If you cannot apply the identical set of principles to two situations, then you are tacitly revealing that you are applying additional, higher priority principles to which you do not wish openly to admit.

In debating societies, students hone their skills by learning to build arguments for or against any given issue. Translated to the real world, this means deciding what you want and making the best possible case to get it. This is also how the criminal justice system works: a defense lawyer will use all the arguments she can muster to get her client acquitted. But in a world where anything matters, it is the assumptions that need to be made explicit in any argument, with the conclusions a logical consequence—*not the other way around*. And as I have argued, the assumptions that matter most if pure, uncompassionate self-interest is not to be the sole driving factor are universal humanitarian values.

Paying lip service to certain principles while carrying out actions that are incompatible with them is a notoriously common feature of politics at all levels and across the political spectrum, and one of the reasons so many people have such disdain for politics. The alleviation of preventable suffering requires transparent argumentation that unmasks hypocrisy for what it is and demands that universal humanitarian values be consistently applied by people, organizations and governments. When we consider the arguments given for courses of action, consistency represents a vital test.

13. WHERE WE ARE HEADED

THE EXISTENTIAL CONSEQUENCES OF TECHNOLOGY

The past is concrete and tangible, the future vague and murky. But there is something uniquely eerie about the present. For many of us today who were lucky enough to be born with the right nationality, the greatest everyday challenge is not physically to survive, but to occupy our time with endeavors that entertain us, provide ourselves with a feeling of self-worth and, over the longer term, provide some sense of significance to our existence. And yet at the same time, there is a pervasive, looming sense of foreboding among many people today that humanity is coming up against an unbreachable wall, an awareness that serious and dramatic troubles are brewing on our planet that may make the present an illusory calm before the storm. Just decades after health and economic prosperity seemed to be within the sights, if not immediate grasp, of most of our fellow humans, new threats of an ominous nature threaten our very survival as a species. Things are changing very rapidly, in a crescendo of potentially apocalyptic convergence. But judging by the comparatively trivial, daily concerns of the average person, it really seems as if civilization has become anesthetized, oblivious to or apathetic about its own potentially imminent demise. Although the word "apocalyptic" would provoke virtual eye rolling among some pundits for being unnecessarily dramatic, many of these observers and commentators are subject to the same phenomenon of compression discussed early on. Sneering in the face of sentimentality and implicitly refusing to recognize the significance of humanity's terrible fragility is akin to yielding to the eventual triumph of banal instinct over both detached reflection and intensely felt meaning.

We know that the sun will burn out in a few billion years after first expanding dramatically in size, a sequence of events that represents a definitive limit to the possibility of life on Earth. That fact may have momentarily blunted your cheerful mood when you first learned about it in science class, but you could console yourself by remembering that that won't happen for a very, very long time—the same thing that parents say to their children when the subject of death comes up. But whether or not we realize it, a comparably significant occurrence for human life on Earth may be almost upon us, within a matter of decades.

Human beings have been living on the planet in essentially their current form as *Homo sapiens* for about 200,000 years. Although the course of an individual life can always come to an abrupt end from one second to the next as the result of an aneurysm, asteroid, or automobile accident, only in the last 50 years—0.03% or so of human history—have we as a species had the ability to completely destroy ourselves, and almost literally with the push of a button. During the Cuban Missile Crisis of 1962, the use of a nuclear weapon by the Soviet Union, which might have led directly to all-out nuclear war, turns out to have hinged on the decision of one single, stressed submarine captain who eventually changed his mind. As mentioned in the introduction, Sir Martin Rees, cosmologist and a recent president of the Royal Society, whose book *Our Final Hour* details the increasing risks we face as a result of the malign or unintentional use of new and existing technologies, has put the odds of human civilization surviving the 21st century at no more than 50%. Of course, what superficially appears to be an abstract numerical prediction actually implies some terrible concrete scenarios. Rees's dire predictions are increasingly being echoed by other prominent scientists, with physicist Stephen Hawking recently suggesting that the future of humanity depends on our ability to colonize space soon enough. Technology will continue to be exploited in increasingly sophisticated global power struggles. And the rapid spread of information and the increasing ease with which people with malevolent intentions or insufficient foresight can use technology to negatively impact the rest of the planet make the future increasingly hard to control by government injunction.

Against the relief of the billions of years of our planet's history, the decisions we make today take on an extraordinary significance. But because we are so focused on the present, we often fail both to learn from the past and to project ourselves into the future, and to reflect on the possible impact of our current decisions or lack thereof, and how they will be judged. We have huge amounts of relevant information at our disposal, but we make poor use of it—in large part, because it is so abundant, scattered and far beyond the digestibility of any one person.

What we call technology and both praise and blame for its consequences is a continuous acceleration in complexity resulting from the human urge to seek status and newness. The rapidity with which the latest technologies are adopted and exploited for the purpose of gaining money and power is a reality that will impact intelligent life on Earth for as long as it exists. Many of the benefits are undeniable, including the development of treatments for otherwise deadly or disabling diseases, global communications that keep people in permanent contact, or the variety of cultural experiences readily available for viewing or listening on demand. But the potentially destructive power of technologies that already exist and others that will come into being in the coming decades, including those specifically developed for military purposes, represent an extremely serious threat to our survival. While the physical constraints of the human brain limit the efficiency with which self-interest can be pursued by uncompassionate individuals, artificial intelligence networks and sophisticated algorithms may provide a deadly supplement to those with access.

Some people act like passengers on the Titanic, living it up in style as the violins play, oblivious to their imminent fate. They downplay or scoff disparagingly at doomsday scenarios or articulated fears about the future of humanity, pointing to humans' great flexibility and adaptability. Or else they simply don't care all that much. It seems that no matter what arguments you present to some people about where we are heading, they will still prefer to squeeze the most out of a hedonistic existence than take a larger interest in what is happening to our world. Like participants in a Ponzi pyramid scheme who expect to profit by getting in early enough, they don't worry about the poor suckers who will lose out when it finally collapses.

But many thoughtful, well-meaning people are simply resigned to a dim future for humanity, paralyzed by a frustrating sense of helplessness as they see all the suffering going on in the world, understand the significance of what is happening to the planet and yet not know what of substance can be done about it, while visionless, power-obsessed politicians drag their feet about instituting half-measures. They resemble the Australians in Nevil Shute's 1957 novel *On the Beach*, waiting with a mixture of fatalism and denial for a radioactive cloud to arrive from a Northern Hemisphere where life has already been extinguished in a massive nuclear war. It increasingly seems like we are being drawn into a mad rush for immediate pleasure in our species' endgame.

Recognizing the destruction we are unleashing on our planet, with climate change and its consequences foremost in the global consciousness, as described by Clive Hamilton in his book *Requiem for a Species*, and hearing even scientist James Lovelock, originator of the Gaia hypothesis, suggest fatalistically that all we can do is "enjoy life while you can"[79], it is hard not to feel deeply sad. Not merely apprehensive, as one might about one's own eventual death, but something more profound, in the awareness that events of far greater significance are occurring, powerfully thwarting our species' hard-wired survival instinct.

Aside from the long-term threats to our existence stemming from its misuse and self-interested exploitation, it is also undeniable that technology is profoundly altering the nature of the human experience for many in the present. Psychoanalyst and author Erich Fromm published a book in 1968 called *The Revolution of Hope*, in which he expressed his concerns about the dangers of dehumanized technology, where we are all sacrificed for a system that constantly demands "more", that shuns serious reflection and demands unquestioned obedience in the interest of progress. These ideas are as relevant today as they were over four decades ago. Politicians' constant bandying about of the word "progress" has an air of Newspeak about it—the attempt to restrict thought through restrictions in language use in George Orwell's *Nineteen Eighty-Four*. What is this progress? Are our lives actually becoming happier and more meaningful, or is the increase in complexity actually having the opposite effect?

Our lives are already merging with computers in a form of technology creep. We outsource much of our general knowledge to the Internet, implicitly using Google and Wikipedia as trustworthy brain extensions—cur-

---

79 "Lovelock: 'We can't save the planet'," BBC, http://news.bbc.co.uk/today/hi/today/newsid_8594000/8594561.stm.

rently accessible through the existing technology of screens and keyboards, but soon enough through processes that will become ever subtler. More ominously, we are already, to an extent, being manipulated by networks of vast computing power at the service of large profit-making corporations, to whose indispensable services we have slowly become enslaved. The selfish underpinnings of society are becoming increasingly explicit, and our lives and relationships risk being dominated by the widespread, brazen use of algorithms that strip us down to simple bearers of status.

As our world undergoes a fundamental, paradigmatic shift from analog to digital processes, we are lured into believing that the various numbers we use to represent reality capture all that matters. But our measurements are not calibrated to an absolute scale of meaning. Without a stable reference point, we fail to recognize the loss of absolute intensity in the meaning that is subjectively experienced.

Virtual reality is also slowly but steadily encroaching on our lives. A virtual world such as Second Life offers a primitive peep at what reality might feel like to residents of the future. Via their avatars, people can pursue humankind's most basic obsession and engage in virtual flirting extending as far as cybersex, and even while their physical bodies may be slumped in chairs positioned in front of computer screens, the firing patterns of their neurons may resemble those of people actually engaged in the rituals of mating. While one can assert that the pleasures of virtual reality will never replace the full sensory experience of "real life", and in moments of lucidity our still-human selves will grasp the drug-like artificialness of it all, technology will find ever more sophisticated ways to trigger the brain's pleasure centers and satisfy people's many other needs, including those for novelty and variety of experience, and the way that many humans behave and interact may continue to evolve.

Even to the extent that technology responds to demand, many of the basic things that people desire—novelty, reduced effort, sensory stimulation, etc.—are not equivalent to what makes them happy in the long run, as discussed earlier. Some of the mechanisms of desire and impulse satisfaction—which evolved to ensure that people fed themselves sufficiently in a rough environment and were sufficiently curious and innovative to compete with their neighbors—are essentially permanently activated, with no apparent "off" switch to push when satiety is reached. The epidemic of obesity in the United States and its encroachment in other developed parts of the world is just one blatant example of the effects of an unchecked desire for more in a plentiful environment. The future is continuously swallowing the past, the nature of life is changing so quickly, and we don't seem to be satisfactorily applying what we know about human nature to a world of accelerating transformation.

How it feels to be alive is continuously undergoing a fundamental drift, but because it happens relatively smoothly and we continuously adapt, we are never faced with a single dramatic moment where major decisions have to be made. Much of the technology-driven change concerns how we occupy our time rather than controversial issues such as cloning babies. Although we may still be able to distinguish intellectually between reality and fantasy, our emotional reactions reflect a subconscious blurring of the two, with more of reality being triggered virtually in our heads, and the worst aspects of external reality no longer able to shock us effectively. Furthermore, with the ever advancing spread of global connectivity, it becomes increasingly difficult to escape it and fully imbibe the immediacy of the present moment in true isolation. What we have gained in quantity of information and contacts we have often lost in intensity, focus and meaning. We are all increasingly connected yet at greater risk of becoming atomized and impoverished emotionally.

THE SINGULARITY

In his landmark book *The Singularity is Near*, the pioneering inventor and futurist Ray Kurzweil builds on the concept of a "Singularity" previously developed by computer scientist Vernor Vinge and details a forecast of dramatic transformation in the dauntingly near future in the very nature of humanity, of which most people are currently unaware or ignorant of the possible extent. Kurzweil argues that, within the next few decades, biological intelligence will increasingly be supplemented and replaced by non-biological (artificial) intelligence to the point that the former becomes essentially insignificant. Our understanding of the brain, aided by the use of increasingly sophisticated nanotechnology, along with computing power and other technologies, will all have advanced to the point where our subjective experiences can be thoroughly induced virtually without the need for "real world" correlates. And crucially, non-biological human intelligence will pursue its own goals at speeds unrestricted by biological substrates, continuously modifying itself along the way and overcoming technical obstacles through expanded knowledge and computing power. It is impossible to predict just what would happen once a Singularity is reached, as our current models of how the world works would no longer hold. Kurzweil nonetheless remains highly optimistic that the non-biological intelligence will remain "human" and therefore represent more of a good thing.

Many of the details of Kurzweil's predictions could prove entirely inaccurate, in particular, the astonishing speed with which he expects this transformation to occur. It depends on a continued, practically unlimited acceleration in brute computing power, which may turn out to be a false assumption, and also on an imminent, minute understanding of the brain's architecture and functioning, which may have greater complexity and therefore be more difficult to reproduce artificially than he assumes. There are other uncertain factors as well, such as the mechanics of intelligence being able to physically re-engineer and improve itself and its ability to gain complete independence from biological intelligence. Kurzweil also does not translate his predictions into a comprehensive explanation of how events would take shape on the ground, including how governments would react to perceived threats and opportunities to gain power as companies, research institutions and military departments develop new technologies. It is unclear just how these developments will play out geopolitically in terms of initial ownership and application of the technologies and the balance between governments and corporations. How the technologies that could lead to a Singularity are managed will depend on their potential to be used, even subtly, as weapons. And the anticipation of the advent of a Singularity could prompt pre-emptive military or terrorist strikes by those who feel threatened.

However, if we do not destroy ourselves beforehand—and that remains a big "if"—, it is perhaps just a matter of time before the transformation he foresees occurs. Kurzweil's thesis reflects what may be an essential truth about the universe, which is that everything can be understood as a form of information, and that in the end, information processing that transits through biological organisms over large spans of time can eventually escape its biological constraints. The idea of computers surpassing humans in intelligence still seems to many like an unrealizable fantasy, a vision directly out of a science fiction novel from the 1950s. But while one can mock this clichéd view of the future, reality continues to creep along unhindered.

And we know how many past predictions have come true. As technology advances, we come closer to a potential moment in time at which things may proceed irreversibly along one path or another. Once a Singularity is reached, phenomenal events could potentially occur at lightning speed, somewhat analogously to how an entire global financial system can rapidly go out of control once a tipping point is reached, but with incomparably more dramatic consequences.

If and when a Singularity takes place, all the musings of philosophers and historians, trying to explain the course of human development from the perspective of political, economic and social systems, might prove in retrospect to have had less long-term explanatory power than a mixture of simple evolutionary theory, based on the replication of competing self-maximizers and the genes they contain, and the more broadly relevant information theory, which encompasses the study of complexity and the replication of competing memes. The predictions of a Singularity, to the extent that they need to be taken seriously, make the narrow focus of current public debate and the issues addressed by international institutions seem hopelessly short-sighted and comparably trivial. Even much of *this* book is based on thinking about a conventional world, whereas a Singularity would be a major game-changer, although the basic considerations—the fundamental importance of subjective experience as well as the role of competitive processes—would remain similarly relevant.

I believe that, at least in his book—which has since spawned considerable commentary and debate—Kurzweil downplays somewhat the extent to which the initially human intelligence, freed from its biological substrate, would itself be likely to evolve, essentially creating a new "species" and transforming the essence of experience—not necessarily for the better. (To take a cue from the REM song that is coincidentally playing as I first write this thought down: a poor "imitation of life".) Once the line between humans and machines blurs into nothing, evolution may quickly begin to play nasty tricks on us. We may be on the verge of being sucked up by a giant vortex of technology that will radically change what it means to be human. In a post-Singularity world where intelligence and, more importantly, consciousness are non-biological, where genes become irrelevant and subjective experience has new ways of manipulating itself and other subjective experience, an entirely new paradigm is set loose, with unforeseeable and even incomprehensible characteristics and consequences. Intelligences may merge with each other or compete by destroying others' access to energy—literally "pulling the plug"—or sabotaging networks and other intelligent substrates. Any remaining biological human beings may be ignored, manipulated or simply destroyed.

How much does all this matter, to the extent that it is still possible to use the word "matter" in reflecting on such radical transformation in who we are? Would it matter if humans continuously re-invented themselves, or found themselves re-invented, dramatically changing the nature of what things feel like, even if the basic constituents and emotions remained intact, which is hardly a given? Perhaps this is simply the inevitable nature of the next stage in the continuum of "life" which we want to feel part of. But even if it does really matter to anyone who cares about the continuity of *Homo sapiens*, and even if we might influence how it happens, have the anxieties of past generations in the face of technological change ever made a difference? Does anyone care enough to do anything about it today? We take for granted surprisingly quickly what were formerly futuristic technologies, adapting readily to change, regarding how things actually are as normal, and hardly stopping to breathe along the way. We forget who and what we once were. In his novel *Diary of a Bad Year*, J.M. Coetzee wrote about how we have lost the ability to understand the emotions that drove the creation of classical music. Similarly, technological advancements may be causing us to lose, possibly forever, an understanding of the meaning people experienced in the past, without us even realizing it.

The present has constantly mocked the past as technology improved quality of life for many. Perhaps in the future, hyper-intelligent, disembodied consciousness may long for the simplicity of a real world, but perhaps it will be able to achieve pleasures we cannot even imagine? Our philosophical reflections about meaning and the value of life and the species may reveal themselves to be both of extreme existential relevance and, at the same time, naïvely limited in their scope and ultimately futile. In the end, the existential questions may just be the conscious correlates of matter evolving, a cry accompanying a phase transition, like the hiss of water as it escapes from burning wood in the form of steam.

However, to be as practical and concrete as possible, any consideration of the promise of future technology and where we are headed risks being falsely optimistic if it does not place subjective experience at the center of the reflections. Darwinian trends will persist as long as there is competition in some way for resources or other factors that can limit freedom, even if these are in the form of bits of information and computing potential rather than barrels of oil, and those centers of information and control with greater access to these will then dominate. If humans are still around, they may be used as slaves, and the physical world subjected to potentially devastating destruction. The potential for suffering will persist as long as consciousness exists—both biological and non-biological—, and avoiding it will depend on compassionate intelligence in a position of power. This requires that no other kind of intelligence has the knowledge and means to subvert compassionate intelligence. To the extent that intelligences converge in the pursuit of common goals, compassion may thrive, as it does among kin due to genetic selection. On the other hand, competing intelligences battling for informational supremacy and the power it conveys risk paying scant attention to the subjective emotional states of their rivals. The war cry of the modern globalized capitalist will persist, as strong as ever: "accumulate, expand, consolidate". Utopian ideals and romantic notions of subjectivity may fall by the wayside as non-biological intelligence dominates.

Even if suffering can be avoided, I would still venture a very subjective opinion. If we evolve to become disembodied information, even if there is a lot of knowledge and virtual pleasure going around, won't there be more than just a slight sense that we have lost something essential from what it is to be human? Ultimately, the loss of the connection existing between two people in love who look into each other's eyes, the loss of physical contact, without its replacement in at least as real a form, cannot be an improvement. Granted, this is a human speaking. But what kind of super-intelligent non-biological consciousness could really be at ease with its situation? I don't think even the greatest optimist regarding artificial intelligence could provide a certain answer. With a nod to Winston Smith and Julia in *Nineteen Eighty-Four*, there are things one should fight to maintain, even if the natural forces of the universe are stacked against you.

For example, part of what makes life worth living for human beings is the curiosity and sense of adventure that comes from not knowing everything. What would a post-Singularity intelligence seek? Indefinite expansion? Continuous pleasure? An eternal orgasm? Humanity must have something more meaningful to anticipate than either an endless loop of mindless hedonism or the humorless domination of power and information. Besides, if a Singularity ultimately results in a single intelligence consuming the energy and matter of the universe, it is likely to be both extremely narcissistic and bored, with no one to talk to. Perhaps for that reason, it would mold a small copy of itself from some of its matter and plant it in a suitable location. But then, that sounds very religious.

If our decisions today about how technology is steered have a direct influence on subjective experience in the future, we need to take a major interest. A Singularity adds a wholly new dimension to the concerns about subjective experience expressed in this book, which will remain as important as ever but take on a new degree of urgency. If we want a future, post-Singularity world to respect humanitarian values, we need to fight for them. The only way to approach a Singularity with tranquility might be for these values to be firmly entrenched beforehand, with subjective experience and the avoidance of suffering given full priority. Human intelligence in biological form—i.e. what we currently call "human beings"...—should remain an option by providing it with protection, preserving the values of freedom and continuity. A post-Singularity world might otherwise contain people who desire the continued preservation of biological humanity, with access to powerful intelligence they still control, battling for their survival against autonomous non-biological intelligence.

There are researchers, such as Eliezer Yudkowsky of the Singularity Institute, studying how to engineer artificial intelligence in a way that ensures that the Singularity is "good".[80] This is a complex issue that goes well beyond computer science, and it will probably demand a broader consensus among humanistic specialists from other disciplines. Many scientists and futurists routinely—and, I think, sometimes far too readily—absolve themselves of responsibility to address the ethical questions associated with new technologies, relegating them to society, which will have decisions to make about where it wants to go. But of course, there is no single decision-making entity called society, but rather, forces militating in favor of different outcomes, often based on untouched beliefs or what they think are likely to yield benefits to them. The net outcome of the process simply reflects the balance of power. And it is critical that the humanists win.

---

80 See the website of the Singularity Institute at www.singinst.org.

To a limited extent, certain characteristics of the post-Singularity world are already appearing, with much thinking already outsourced to computers, as mentioned above, and much of how our time is occupied is already tied to digital platforms. As information as well as computer processing power continue to grow exponentially, power disequilibria may be exploited in ways that will have huge consequences, and the motives of those with access to this incremental information will become critical. This is a crux of the problem with the Singularity. And because upcoming events may be of such overwhelming significance, we may be forced to "play God" if we don't want harmful processes to dominate.

The earlier reflection on the nature of identity becomes extremely pertinent when we talk about the future and the potential substitution of human intelligence by machines. The onslaught of technology forces us once again to come to terms with underlying reality and the illusions that keep it hidden. The divide between individual identities becomes very vague indeed, even as the principle of respecting subjective experience becomes as all-important as ever. As the physical correlates of "life" fade into irrelevance, we will be forced to re-evaluate the traditionally sacred boundary between life and death. How can conscious beings whose existence depends more on electronic processes than on organic substrates be assured they will not be "killed" and thus be able to live in peace without fear?

The occurrence of a Singularity may be, if not intentionally impeded—and some scientists believe it probably cannot be, even if this were desirable—, both an inevitable outcome of a long, continuous evolutionary process, and a major discontinuity in the existence of our species and consciousness. The paradigmatic change in the nature of our existence that it would represent makes it almost vertiginously difficult to think meaningfully about our priorities. Does everything that is happening right now on our planet take on far greater importance as the future of traditional human existence suddenly appears very finite? Or would the Singularity be a new beginning, the opportunity we've been waiting for all along to see suffering relieved and continuity in our existence freed of the risks of a global catastrophe, but one we must ensure we get right?

But present suffering and the future of consciousness are closely related issues, as they both relate to the importance we attribute to subjective experience—our scale of caring. We shouldn't have to make a choice. The future starts now, and with it events we can strive to affect. The primacy of subjective experience and the need for compassion remain guiding values we should be endeavoring to implement as widely and deeply as possible. The challenge of ending preventable suffering caused by human cruelty, conflict, disease and gaping wealth disparities is radically different from that of making the best out of a Singularity. The first challenge is mundane but colossal, while the second is über-existential but potentially surmount-able. Yet the underlying goals are the same.

14. As Good as It Can Get

Throughout this book, I have been seeking to offer a fresh, less intuitive perspective on our existence and the fragile situation in which we find ourselves that might provide some additional insight to people interested in making a difference. If we open our eyes widely, we cannot avoid recognizing the absurdity of our situation: conscious creatures that emerged by chance in this remote corner of an apathetic universe that produces beauty and pain, playthings of an apparently soulless cosmos, tossed about in a complex web of interactions, under the illusion of having absolute control while subject to larger-scale forces of which we are often just dimly aware. All our subjective experiences, the things that matter, are determined by objective reality, ultimately making our emotions prisoners of a physical world.

Descendants of a long line of often suffering creatures reaching back hundreds of millions of years, we are all victims of innate urges that condemn us to compete and sometimes subject one another to pain. A program originally designed through spontaneous processes to pursue self-interest, running simultaneously in all our brains, though a driver of innovation and wealth creation, causes or contributes to the persistence of widespread major suffering. Without a concerted effort to make appropriate changes to the environment in which it finds itself, it will continue to do so. This hardwired impulse represents a constant threat to stable cooperation. While we focus on small-scale details and short-term crises, power appears to be continuously consolidating itself in small steps as globalization and technology march ever onward. The same forces may also lead to dramatically new forms of consciousness in the near future, while threatening our existence as a species.

We are much more similar to each other than we realize, in a deep, existential sense. And yet, because subjective experience is opaque, and individuals often do not share the same experiences, the sometimes intense suffering experienced by some brains frequently goes undetected by other brains or is only understood abstractly, and the quality of distress at the extreme end of the scale is rarely appreciated for its true, terrible significance. Furthermore, it is very difficult for most people to remain fully aware of and navigate the phenomenal conceptual gap between their everyday bubbles of subjective experience, often saturated with positive and negative hedonic triggers, and the profound significance of the risks to our existence.

Those of us alive today are, to repeat the phrase, existing in a uniquely critical sliver of time. Technology has just now reached the point where we could spread messages of choice and initiate new processes in a way that could possibly have dramatic, sustained, positive global impact if planned minutely, but where the wrong decisions, or the simple lack of the right ones, could very soon lead us down an irreversible path towards self-destruction, or towards a situation where uncompassionate technology takes over the relay from its human creators. Will we seize the opportunity we now have? Is it even possible?

A VISION OF UTOPIA

> Our task must be to free ourselves from the prison by widening our circle of compassion to embrace all living creatures and the whole of nature in its beauty.
>
> —Albert Einstein

Any attempt to shape the future needs a vision to guide it. Given what we know about human nature—our innate drive to compete, our need for connections with others, for happiness and for meaning, as well as our desire for continuity—what might a more utopian world in the not-too-distant future look like? Let's be idealistic and imagine some likely practical elements.

• Subjective experience would be universally recognized as the core locus of meaning, with the highest priority given to how individual people feel, not to cultural concepts that people may or may not want to be part of.

• People's individual freedoms and human rights would be universally respected and applied around the globe.

• Society would show solidarity to those in difficult situations, and preventable suffering, especially of the worst kinds, would be essentially eliminated.

• Acts without real or reasonably foreseeable victims would not be punishable as crimes.

• Judicial systems would administer sentences in a pragmatic, humane and minimally vengeful manner. Sentences would be sufficient to dissuade crime, protect society and change bad behavior, but more creative, respectful ways would be employed to deal with criminals.

• Torture would not be authorized in any jurisdiction, even surreptitiously, including for the extraction of information from captives.

• Armed conflicts would be averted through an international system that aimed to satisfy conflicting parties with their most important needs, employed impartial mediation, and used concrete enticements to make enforceable peace deals more attractive.

• Concentrations of ethnic and culturally related groups living in defined geographical areas would be given significant political autonomy, with minorities and their human rights accorded full protection.

• People would enjoy the freedom to travel around the globe without excessive barriers.

• Scientific and intellectual inquiry would be carried out freely without fear of persecution, and rationalism would be respected by governments as the most dependable and direct means of making sense of external reality.

• Spiritual freedom and the right to engage in religious practices would be entrenched, as long as they do not seek to infringe on universal humanitarian values.

• Health would be a universal priority. Diseases for which prophylactics or treatments existed would no longer cause people to suffer and die, including in the developing world, as the appropriate medications and vaccines would be made available through the mobilization of resources and the resolution of logistical problems. Universal healthcare would be provided. Increased funding of medical research would aim to radically reduce suffering due to disease.

• Poverty would be eliminated in the developed world through social safety nets that ensured that no one is allowed to fall off the edge.

• Extreme poverty in developing countries would be eliminated as a result of sustained economic growth, through a shrinking of corruption and the multiplication of local entrepreneurial initiatives increasingly linked to the global economy, while effective aid programs would come to the assistance of the neediest. Eventually, developing countries would achieve sufficient prosperity to eliminate poverty as well.

• Reasonable limits would be placed on average income disparities within and between societies, with taxes and other measures used to ensure a sufficient distribution of wealth so that the benefits of an incentive-based, globalized, capitalist society would no longer be accompanied by marginalization and social tension.

• Corporations would play a constructive role in the support of universal humanitarian values.

• A major goal of compulsory education throughout the world would be to provide people with effective tools to be happy and compassionate towards other conscious beings, instilling in them a respect for universal humanitarian values.

• A universal code of animal rights would be globally adopted and applied, ensuring that animals are respected as conscious beings, raised under comfortable conditions and, if used for human consumption, only killed in a way that essentially eliminated both physical and emotional distress. Over the longer term, as our cultural mindset evolved, our use of animals would be phased out and, ideally, eliminated.

• Countries would cooperate in an increasingly trustful way that explicitly acknowledged the validity of universal humanitarian values.

• Diversity in the world would be universally recognized by the global community as a principal source of meaning, and effective steps would be taken to preserve the variety of species and cultures in existence.

• The continuity of human life, intelligence and consciousness would be respected as a fundamentally important objective, and the preservation of the planet and its protection from such threats as climate change would be a global priority.

• If a Singularity turned out to be inevitable, it would be engineered to ensure that the quality of subjective experience was the overriding priority, whether biological or non-biological, and that universal humanitarian values were protected. Human beings would never be threatened by non-biological intelligence.

Even in a utopia that successfully incorporated all the above features, equal happiness for everyone might not be an attainable goal, as it would sometimes come into direct conflict with our primeval need to compete with one another—one of the reasons for the catastrophic failings of communism. There will always be differences in perceived status. But a minimum level of happiness is a theoretically possible vision to work towards. And as long as there are people made or allowed to suffer excruciatingly, this has to be our primary focus.

One existential question remains. How would we preserve meaning in a utopian world where everything was controlled through technology and carefully engineered to avoid threats to people's well-being, and the only struggle was to raise one's status in society, within defined constraints? With the loss of mystery, adventure and risk, would large numbers of people float aimlessly in search of ways to fill a meaningless void in their lives? Does low uncertainty imply less magic? I don't know the answer. But if we could ever get to this stage, we might conceivably rise to any accompanying challenges, the world's inhabitants learning to take full advantage of the potential contained in consciousness to achieve sublime states-of-mind and connect with others in a way that many do not realize is possible.

REALITY

Generations of philosophers have drawn up blueprints for a utopia. Although none has seen their vision stably realized on any large scale, modern Western democracies have come closer than ever before. But in today's high-tech, globalized and unstable world, where things are changing so quickly, where the planet we call home is like a giant powder keg attached to a profusion of fuses, and where extremes of good and evil are conceivable, how close to a stable utopia could we really get?

The characteristics of the hypothetical utopia outlined above address many of the varied causes of preventable suffering on our planet. The issues differ widely from one another and obviously require very different types of solutions. Many of the challenges, including how best to eradicate poverty and infectious diseases in Africa, have major logistical aspects, such as how to attract investment in a way that supports improvements in infrastructure and the creation of job opportunities. But over the long run, the more persistent challenges probably regard the harm humans intentionally or indifferently cause to others through the pursuit of self-interest and power, whether through the waging of war and terrorism, entrenched corruption at the highest levels of government, disregard for our ecosphere and the well-being of future generations, incarceration and torture of prisoners for political reasons, a rabid administration of justice and sheer lack of compassion for others—including the losers in a globalized, liberalized economy.

Is a stable utopia theoretically impossible to achieve because the nature of the universe and its laws are firmly stacked against us, as impossible as trying to escape the boundaries of space-time? And even if it is not theoretically impossible, is it simply too complex a problem for us to solve? Have the pragmatists already resigned themselves to this fate? Is humanity therefore condemned to live out its remaining days through the unwavering exercise of basic human nature and a realpolitik of self-interest and threat of force? Will the dark side of our Darwinian past always return to haunt us, disregarding compassion as it follows a path towards domination and pain, with the latest technology at its disposal? Will there always be a risk of countries and their leaders flouting international agreements and human rights when they perceive it to be to their immediate benefit? Are any efforts by activists to knock some sense into the minds of world leaders unlikely to leave their mark on history as anything other than insignificant noise or minor fluctuations against the triumphant beating of the war drums of evolution and competition? Is the fate of the world akin to that of a chess game, with at most one residual winner on a battlefield of decimated pieces? Must we throw our hands up in the air and concede that the engineering of compassion on a massive scale is something we're not capable of doing? That even major catastrophes can only shock people into changing their behavior temporarily?

Or do the large-scale trends occurring on our planet still leave us with enough leeway for promoting lasting positive change in the world? Is it possible that a minutely contemplated, multi-disciplinary and creative approach to promoting compassion—like a chess program with a far greater number of parameters to consider and great uncertainty associated with each move—really could develop a successful strategy that would lead humanity towards a stable, robust state of peace and happiness grounded in universal humanitarian values? Could some kind of utopia be achieved with the right knowledge? What would it take?

Let's take a concrete example from recent history to put the question into another perspective. Imagine that achieving a stable humanitarian utopia and protecting humanity from extinction were a challenge for the world equivalent in difficulty to avoiding bloodshed as Yugoslavia disintegrated in the 1990s—a much more limited problem which nonetheless was not successfully solved. Could we possibly have managed to do that with the right ideas and collective willpower? What would it have taken? Or was the bloodshed simply inevitable?

Although the answer is obviously unavailable, it would be illuminating to know the objectively probable outcome for the Earth-humanity system. In other words, if you replayed the same "game" on 1,000 planets identical to Earth, allowing humanity to evolve separately on each, with random variability in details such as the individual personalities that emerged, on what fraction of them would human life be wiped out relatively soon after the development of weapons of mass destruction, globalization, rapidly advancing technology and perhaps a Singularity, and how many would achieve stable peace and widespread happiness, possibly through the triumph of massive social activism, guided by a team of powerful humanists? And on those—if any—where peace and happiness finally triumphed, what would be the defining event(s)? In other words, what kind of odds are we really up against, and what might improve them?

I believe these are questions worth asking, and even making rough attempts to answer. People need a reason to hope, to believe that their efforts have a chance of succeeding. But hope must not blind us to a realistic assessment of what needs to be done and the scale of the enterprise. The famous doomsday clock of the *Bulletin of the Atomic Scientists*, which represented the estimated degree of threat of nuclear war over the years, arguably served a more useful purpose then than the sometimes boundless enthusiasm we see today among some (though probably ever fewer) scientists, writers and journalists, eager to tell the world about the promises of new technologies and of the glorious future awaiting humanity just around the corner.

In theory, countless solutions must really exist, series of precise, concrete steps that, if followed, would allow compassionate, intelligent agents to initiate appropriate processes that would dramatically improve our odds.

But in practice, these solutions are unknowable, like the key to a sophisticated, unbreakable code. The world is just far too complex and chaotic, there is too much relevant information available for any single human brain to make sense of, and there is too much unavailable information that can influence events. We are unable to predict even individuals' reactions to things we say or do, whether an influential president or company CEO or a stranger one is chatting to in a bar. The only scenarios that could assure us of a stable future would be for an omniscient, compassionate God to have planned everything carefully in advance, or alternatively, for an infinitely wise, benevolent and, ideally, immortal dictator to take over the world. Unfortunately, neither scenario seems particularly likely. And so we have no choice but to make some very good, educated estimates about what the best-possible solutions might look like, making full use of what reason and empiricism tell us, and hope that we are not far off.

Game theorists have attempted to get at the heart of the problem of achieving optimal outcomes for all in a self-interested world by using a mathematical approach to see whether cooperation can theoretically triumph. Over the years, they have performed a wide range of computer simulations of "prisoner's dilemma"-type situations, with populations of simple agents each aiming for self-maximization, and have tried to determine what strategies might lead to stable, indefinite cooperation—a state in which, on average and over the long run, everyone benefits the most.[81] The short answer is that it is complicated, and the best long-term strategy depends on what the other is doing, but a state of cooperation can—eventually—persist. Although strategies of reciprocation—cooperate when your rival cooperates, defect (betray) when they defect—, with a slight bias towards cooperation, tend to do well, when agents can modify their strategies over time, the strategies that dominate and also lead to cooperation in the long run tend to be more opportunistic ones. This result is, perhaps not coincidentally, what one might have expected based on raw human nature, which evolved under essentially similar conditions. Simply put, if everyone is al-

---

81 The prisoner's dilemma is a classic game theory scenario where two players have to decide independently whether to cooperate with or betray the other. The best outcome for either (and the worst for the other) comes from betraying while the other cooperates, but if each betrays the other, the outcome for both is more severe than if they both cooperated. A detailed summary of many of these studies is provided in Philip Ball's *Critical Mass*.

ways cooperating, emergent rogues will "get away with murder" if they can, eventually forcing all the survivors to play the same game.

One of the hopes in carrying out these simulations was to ascertain whether a stable end to conflict is a theoretically achievable goal. The agents' strategies are determined uniquely by the goal of self-interest, defined as maximizing one specific payout, and they reflect the fact that opportunism is a staple trait of our species. Nonetheless, these simulations are clearly far too simplistic a model for our world. There are two considerations in particular that I think are especially important for the threat and the promise they represent, respectively, for long-term stable peace. The first is that even how these simulations played out was still very sensitive to small changes in some agents' strategies. In the real world, the enormous complexity of a virtually infinite number of permutations of various factors, including the vagaries of decision-making by an individual leader who might have had a bad night's sleep, make solid predictions of outcomes impossible and statecraft an extremely intricate and uncertain exercise. Furthermore, the world is in a constant state of change. New technologies can upset geopolitical balances if they give one country a decisive advantage that it can be tempted to exploit. The discovery of valuable natural resources can tempt a country or local population to behave aggressively. As long as change is occurring in the decisive factors that define a situation, long-term stable cooperation among potential rivals may remain a dream, conflict and bloodshed a persistent risk. During periods of stability, we are too easily lured into believing that we are destined to cooperate happily ever after.

A second consideration, however, is that the simulations are based on a closed system of independent, self-interested agents. In reality, the world is affected by the actions of countless individuals outside of governments, and many of them are driven principally by motives other than crude self-interest. If the global system of international relations can be sufficiently influenced by "external" agents with other goals than the maximization of personal wealth and power, such as the achievement of sustainable cooperation, the nature and outcome of the game can be shifted. In a system where the self-interested agents are represented by countries, this is where people and organizations with strongly anchored humanitarian principles, armed with creativity and intelligence, can strive to engineer sustainable well-being. History has shown how the repeated chance emergence of evil men who exploit favorable political, economic and social circumstances can utterly destroy the well-being of huge numbers of people. Preventing such events from happening and promoting general well-being may also depend on the chance emergence of individuals able to intelligently exploit the circumstances and mobilize large numbers of other people to pressure their own and other governments into acting compassionately.

The growing field of complexity theory, which studies the behaviors of complex systems and the new, emergent properties they exhibit compared to their components, offers some further insights into the challenges we face in engineering a better future, though they are not necessarily encouraging. Beyond a certain degree of complexity, a system becomes self-organizing, and it becomes increasingly difficult for any one agent, whether a person or organization, to manage. Some researchers in the field conclude that civilization—though not necessarily all of humanity—is therefore, by its very nature, doomed, as it takes on the characteristics of a large, increasingly vulnerable organism.[82] However, not all researchers are equally pessimistic, and some believe we still have time to act. It seems clear, in any case, that any effective large-scale approaches to achieving stable solutions will be heavily dependent on the use of this field's methodologies and findings.

How long any pseudo-stable peace could be maintained before countries, acting in their role of self-maximizing agents, exploit imbalances and upset the whole equilibrium is an open question. The meme of universal values will always have to compete with our biological predispositions. Any long-term stable solution has to be compatible with both. In a system that is inherently compassionate, the trespassing of universal values must always be contrary to countries' and other agents' self-interest. In many Western democracies with a strong civil society, this situation seems to have been approached, although we easily downplay the dangers of latent nationalism. Globally it is still a dream.

Where do we stand today? Is the trend towards a sufficiently frequent and spontaneous sprouting of poles of activism to eventually reach a critical mass and push a global wave of humanism beyond the tipping point? So far, the net effect of global activism seems more like damage control. But how do we engineer our concrete vision for a better world when ordinary citizens' room for maneuver often seems so constrained? How can we achieve real impact in a world of globalization, resurgent nationalism, corporate

---

82 Debora MacKenzie, "Why the demise of civilisation may be inevitable," *New Scientist* (2 April 2008).

power consolidation, financial and economic crises, partisan politics, corrupt governments, religious fanaticism, wanton consumerism, greed and cynicism? And what can we contribute to all the existing endeavors and ongoing strategies being carried out by countless NGOs, international bodies and individuals to reduce suffering and improve well-being in the world? Is there anything fundamentally new to learn in trying to make the world a more humane and cooperative place, or have most of the reflections in this book already implicitly been taken into account—or proven to be irrelevant?—by those working on the ground? Are we already doing as well as we can? And if not, is the problem mainly one of execution and of tinkering with existing tactics? Or do we need new ways of thinking to spread the message and put it into practice?

However challenging the issues we face, I am convinced that we can improve the odds. This will require a great deal of idealism combined with hard realism. In the chapter "Making an Impact", I develop some thoughts on the kind of thinking and approaches that might be needed.

15. Down to Earth

What does the utopian vision described in the previous chapter imply in practice? It is well beyond the scope and ambition of this book to wade very far into the thick, murky waters of domestic and international politics and economics, and to attempt to offer detailed recommendations for change. I will stick here with the old maxim that it is better to be vaguely right than precisely wrong. But the overriding conclusion is that the respect for universal humanitarian values needs to be implemented and reinforced throughout global society and serve as a universal reference for how we should conduct ourselves. This chapter briefly explores some of the concrete implications of implementing these values for a range of relevant issues and the role that governments and corporate institutions need to play.

The Role of Governments in Defending Universal Humanitarian Values

For all the different loci of power in the world and the wealthy individuals and corporations exerting influence from the back corridors, the ultimate guarantors of humanitarian values are still usually governments, responsible for law enforcement within their jurisdictions and with police and military forces under their control. There will always be debates about the reasonable size of the public sector, and the execution of some responsibilities assumed by governments can often be taken over more efficiently by the private sector. But there is nothing fundamentally more important for a government to do than to defend universal humanitarian values, by force if necessary.

Political and economic systems should be judged by the real effects they have on people's lives. Any political system that exercises cruelty against even a very tiny proportion of its population, whether political dissenters or a cultural minority, and even one that does not intrinsically try to provide a context in which every one of its residents can be happy, implicitly considers some people's well-being as expendable. This is precisely why universal humanitarian values need to be defended.

Governments need to make more explicit the principle of upholding these values, and they must be challenged to ensure that the law and the way it is enforced are based on compassion and compatible with them. Pragmatism is essential and can often lead to better outcomes than blindly applying strict moral principles regardless of the cost. However, pragmatism makes the adherence to universal humanitarian values all the more important to affirm and any actions that appear to contradict them all the more important to justify. Governments must be held to moral accountability and, where this is not a given, persuaded through all possible means to acknowledge the importance of universal humanitarian values and to fully abide by the UDHR.

Because power tends to corrupt[83] and politics naturally attracts people with a desire for power, there is often a legitimate mistrust of governments as honest brokers. Furthermore, retaining power is usually attributed higher priority than arguing for unpopular measures, and democratic governments tend to follow public opinion more than they attempt to influence it. There is at times a necessary tradeoff, of course, as a politician who is not elected will not be able to implement policies. But humanitarian values and courageous political leadership are not a combination found in abundance. Strong leadership in translating compassion into policy requires serving as a moral compass to the population rather than simply echoing the howl of the prevailing political winds.

Countries should also be persuaded to calibrate national practices to make sure they are in keeping with universal humanitarian values. Maintaining the essence of one's culture should not require disrespecting these values and causing preventable suffering through the exercising of atavis-

---

83 "Absolutely," *The Economist* (21 January 2010), www.economist.com/node/15328544.

tic customs, whether female genital mutilation or any of countless barbaric acts performed on animals. Countries should be encouraged to make the leap, shedding customs that are incompatible with these values and developing the more beautiful aspects of their cultural identity that do not depend on suffering.

The left-wing/right-wing political divide within democracies is, to a degree, about the size of government and its degree of intervention in society, but there is often a strong corresponding social component, with those favoring less government involvement also, perhaps counterintuitively, tending to be more authoritative about social issues. The fact that people's views on political and social issues tend to cluster together is partly a reflection of people's character traits, which have a marked genetic component.[84] These traits include degree of openness to experience, more pronounced on the left side of the political spectrum, and conscientiousness, more pronounced on the right. But especially in a country like the United States, with an essentially two-party system, each party has to accommodate a relatively wide spectrum of views and combinations of positions on economic and social issues, with the official party line belying the diversity of individual stances. However, camouflaged among the political issues is the deeper question of compassion and the limits to the suffering that can be tolerated by a society. It is essential to distinguish between conservative opposition to big government that reflects a frustration with wasteful spending more than a lack of compassion, and the far right of the political scale, harboring angry individuals for whom anyone's misery is merely a consequence of their own lack of responsibility or initiative.

If people were not allowed to suffer needlessly, the degree of government involvement in our lives would be an issue of much less relevance, and could be debated on the basis of hard data and questions of efficiency. Government is only needed in areas where the private sector cannot do the job sufficiently well alone. But nowhere is this more pertinent than in ensuring a humane society and coming to the aid of people in need. Since the pure pursuit of self-interest not only can marginalize people but can also be used to manipulate them into harming themselves, the government also has a legitimate responsibility to protect its citizens without being accused of running a "nanny state", although it should not go so far as to stop people from

---

84 Jim Giles, "Are political leanings all in the genes?" *New Scientist* (2 February 2008).

harming themselves if they desire. Banning the advertising of cigarettes but not their actual production is one such example.

Because governments' respect for universal humanitarian values is often so fragile, a population's ability to think rationally and critically is all the more important, and the modern assault on reason represents a major threat. If only government leaders and those politically close to them are doing the thinking and then manipulating the masses through TV and other media, they can get away with pushing whatever self-serving agenda they want. For example, some influential politicians continue to throw into question the conclusions from carefully accumulated and analyzed scientific data while the world continues to pump enormous quantities of carbon dioxide into the atmosphere. By doing so, they impede efforts to bring the world together and implement effective measures to save our planet from irreversible changes that will dramatically upset existing equilibria and potentially destroy millions of lives.

People who have been exposed to what humans are capable of doing to each other without becoming desensitized, and who have already thought carefully about humanitarian issues, should not be penalized for trying to promote the appropriate ideas and policies to thwart the recurrence of such events. But unless they take other people through the reasoning process, they may be perceived as run-of-the-mill politicians or activists simply fighting for power or for the dogma of their intellectual clan. Especially in a country like the United States, with so much potential to serve as a source of leadership in the world, there is a pressing need to break down the partisanship and agree on efficient measures to implement more compassionate policies. But this will not happen spontaneously. It requires the initiative of powerful people who place the rational pursuit of universal values ahead of partisan politics and clan warfare, and who can create a vision for a more stable, less polarized society.

Preserving Freedom

Many of the major issues we are confronted with today and which are being addressed by various international organizations relate to the universal humanitarian values of solidarity (ending torture, wrongful imprisonment, poverty, disease, climate change), continuity (preventing nuclear proliferation, terrorism and the spread of infectious diseases) and diversity (support for threatened cultures, protection of endangered species). Every action to control the state of the world intrinsically seeks to avoid alternative scenarios, and this often entails some corresponding limits to personal freedoms, even when these are minor and indirect. Although seen objectively, freedom from the rest of the universe and from the dynamics of the system we are part of is an illusion, the subjective sense of having options and, within the constraints and opportunities of the environment in which we live, of having a choice of immediate and long-term futures available, is essential for happiness and a sense of meaning. As governments have increasing access to information that allows them to control the lives of their citizens, it will remain an existential challenge of the highest order to preserve the sense of freedom from the encroachment of invisible walls. Even in a world that increasingly resembles that of *Nineteen Eighty-Four*, the principle of "elbow room" needs to be firmly engineered in. Preserving freedom also implies that there are points at which the preservation of the other values would necessitate an inacceptable tradeoff. However, the greatest threat to freedom comes not from attempts to reduce suffering or maintain diversity in the world, nor from efforts to preserve the future, but from the concentration of power in the hands of forces that do not uphold universal humanitarian values.

Governments are being faced with an increasingly diverse range of risks of catastrophic scenarios posed by advances in technology, widely and readily available information that can be used malevolently, and disgruntled individuals and groups seeking an outlet for their frustrations and perhaps a perverse sense of meaning in their lives through terrorist acts. There may be a legitimate case for governments to keep closer tabs on their citizens in order to protect them. But the degree of possible surveillance could extend as far as super-intelligent networks monitoring citizens' every movement. Under these conditions, the dangers of sliding closer towards a totalitarian society in which citizens can no longer trust their governments to safeguard their right to freedom, and in which law enforcement officers are conferred broad powers, are extremely serious. Citizens risk becoming prisoners of a faceless, Kafkaesque system that subordinates human freedoms to order and security. It is therefore becoming ever more critical that universal humanitarian values be firmly and thoroughly entrenched in the system, at all levels of government. This is an area where the United States could learn something useful from the spirit of the European system. In a society where individual privacy becomes increasingly precious, individuals should have nothing to fear from their own governments, and victimless acts related to individuals' personal habits, views, and choices of subjective experience should be fundamentally and explicitly permitted and respected. As the sense of what it is like to be human risks being transformed in fundamental ways, due to the curtailing of some freedoms and to the evolution of new means for humans to use and even be dominated by technology, remaining autonomously human in a meaningful way will require a strong assertion of all the core values, including individual freedoms.

With information that can be used to carry out devastating terrorist attacks often available in the public domain, and with scientists increasingly understanding the various determinants of behavior, the issue of determinism and free will is likely to become ever less abstract as governments seek to anticipate and pre-empt crime and terrorism by studying people's behavioral tendencies and profiling them through the measurement of physical parameters without their explicit consent. There is the real danger that a person may in the future no longer enjoy the right to be treated by default as innocent if they have not actually committed a crime, a situation that served as the basis for the film "Minority Report". Deprivation of liberty may no longer be limited to those who can be classically diagnosed as mentally ill, but include those with genetic predispositions to psychopathic behavior. The freedom of movement and of action that permits the illusion of free will and that is so essential for people to feel like autonomous, responsible, motivated members of society actually risks being taken away from them. Our brains may no longer enjoy their status as safe havens of private thought.

Again, a principal bulwark against such a scenario is a strongly anchored commitment by governments to respect and rigorously adhere to universal humanitarian values, even when legitimate measures are needed to protect society. Creative approaches may be needed, such as providing free, facultative counseling to those with genetic predispositions and others in need, so that criminal behavior can be averted without incarcerating innocent people.

A subjective sense of freedom also requires that a certain degree of tolerance be built into the system, rather than establishing cold, hard boundaries like electric fences that keep cows tightly contained within a field. A real sense of freedom requires that one does not perceive powerful, intelligent beings tracking one's moves, nor fear major punishment for slight changes in behavior. The imposition of steep penalties for minor trespassing of the rules, while perhaps effective for its dissuasiveness, is the hallmark of a rigid, authoritarian mindset rather than of a compassionate society. Ensuring personal breathing space also requires tolerance of unusual behaviors that would only be problematic if carried out by many people on a large scale.

Freedom of expression represents a particularly challenging issue, lying as it does at the boundary between thought and action. It is considered a fundamental of democracy and is defended most vigorously in Anglo-Saxon cultures. But there are recognized limits. Even in the United States, where hate-mongers have the greatest legal protection, one cannot say whatever one wants about someone else, at the risk of being sued for libel. The spreading of hatred can be seen as contradicting the core value of solidarity, and there is arguably little lost in keeping this kind of activity outside the sphere of legality. We accept all kinds of restrictions on our behavior when they directly interfere with others' ability to enjoy life. Although any restrictions on our behavior and especially our speech need to be very carefully evaluated and cautiously applied, hateful speech can cause far more damage than many other kinds of behavior, and some restrictions on what one can say in public are arguably a lesser evil. Freedom of expression can only be regarded as sacred when it doesn't willfully lead to hate and behavior that threatens people's well-being. If hateful speech that incites discrimination or violence cannot be sufficiently drowned out by compassionate voices, more effective measures need to be applied. Values are fragile and need to be fought for. A right to intentionally spread hatred is not one of them.

The Limits of Justice

Imprisoning criminals protects society by preventing them from committing further crimes while deterring others from doing the same. In theory, though often a failure in practice, it is also meant to reform criminals by encouraging a change in their thinking and behavior. And most viscerally, under the noble banner of "justice", it also represents a form of institutionalized revenge. Given the hardwiring of this instinct, the delivery of what is perceived as justice understandably helps to appease the suffering of victims and their families and meets a need demanded by society, regardless of any other practical benefits.

But while putting criminals behind bars may provide victims with a necessary sense of relief, the way the practice is often carried out harks back to an archaic, Biblical worldview rather than reflecting a modern, progressive understanding of human nature. The demonization of some convicted criminals as sub-human reflects an almost animalistic emotional response. By punishing criminals severely we are also, ironically, attributing to them full responsibility for their actions and yet, at another level, relenting to our own primitive instincts that demand revenge.

Systems weighted heavily towards retributive justice are out of focus and distract us from pragmatic solutions. An attempt to create a gentler world based on an understanding of human nature would necessarily acknowledge the need for punishment as a means of shaping behavior while diminishing the emotional, retributive component. Governments should place their primary emphasis on the conditions that lead to crimes, reducing the likelihood that they will be repeated in the future. Simply imprisoning people without providing them with psychological counseling that can help them gain self-confidence and a more positive perspective is unlikely to be sufficient for breaking the cycle of crime and punishment. The Finnish prison system, one that treats prisoners with dignity and respect and aims to shape their values in a more pro-social direction, is a successful model that should be widely emulated.[85]

Increasing the severity of sentencing for purely political aims sends less of a practically effective warning to potential criminals than a bleak message to all of us about the kind of society we are living in. The core value of solidarity implies a humane justice system that regards criminals as humans who represent the intersection of an unfortunate combination of causes. Although this perspective is often unintuitive and runs up against our primal instincts, its adoption will become more important than ever if we move to a society that is more intrusive. Otherwise, even liberal democracies[86] may drift increasingly towards Big Brother police states. This is not just fantasy.

Capital punishment represents a step in the other direction. The characteristic feature of this form of justice is a fundamental lack of compassion for another human being by taking away his life even after he has been removed from society and no longer poses a danger. The absurdity of a government stamping out the life of one of its citizens comes into sharp relief when one considers the supposedly humane gestures preceding the execution, such as providing him with his favorite meal and perhaps a last cigarette. It is

---

85 Warren Hoge, "Finnish Prisons: No Gates or Armed Guards," *New York Times* (2 January 2003), www.nytimes.com/2003/01/02/international/europe/02FINL. html.

86 Also known as constitutional democracies, the political system found in the United States and most European countries.

not inconsistent to consider a crime to be reprehensible or even an atrocity and yet still understand the mechanism that led to it and show a minimum of detached respect towards the deranged character who committed it, in the same way that one shows respect towards the mentally ill. A system that does not display a markedly more humanistic spirit than the people it judges cannot aspire to shape society for the better.

Of course, the co-habitation of the subjective and the objective can be extremely difficult. For example, confronted with a crime victim's suffering, experiencing intense, heartfelt emotions, including sadness, pain and anger, and at the same time recognizing that, from a purely objective point of view, criminal behavior is a consequence of defined causes, is challenging to the point of impossibility if one hasn't really reflected on it in this way. As expressed by the character Michael Berg in Bernhard Schlink's novel *The Reader*, after he uncovers the shadowy past of his older lover: "I could not resolve this. I wanted to pass myself both tasks—understanding and condemnation. But it was impossible to do both." Perhaps at the same instant it is. But we need to retain both these subjective and objective capacities. We cannot *feel* what is important without embracing our emotions, including an inherent disgust at inflicted suffering, but we cannot *achieve* what is important without taking a detached view of it all through the lenses of science and empiricism, including the elucidation of pragmatic, effective solutions.

By not letting strong emotional reactions dominate our behavior and our administration of justice, we might feel we are losing something essential from our humanity. Indeed, a basis for compassion itself serving as a driver of values is that we open ourselves up to experiencing others' emotions. But we need to defend our ability to understand and act intelligently without succumbing to our violent urges. Our human instincts require justice, but it should not be sadistic.

There is something to learn from the history of Europe in the last century about the usefulness of pragmatism and resisting the instinct for revenge. Consider the contrast in how Germany was treated after World War I and after World War II, crushed as a form of punishment after the former, helped to rebuild itself after the latter despite the massive atrocities committed by large numbers of ordinary Germans. The uncomfortable fact is that other countries in similar circumstances to Germany's in the late 1920s might have followed a similar downward spiral. The pragmatic treatment of Germany after World War II aimed in part to avoid the mistakes of the Treaty of Versailles and turn a page on the past in favor of a better future. Of course, the geopolitical situation at the time demanded a strong Western ally. And you cannot put a country in prison the way you can put an individual. But Germany has since proven itself one of the strongest defenders of human rights and democracy in the world, as well as a driver of European integration and stability. There would hardly be less genocide and torture in the world today if the Germans had been collectively punished after World War II. Shouldn't we also consider the merits of this kind of thinking when we reflect on how to create a gentler, safer society?

Drugs and Other Victimless "Crimes"

There is no rational, humane basis for criminalizing and punishing behaviors that involve no victims. A free society that respects universal humanitarian values should allow people to experience a variety of mental states if they desire, carry out the behaviors of their choice in the privacy of their homes, including sexual acts with consenting adults, and carry out peaceful self-expression in public. The potentially frightening consequences of entrusting law enforcement officials with the power to fight victimless "crimes" are described by Sam Harris in a short section of his book *The End of Faith.*

The controversial subject of drug use, one of the most criminalized of victimless acts, can hardly be circumvented in a book about respecting others' subjective experience. It is probable that people have been using mind-altering substances for as long as our species has existed. Although we tend to reserve the politically charged word "drugs" for substances like white powder smuggled in cargo containers and bodily orifices, good old ethanol has as significant an impact on the brain's functioning as many more vilified chemicals. The universality of fermented fruit and grain has allowed alcohol to become firmly intertwined in the fabric of human civilization, accounting perhaps for why fermented grapes were found to be a more appropriate religious offering than freshly squeezed grape juice. Other substances with a more limited geographical distribution have today failed to compete for global society's favors, although dozens of plant species have been providing pleasure to local human populations for countless generations, and some, perhaps, to animal species for millions of years. Although in many cases it may be an evolutionary artifact, it may not be mere chance that so many plants have pleasant psychoactive effects when consumed—possibly an alternative survival strategy to providing a sweet taste and calories that encouraged consumption and the spreading of seeds.

For various reasons, including preserving a strong work ethic and minimizing threats to organized religion, societies today are squeamish or even terrified about people spending too much time triggering the pleasure centers of their brains and thinking too differently. Since it is far too late to do much about alcohol except take a share of the fun and tax it, it is the next tier of mind-altering substances that are the target of lawmakers, and what cannot be done with alcohol is done all the more vigorously with its distant cousins. And so while wine and beer are to be had almost ubiquitously around the globe, including at publicly sponsored events, the smoking of weed is illegal in most countries and grounds for confiscation, a fine, imprisonment or execution, depending on the location.

An ironic aspect of society's battle against drugs is that their use may have contributed to an important though unquantifiable portion of its creations throughout history. The fact that some of the most famous artists, musicians, writers and scientists have used drugs to expand their creative horizons is ignored or commented on with detached interest, although the paintings auctioned off for millions of dollars or the written works studied in university literature courses may never have seen the light of day or attained the value that they are now attributed had their creators not taken mind-altering substances. The highly prevalent, discreet use of marijuana in much of the world suggests a much larger influence on our artistic culture than most people would readily acknowledge or even recognize.

The positive features of drugs such as marijuana extend beyond the artistic realm, providing potential insight into aspects of existence that are often hidden from view. It is well documented that some drugs make life feel more meaningful and beautiful, promoting empathy and connections between people, helping to break down barriers and allow a more vivid understanding of how others see the world. These are effects that would not be without merit in trying to bring about reconciliation between conflicting parties, although smoking the peace pipe would likely breach standard diplomatic protocol. Carl Sagan, the brilliant and highly respected cosmologist and humanist, wrote an anonymous essay many years ago, long before he admitted to marijuana use, that provides a fascinating perspective on the issue from a highly perceptive scientist with a gift for communication. Sagan concluded, "The illegality of cannabis is outrageous, an impediment to full utilization of a drug which helps produce the serenity and insight, sensitivity and fellowship so desperately needed in this increasingly mad and dangerous world."[87]

The overall picture is, of course, hardly that rosy. Substance abuse ravages lives, both of users and of people who are dependent on them. Even heavy use of "soft" drugs such as marijuana can have long-term nefarious consequences. The point of this section is not to idealize the use of chemicals with negative side effects.

The essential issue, however, is that freedom includes the ability to experience life on one's own terms, potentially including mental states achievable through mind-altering substances. What one does with one's own body is one's own business, provided one does not cause harm to others, and the same is true for one's brain. The state entirely oversteps its role when it punishes people for committing victimless "crimes", even when the behavior is self-destructive.

There is also, somehow, a fundamental incongruity between the ideology of unrestricted free market capitalism, where the most able and ambitious are allowed to accumulate increasing amounts of relative wealth and thereby come to exert power over others' lives, and the restriction on people's freedom to influence their own internal mental states, including those at the bottom rung of society with low-paid jobs seeking a certain degree of escapism from an otherwise mundane existence. And there is something hypocritical about the fact that powerful, organized religions that present as the truth events that did not literally happen in the way described often receive some degree of support from the state, whereas the private use of substances that can sometimes make life in this absurd universe more enjoyable is often legal grounds for incarceration.

One of the principal objections to a decriminalization of drugs is the fear of facilitated access to adolescents, for whom society's efforts to educate them by sending them off to school for many years will not be properly served if they spend their time dreaming of pink elephants instead of paying attention to their history teacher. But there are numerous activities that adults have the right to carry out which would not be in the interest of children. There are many ways of providing an acceptable level of protection, and legalization provides a much wider range of means of control than

---

87 The full essay is on the website of Lester Grinspoon, Assoc. Professor Emeritus of Psychiatry at Harvard Medical School, at http://marijuana-uses.com/mr-x.

criminalization. The various practical consequences of legalization, includ-ing the virtual elimination of the huge, violently criminal black market, have been amply described, including in The Economist.[88]

The drug laws in place in most of the world, including in supposedly progressive Western democracies, are generally far broader in scope than what would be needed to protect children, and they are incompatible with basic humanitarian values. That such laws are still so widely maintained is a wrong waiting to be righted.

Animal Rights

At present, giving up meat consumption is still probably inconceivable for most people. Even many in the developing world who eat meat only on special occasions aspire to eat it more regularly. If it is a challenge to stop human beings from going to war with each other, it is currently a sheer impossibility to prevent most of them from killing animals, directly or by proxy, for food. Of course, there are also many new converts to veganism, an admirable step driven by compassion. But vegans still remain a small frac-tion of the world's population and, realistically, this is unlikely to change very dramatically in the near future.

As long as humans consume animals, it is essential that we focus on the critical and more readily addressable issue, which is the suffering inflicted on animals through inhumane living conditions and slaughter. Some suffer-ing is so extreme that there is no economic justification for not taking the necessary measures to eliminate it. This requires widespread sensitization of people to the pain that other living creatures can experience, relating it to human pain they can relate to. It means imposing measures that ensure that animals used for human benefit—whether for food consumption, body parts or scientific research—are treated with respect for their subjective ex-perience and not made to suffer. It requires, in particular, that the horrors of factory farming be eradicated, including also the cruelty of high density fish farming, and that slaughter be carried out painlessly and with absolutely minimal stress.[89]

Veganism remains the most certain way to ensure that one's own per-sonal eating habits do not directly or indirectly entail the suffering of ani-

88 "How to stop the drug wars," The Economist (5 March 2009), www.economist. com/node/13237193.

89 Rebecca Marx, "Humane Slaughterhouses," Gourmet (June 2009), www.gour-met.com/foodpolitics/2009/06/humane-slaughterhouses.

mals. Of course, legally imposing veganism on individuals is hardly a realistic solution, and even stigmatizing those who have not converted to pure veganism for persisting with a lifestyle they grew up with is likely to be counter-productive. But consuming products that require sustained or intense animal suffering should not be left to personal choice. As Jonathan Safran Foer, author of *Eating Animals*, has asked rhetorically, "Is it right to eat animals given the ways we are actually raising and killing them?"[90] If one accepts that the primary concern is any suffering and fear they experience while alive rather than the end of their existence per se, then one has to acknowledge, even if one personally finds the concept distasteful, that there is a reasonable and pragmatic case to be made for so-called "compassionate omnivorism", in which food is sourced from farms that strictly respect animal welfare. But as long as a society remains omnivorous, this is the only kind of omnivorism we should retain. And the legal system itself has to entrench this compassion. In heavily meat-based cultures, it is unrealistic to expect even well-meaning people to define compassionate limits to their own eating habits on a daily basis and that a resulting change in consumer demand will do the job.

The issue of animal rights is of dramatically greater importance than the short space devoted to it here might suggest, and the implications are wide-ranging. The extent to which it is taken seriously reflects the degree of consistency in one's belief in the avoidance of suffering as a basis for our entire value system. The only way forward is through the achievement of agreed upon international standards, changes in national legislation and rigorous enforcement.

Economics

Ingenuity, hard work and trade have brought the world the material comforts and physical and emotional well-being that many of its inhabitants now enjoy. Technological advances continuously surprise us with the new possibilities they offer to interact with the world and spend our time. But, as reflected on earlier in the section "Happiness", is there a point at which we can we fairly ask whether indefinite, continuous, maximal economic growth makes sense, and whether as a society we couldn't start to

---

90 "Jonathan Safran Foer on 'Eating Animals'," *The Washington Post* (19 November 2009), www.washingtonpost.com/wp-dyn/content/discussion/2009/11/13/DI2009111303078.html.

devote more attention to enjoying life? Globally, of course, wealth has not been distributed widely enough for everyone to have clean water, nutritious food, good health, realizable dreams and, perhaps, an iPod. But for those of us in the developed world, how much more growth do we need? And, just as importantly, where is this growth actually leading?

We are encouraged by politicians and economists to believe in unlimited economic growth as a principle, without a convincing, concrete vision to accompany it. The spiritually attuned practitioner of meditation is implicitly dismissed as unproductive while the hyperactive, globe-trotting manager at a multinational corporation is admired for his or her work ethic. Our modern international financial and economic system has created opacity in seeing what really matters. The obsessive focus on economic indicators such as GDP growth and stock market indices induces people to think that these are what matter most and forget that these metrics are merely a means to an end. When one reads articles that refer to the "lost earning potential of the dead"[91], isn't there a legitimate concern, despite the probable validity of that concept within an economic framework, that, in a larger sense, we have somehow lost our bearings? That the health of the economy, though a critical part of the puzzle, is itself more important than the health and happiness of individuals?

The work ethic of many cultures, while effective in ensuring that food and other goods and services are produced, institutionalizes the eternal drive for higher status and implicitly attributes highest priority to being a "productive citizen". We are shielded from a more objective perspective, a sense of what life can be about and where we are going. The principle of unlimited economic growth and the excessive promotion of a competitive mentality to support it are perversely pushing us faster towards the transformation and exhaustion of our planet. Drawn into the system, insufficiently aware of the forces driving our own behavior, we are allowing ourselves to be undermined by the congenital satisfaction in having something that our neighbor does not, even if it ends up destroying us all.

Furthermore, many people in the world's largest economy still regard anything too closely resembling collective help for the poorest with the disdain one might expect to be reserved for oppressive totalitarian regimes. We can all go down with the ship professing the dogma of "eternal maximal

---

91 "In a flap", *The Economist* (20 October 2005), www.economist.com/node/5053648?story_id=5053648.

economic growth", but after the last words disappear as air bubbles at the surface, there will only be silence. Or maybe an echo of Alan Greenspan's famous testimony before a United States House Committee in October 2008, where he admitted he found a flaw in his model. Oops, too late.

Respect for universal humanitarian values, and for limits to freedom when it leads to others' suffering, means acknowledging that any other assumptions you have made about how the world works or how we should act may prove to be inconsistent. This includes the assumption that the markets will eventually solve all our problems. When unrestricted free market capitalism is seen as a fundamental value in itself and not subordinate to universal humanitarian values, the result will be consequential. By equating human nature and the behavior that stems from it if it is left unrestricted with how things *should* be, we leave no more room for compassion than what is ultimately in people's self-interest. And as we know, people will get away with whatever they can—even when cloaked in the respectability of business suits.

There are also limits to the ability of free trade to bring happiness to the world's poorest populations. Where interests converge, free trade enables transactions that are to parties' mutual benefit. But human beings living in poverty in underdeveloped parts of the world may initially, in the absence of innovative businesses and infrastructure, have little or nothing to contribute to others' material well-being, and thus represent no immediate value, economically speaking. A strict free trade philosophy that embodies blind faith in the intrinsic power of the markets—if such a blind faith indeed still exists today—has little to offer these human beings, whose struggle for happiness is also dependent on the activation of an evolutionarily derived but unreliable emotional state called empathy.

Relatively few people seriously imagine trying to radically transform our current Western economic system, which has proven its formidable ability to harness human nature to spur innovation and generate wealth, and is also the one that much of the world aspires to. A radical transformation would probably be impossible to achieve and, in any case, both undesirable and unsustainable if human freedom to innovate and reap the benefits was not respected. The challenge is to adapt the system sufficiently so that, while respecting the human urge to create and accumulate, it places more explicit limits on wealth disparities and incorporates a host of measures that ensure greater sustainable happiness as an outcome. The heterogeneous spending of money by federal governments within their jurisdictions, including the use of European Union money to support poorer regions and the social safety nets typified by northern European countries, are examples of how some degree of wealth redistribution can be carried out in a way that is generally perceived as fair by the net contributors. Ultimately, one of the essential questions for a society is settling on a degree of polarization that the vast majority can live with.

Limiting wealth disparities doesn't even mean that one can't get really, "stinking" rich. It is almost unquestionably true that one of the greatest feelings of ecstasy in life must be to achieve a position of power and dominance, where one feels that the world is one's oyster, and that one can even shape it for one's personal benefit. The possibility of feeling powerful and desired cannot be denied to people who seek it as a goal. But there are necessary limits to the economic polarization that this dominance implies, even if it feels good at the top. Again, it's a question of degree and of not allowing the averages at the top and bottom to drift too far apart. The difficulty of determining reasonable boundaries is no excuse for promoting a bogus slippery slope argument that the end result will be a slide into some form of communism.

Until technology makes humans superfluous as physical manipulators of their environment—and even then, how this is carried out will depend on who controls the technology—we will still need people to clean our toilets and mine our minerals. Few investment bankers would agree to perform such tasks part time, so the principle of equal opportunity is only valid with the caveat that some people will necessarily get left at the bottom, like on a curved college exam.

The value that traditional United States Republicans accorded to liberty, personal initiative and self-reliance is the attitude that is most likely to make people successful and happy, and in that respect cannot be faulted. But this perspective is incomplete if it ignores the bigger picture and the mechanics of the system that we are all part of. Wanting the whole world to be full of self-reliant people working as hard as they can to be successful—if that is indeed the desire—, and blaming those who are not for lack of initiative, reflects a severely distorted perspective on reality.

Meritocracy is a good thing when it allows people the freedom to create, unlock their potential and derive personal benefit from it, and it helps ensure that the most capable people rise to the positions of highest responsibility. But the principle is misguided when used as a justification to continuously increase disparities in wealth and power and erode solidarity with the least well off, while it is cynically argued that others are theoretically free to compete. And the argument that people deserve a reward for hard work is sometimes used disingenuously by high-earning professionals, as many people work hard at menial tasks and never move upwards or receive recognition. Success depends on a range of factors. The path of many achievers can be traced to chance opportunities, or to genetic predispositions to be persistent or smart, or both.

If even a small minority of people are implicitly sacrificed by economic and political policies that improve overall living standards but cause harm to a few, with little immediate means of redress, one cannot expect the few to simply accept their fate and suffer the consequences. Within a Western democracy, those who are left out have at least the means of expressing their opinions peacefully and demanding, though perhaps futilely, that their concerns be addressed. Short-sighted, uncompassionate policies that lead to increased wealth concentration and inequality are virtually certain to lead to increased tensions that are eventually eased by a leftward swing in the political barometer. But when the same kinds of policies are pursued on a global scale, the losers may feel powerless to make their voices heard effectively. People whose survival is threatened or who have little basis for hope of improvement cannot be expected to docilely adopt the worldview of those who have power and security on their side.

Furthermore, transposed to the level of international politics and economics, there is an inherent contradiction between unrestrained free market capitalism and its "may the best one win" philosophy, and an expectation that nations will cooperate in the interest of the greater good. If countries' domestic policies accord relatively low priority to the welfare of the poorest, why should the same countries' authorities be trusted to secure the welfare of the planet's most miserable, or to preserve the future? Rampant, unrestrained capitalism is a poor ideological basis for international cooperation on humanitarian issues.

Recently, there have been increased efforts to sensitize people to the intrinsic value of "soft" factors such as environmental protection and sustainability, and to achieve a fundamental shift in the focus of society and in the policies that are officially pursued. For example, the New Economics Foundation (NEF) is a think tank that aims "to redefine 'wealth' and 'progress': to judge our systems and economies on how much they create the world we actually want, rather than how much money they generate."[92] Essentially, then, NEF also functions as an advocacy organization attempting to persuade people to attribute greater value to things that matter, even if these are difficult to measure, in the interest of a happier world.

These efforts need to be given greater momentum. The goal should be decreased polarization and a markedly increased commitment to universal humanitarian values in how we allow the world economy to progress. The choice is not between one extreme economic system and another, but how to make a relatively free market economic system satisfy the needs of everyone, rather than allowing a subset of global society to be abandoned to their misery in order to satisfy the unlimited cravings of a meritocratic elite.

Corporate Social Responsibility

Large corporations are often viewed by social activists as self-serving, greedy behemoths whose sole interest is profit and growth. Sometimes, this caricature does undoubtedly come very close to the truth. But demonization should not hinder an understanding of how companies can best be guided towards playing a more positive role as a force for social change in the world. With corporations de facto often wielding more power over people's lives than governments, it is becoming ever more important that their conduct and activities be supportive of humanitarian values.

The existence of large corporations is a direct consequence of human nature—the competitive drive to gain status and resources, achieved more effectively through the collaboration of individuals with a common purpose. While making profit through the fulfillment of people's needs for goods and services, companies can help generate wealth for society, although in the absence of any external pressure they are often apathetic about collateral damage they cause, or even, in some cases, cynically destructive.

Corporations are part of the system and take full advantage of the defined rules of the game, just as citizens exercise their own individual freedoms within the limits of the law. While some exceptional companies have deep-seated humanitarian values, large publicly held companies with many profit-maximizing shareholders to answer to cannot realistically be expected to spontaneously "do the right thing" if it does not make good business sense, unless they are obliged to, or if public pressure actually

---

92 www.neweconomics.org

makes shifting course a good business decision. Companies operate under the constraints of their environment, including changes in consumer behavior and in society's expectations. They adapt to legislation and the market and, where money is to be made, are usually resourceful in finding solutions. What they can legitimately demand is a level playing field in which the same rules apply to all.

Preventing companies from conducting behavior with negative consequences for human welfare, whether direct or indirect, requires rational argumentation, objective scientific data and an appeal to universal humanitarian values, as well as a readiness to take the arguments "to the street" in an effort to raise awareness and apply public pressure, if necessary. Brand image is one of companies' greatest assets and sources of value and, today more than ever before, most will seek to maintain a reputation as good corporate citizens. Transparency as well as initiatives and audits carried out by external organizations can help distinguish practices such as "greenwashing"—the disingenuous highlighting of superficial measures as being environmentally motivated or effective—from those with substance.

Working with companies to actively promote positive change is, perhaps, the more interesting challenge. Encouraging companies to promote human welfare, incorporating the respect of universal values into their brand value and thereby gaining a competitive advantage among socially conscious consumers is an indispensable tool for change in a world where corporations command so much power.

Employees themselves have a role to play in helping the companies they work for to become more responsible citizens and create sustainability. By helping their employers to adapt their procedures to the demands of a more socially conscious world, they can promote change from within while increasing their companies' value proposition. And for cases of serious wrongdoing, laws that protect and even reward whistleblowers are essential to keep companies honest.

Because employees tend to be loyal to the organization that pays them, especially when they are well looked after and provided with a sense of security, stability and defined objectives, they will tend to identify with their employer and even align some of their values with those of the organization. Large companies with a socially conscious management therefore also have a potentially powerful and useful role to play in raising awareness among their employees about the importance of abiding by universal values, through the development of a humanistic corporate culture.

INTERNATIONAL RELATIONS

People's pursuit of their own interests and those of their family and tribe, extended to the world arena, means that countries themselves can often be best regarded as self-maximizers, like the individual citizens they represent. Although the individuals that make up a population display a broad range of characteristics and desires, and many embark on lifestyles that explicitly shun aggression and exploitation of others, at the level of national government, the principle of self-interested agents holds very well. It is a truism of international politics that every country looks after its own national interests, and American statesmen in particular are constantly defending their country's foreign policy on this basis. John Bolton, former United States ambassador to the United Nations, angrily exclaimed in 1994, "The *only* question for the United States is, 'What's in our national interest?'"

But when a powerful country repeatedly uses language that implies that its national interests are more important than any other, universal principles, it is not surprising that resentment builds elsewhere. It implies that the guiding principle is "each for his own", and that suffering in other countries need not unduly constrain the exercising of power. Many Americans view their country as a beacon of morality spreading goodwill and freedom to the rest of the world, and are perplexed that the rest of the world does not always share this opinion. Yet it is likely that if the United States explicitly made the global preservation of universal humanitarian values its highest international priority, there would be much greater acceptance in many parts of the world of the exercising of American influence.

Much of the language used by politicians at international summits is official-sounding, legalistic and devoid of passion. Statesmen cautiously evoke the phrase "human rights" when meeting foreign counterparts. Again, there is a lack of leadership based on universal values, a compelling vision for humanity and the insistence on practical steps forward based on co-operation. Behind much of the diplomatic language often lies a degree of self-interest that would severely hinder progress on humanitarian issues if left unchallenged. The difficulties in getting the world's leaders to agree on robust measures to avert the worst consequences of climate change are proof enough.

A practical obstacle and the crux of many of the world's problems today is the higher priority accorded to the inviolability of state borders than to the protection of human rights. A legitimate, universally accepted world government with policing powers is still far from becoming a reality. In Sudan, the United Nations needed to request permission to introduce a peace-keeping force to protect tribal populations from massacres. The same principle also helps explain why the Jews fought for an internationally recognized country of their own where their physical integrity could be better defended after centuries of persecution and massacres, and why, as of this writing, they are still locked in a sometimes bitter struggle with the Palestinians, who strive for respect and self-determination within their own defined borders. Preserving internationally agreed upon borders is a practical prerequisite to having other aspects of international law respected by national governments. The consequences, however, are often that major human rights abuses are viewed as lying outside the jurisdiction of the international community. Fortunately, the responsibility to protect (R2P or RtoP) has emerged in the past few years as an international norm that explicitly permits intervention when states gravely fail to protect their own citizens. In practice, this principle is only selectively applied to situations where the military advantage is sufficient to keep the risks of intervention acceptably low.

Increased pressure needs to come from outside the system of international diplomacy. As is the case for domestic politics, countries need to be pressured to respect and apply universal humanitarian values, including the UDHR, as an overriding priority. Creativity among NGOs is needed to incentivize countries to comply. In some cases, persuading countries to respect universal values and the UDHR might be achieved by large groups of people who can function like consumer blocs and wield economic power in a way that might be more effective and less likely to create counter-productive tensions than government-imposed economic sanctions. It should always be made clear that the objective is the defense of human beings rather than an attack on other countries' cultural customs, beliefs or integrity. There are ways of depoliticizing the issues by carrying out initiatives in a spirit of transparency and putting the entire focus on human beings. Such approaches may be a key to the success of international relations and the spreading of universal values in the coming years and decades.

It is sometimes said that it is up to countries to determine their own destinies and find their own solutions. This principle matters when it concerns the approach with which developmental aid is offered, sometimes imposed condescendingly by outsiders with little knowledge of the realities on the ground. But it should not be used as an excuse to shirk solidarity with innocent people and avoid protecting them from cruel political systems they did not choose. The international community should not swoop in to meddle in local practices that are relatively benign. But where people are suffering substantially, including due to the corruption or violence of their governments, compassion for other human beings trumps any charge of interfering in other countries' affairs.

War and Self-Determination

The issue underlying many of the world's conflicts is the control of land: who gets to live where, and who gets to exploit the resources and other advantages of any particular territory. In the past, the principal determining factor was physical force: if you were strong and numerous enough, you could take over a territory, rule, enslave, rape, assimilate, expel and murder its current inhabitants, and assert ownership of its riches. Indeed, the history of the world is one of a continuous series of slaughters and conquests, conducted even in recent memory by Western countries that now portray themselves as bastions of humanistic ideals. Given the intrinsic human quest for power and the propensity to use violence to obtain or secure desired resources and (ultimately) spread genes, it is inconceivable that the world could have reached its current state without the hundreds of millions of lives lost in warfare over the millennia and the vast amounts of suffering entailed. That is a terrible and sobering realization. As reflected on earlier, it means that if we started everything from scratch, we would end up slaughtering and torturing each other by the millions all over again.

The relative peaceful stability in many parts of the world today is in large part a consequence of boundaries of control—in many cases consolidated through centuries of bloodshed—being crystallized into internationally recognized borders, a process often complicated by arbitrary lines drawn by colonial powers that later retreated. The existence of an international treaty system, rapid communications and transport, economic integration and prosperity, as well as modern weaponry, all tend to make warfare more costly and less attractive than negotiation and in many cases, such as within much of western and central Europe today, almost inconceivable as a means to an end. From a big-picture historical perspective, it seems that it is only once human populations multiply, achieve economic prosperity and integration, and have little to gain by killing each other that some degree of true stability can be achieved. It is also, arguably, only with the advent of modern communications that non-state actors with motives other than self-interest can realistically aspire to influence events on a global scale.

However, while borders tend to follow cultural lines, they often leave some cultural groups under the control of, or warily sharing power with, others. The deeply rooted desire to be master in one's own home extends to groups of culturally and ethnically related people. The tensions that can potentially explode into violent conflict will never be dissipated as long as some groups' human rights are suppressed by the rule of others, including the right to exercise their own customs, use their own language, and preserve their identity, through controls on immigration if necessary.

Countries and their dominant populations are understandably reluctant to cede territories, especially when these are resource-rich, represent a net source of tax revenue, and contribute to their overall size and international clout. In an ideal world where humanitarian values were universally respected and, through a greater degree of international solidarity, people's prosperity was not overly dependent on the vagaries of history and which pieces of the Earth's surface they happened to occupy, none of this would matter very much. But in the real world, where international borders often command greater respect than the people living within them, reducing the risk of conflict requires maintaining the above vision, respecting local cultural freedoms and, in some cases, finding creative and equitable ways of distributing the wealth arising from localized natural resources.

Even where the physical stakes are minimal, tempers flare, national pride is slighted, and countries poke each other aggressively. The United Kingdom sent 255 of its citizens to their deaths as recently as 1982 to defend a far-away territory, the Falkland Islands, essentially on a matter of principle rather than as a calculated means to avoid human suffering. As much as one may crave a peaceful, non-violent world, the threat of military retaliation unfortunately remains an inevitable requirement for a country or population to avoid being bullied around by others. Any country governed by extreme pacifists, at least in the absence of an alliance with others that can guarantee its security, risks losing control of its destiny and, consequently, its ability to ensure that universal values are respected within its borders. As long as an independent, international police force with a universally recognized global jurisdiction does not exist, a certain level of mutual threat among heavyweights may remain necessary, and this principle will continue to play a major role in attempts to achieve a stable resolution to conflicts.

Most people living in the West today have never directly experienced war, while at the same time, we have become conditioned to accepting faraway wars as normal, including those supposedly being waged to protect us from future harm. As a result, we fail to experience a sufficiently strong emotional reaction to the horrors that accompany them. We allow armies to knowingly subject others to terrible suffering and death, even under the label of collateral damage, in order to reduce the risk of us eventually experiencing the same fate. Even a euphemistically titled "just war" is an appalling thing, regardless of the fact that it is sometimes inevitable, as it has consequences equivalent to, or even worse than, situations it is intended to prevent. Aside from civilian casualties, there remains something intrinsically grotesque about the institutionalization of men killing other men (and sometimes women), each believing their actions to be justified. And although the elimination of other humans is awful enough, in practice, of course, hits are rarely as clean as in video games.

One can provide all the justifications in the world for going to war, and there are many cases where even the staunchest humanitarians would agree to its necessity. But there will always be something deeply disturbing about inflicting extreme suffering on innocent people in the name of a just world. It is very difficult to maintain a consistent argument in favor of war by claiming that reducing suffering—including the potential consequences of submitting to others' culture and rule—is the highest value and ultimate objective. The very act of intentionally participating in warfare, sending young people to their deaths and inflicting certain death and great suffering upon innocent populations—even if the identity of the specific victims is a matter of probability—undermines our efforts to defend a value-based global society predicated on the fundamental importance of reducing suffering. The professed need to carry out just wars with the aim of preserving the well-being of one's own tribe, while understandable from the point-of-view of our deepest survivalist instincts, can easily lead to a cycle of terror that reveals the fragility of the ethical argumentation.

The doubts and ambiguity about one's country's actions that this think-ing can trigger are certainly a reason why we often suppress it and accept the reasoning offered by the authorities. But beneath the appearance of re-spectability and official international approval that an action can elicit in a world where the boundaries between legality and illegality are fairly clearly defined, there is the eternal tug-of-war between self-interest and compas-sion, and when push comes to shove, we know which one usually wins. The Geneva Conventions were a welcome move to imbue institutionalized kill-ing with a modicum of civility, cordoning off the field in which horror can be committed, but they do not solve the underlying problem. In a smarter, more creative world, reason and empathy would prevail and obviate the need for killing.

If we accord a high value to human life in practice and not just in theory, intentionally imposing on humans a high probability of death, as govern-ments do when sending soldiers to engage in combat, should only be done as a last resort, when negotiations have failed and the risks of not going to war are too high. In today's world there are fortunately more creative ways of achieving an acceptable, peaceful outcome than by resorting to force, even though the latter can never be ruled out as a necessity in some cases.

There need to be greater means employed to anticipate wars and take evasive actions before tensions explode. Wars do not usually occur without warning, and they are inevitably preceded by a perceived lack of respect by at least one group, increased polarization, and a reversion to primitive, nationalistic emotions. Within the West, we can no longer imagine that happening, perhaps naïvely and to our future detriment. But we need to keep the images of war alive and institute trust-building measures wher-ever conflicts seem likely in order to avoid new, dangerous tipping points ever being reached.

Negotiating

If the preservation of individual freedoms and the reduction in suffer-ing are our highest priorities, then we must acknowledge that it is often necessary to talk to people who have done some very bad things, regardless of how distasteful we may find it, and to carry out negotiations whenever these bear hope for a more peaceful future. Pragmatism must support ideal-ism, and only when negotiations are likely to be a tactical error should they be delayed.

A reluctance to talk to criminals, murderers and enemies for fear of becoming morally tainted is misguided and ultimately tragic when this stubbornness prevents the reaching of agreements that can reduce human misery. Neville Chamberlain's failed appeasement of Adolf Hitler in 1938 is often regarded in hindsight with disdain for a lack of moral resolve. Yet had the policy actually worked in practice, the tactic might have saved over 70 million human beings from death through sadistic violence, war, disease and famine, even though a psychopath would have remained in power. Moral courage is admirable and of the highest importance for defending humanitarian values, but where human lives and welfare are at stake, it should not exclude pragmatic solutions.

Pragmatism also sometimes requires a certain dose of cynicism in support of higher ideals, such as compensating disreputable people for doing the right thing. Admittedly, this practice carries risks. If it becomes commonplace, it risks eroding a culture of compassion. And it can trigger more wrong-doing by those seeking to profit. But where other approaches are impotent and the alternative is more suffering, it needs to be contemplated as a serious option. The ends may often justify the means, so long as everyone shares the same explicit, transparent vision of the ends, and idealism is protected from the slow encroachment of cynicism.

Where a choice has to be made, ending conflict and bringing peace and security to populations is more important than putting even barbaric dictators behind bars. South Africa's post-apartheid Truth and Reconciliation Commission provides an example of a potentially useful approach, despite its actual shortcomings, where victims were given the opportunity to be heard and respected, without an endless witch hunt that might have caused greater instability.

Many armed conflicts today are less about defending racist philosophies than about self-determination and access to resources, though ethnic tensions invariably play a role. On the basis of what moral high ground should one shun dialogue if the alternative is conflict and suffering? Even the doctrine espoused by many Western democracies of not talking to terrorists, rooted in part in the desire not to provide a political reward to those who attack civilians, is often more ideological than pragmatic. It is not inconsistent to condemn murder in the strongest terms and to feel disgust with the perpetrators, while still seeking practical solutions that will lead to a stable peace. Intelligent people with emotional control should not allow the psychological predispositions of the human brain to hijack rational decision-making that will lead to reduced suffering, regardless of how understandable the instinct may be.

The difficulty is that the average person is likely to cringe seeing one of their political leaders shaking hands with a murderous head of state or terrorist mastermind while common criminals languish in prison, viewing it as both an example of a double standard and as a symbolic moral failing of a figure who should be setting an example. When mass murderers are greeted warmly—and one cannot help but remember Muammar Qaddafi's state visit to the Elysée Palace in late 2007—, there is an inevitable, wearying sense that anything goes, that there are no moral bearings anymore, and that we are being governed by an elite that pays lip service to values. Similarly, it is a great burden for a victimized population to accept that a high-ranking slaughterer be allowed to go free, even after the negotiated end to a conflict. People have a deeply rooted need for justice that cannot be brushed aside.

It is therefore essential, once again, that leaders continuously demonstrate genuine, explicit commitment to universal humanitarian values. Wherever possible, any meetings with other political leaders who are guilty of major crimes should be carried out with discretion, and with explicit caveats that the meetings in no way condone the crimes of the past. This behavior is necessarily a tightrope act, with populations judging their leaders by their acts, and leaders' true motives themselves often murky. But when more lives can be saved and more suffering prevented by negotiating with tyrants than by seeking to cart them off to a criminal court, it becomes all the more important to explain the rationale to a public that demands justice, and reassure it of the commitment to preserving people's well-being. This approach requires a high level of trustworthiness as well as effective communications in order to be credible and effective.

Clearly there are situations that have no perfect win-win solution: sometimes two parties simply want the same thing. And from cases ranging from King Solomon's famous judgment to modern day custody battles, you cannot divide a baby. But there are always creative solutions possible— even for the city where King Solomon once reigned—where each party can obtain the essence of what it needs.

Life partners sometimes engage in senseless arguments that lead to bitter feelings. How can one expect countries that didn't choose each other as neighbors to resolve their differences easily? But if the key to a successful relationship is the ability to understand the other's perspective and to make compromises, the same is true in international relations. Because in the end, relations between countries are strongly swayed by the sensibilities of individual human beings. The importance attributed to other individuals' subjective experience is often as important in resolving international disputes as in solving interpersonal conflicts.

Although it is practically a platitude that countries' first priority is the pursuit of self-interest, we are fortunately in an age where violence is less likely than ever to be rewarding, with the large majority of recent conflicts resolved through negotiation.[93] The promise of confidence-building measures to increase the chances of negotiated settlements is testament to the very real human component of conflicts. While the resolution of conflicts through attention to minute practical details depends strongly on the strength of the respective bargaining positions, the willingness to compromise remains dependent on goodwill towards the adversary.

Negotiations are more likely to succeed when adversaries are respectful of each other's emotional states. Because ultimately, what people want are solutions that make them happy and that take into account their needs, not simply land and resources per se—although sometimes the two can seem inextricably linked. When subjective experience and happiness, including physical prosperity, are placed at the center of considerations, more creative solutions can be arrived at that expand the possibilities beyond a one-dimensional tug-of-war. If you meet people's needs and desires for freedom, respect and some comfort, you relieve much of the frustration that leads to unhappiness and conflict. Neutral mediators can help to judge the fairness of a situation in a supple, non-arbitrary way.

The standard current of thought related to conflict resolution holds that first you negotiate peace, *then* you sell it to the local populations through a PR campaign. The potential role of communications in creating the trust that is necessary to negotiate a lasting peace seems to be overly neglected. Increasingly, initiatives have been taken to help the respective populations envision what their immediate world would come to look like if peace took

---

93 "The discreet charms of the international go-between," *The Economist* (3 July 2008), www.economist.com/node/11670918.

hold, such as the OneVoice movement in the context of the Arab–Israeli conflict. These kinds of initiatives need to be greatly expanded.

How many conflicts are being fought today between groups who, in principle, would adhere to universal values if their adversaries' respect for them were guaranteed? And yet, in how many cases have these universal values been explicitly voiced as part of the framework for a solution? And to what extent are steps taken to bootstrap peace negotiation processes with signs of desire for reconciliation?

Again, we cannot change the past. And if we are prepared to observe our situation with detachment and extreme lucidity, we even have to acknowledge that the past was an inevitable outcome of the forces of fate. Even if we know this intellectually, we still have trouble fully accepting it. It emphatically does not mean ignoring people's and groups' sense of being wronged— one cannot will away deeply held resentment with a few feel-good phrases. Claims need to be acknowledged and addressed pragmatically. But there has to be a willingness to free oneself from the bonds of the past and work towards a promising future in which all parties' true underlying needs are taken into account.

EDUCATION

The global entrenchment and application of universal values require that they matter to the world's population and not just to a subset of statesmen who happen to be in power at a given time. Because values are ultimately relative, and because the details of one's moral sense depend so greatly on what one was exposed to while growing up, the educational system has a critical role to play in sensitizing children to the consequences of pure self-interest, developing their sense of empathy, and teaching them how they can contribute to making the world a better place. We cannot allow the set of laws we have inherited to become an empty shell from within which the emotions and empathy which originally sustained them have meanwhile slowly disintegrated.

Some of the important decision-makers in a few decades' time, and much of the population whose support they will depend on, are going through the compulsory educational system at the present. The extent to which they are impressed with the need to promote universal humanitarian values may have a marked influence on the priorities of the next generation and, consequently, on the fate of the world. This principle was defended by philosopher Richard Rorty, who stated that we need to create a global human rights culture in order to stop violations from happening, through so-called "sentimental education". He argued for the need to create a sense of empathy to promote an understanding of others' suffering.[94]

The educational system is still seen in most places as responsible mainly for preparing children for a tough, competitive world by providing them with the necessary skills. It is also used to instill a sense of national pride and identification. Too often it remains steeped in conservatism in the choice of curriculum and the priorities regarding what tomorrow's adults will need to know.

Many insist that the teaching of values is a private matter that should be left to parents and not assumed by the state. Indeed, values cannot be taught merely as theoretical concepts: they need to be experienced and lived. But there are several reasons why the state has an essential role to play. Parents can serve as important role models, but many are not sufficiently equipped or motivated to teach humanitarian values as effectively as possible to their children. The relevance of others' subjective experience, and what humans are capable of doing to one another, are vitally important messages to be taught. Ensuring that the next generation of adults cares deeply about human welfare and reducing future threats requires the impact of large-scale educational campaigns on a global scale. Centralized initiatives taken by those who have thought deeply about the issues are the way to ensure broad impact, rather than hoping futilely that these values will be taught spontaneously by the vast majority of parents. Furthermore, as children are expected to grow up to become law-abiding citizens, explaining to them the basic values and principles on which democratic institutions and international humanitarian law are based is an obligation if we expect them to grow up to be responsible, caring world citizens. It is hard to imagine a more important use of students' time than helping them to discover compassion, empathy and respect.

While I was in primary school, the students were on several occasions shown explicit films about the Holocaust, including graphic images of the bodies of concentration camp victims, scattered like piles of detritus in deep

94 Richard Rorty, "Human Rights, Rationality, and Sentimentality," in *On Human Rights: The 1993 Oxford Amnesty Lectures*, edited by Susan Hurley and Stephen Shute (New York: Basic Books, 1993). Available at http://usm.maine.edu/-bcj/issues/three/rorty.html.

pits. These films created in me a deep-seated awareness, at an age where I was forming impressions of how the world works, of the horrors that people had been forced to experience, and these events have since remained for me the epitome of evil. The lesson we were taught was that the events from this terrible period in human history should never happen again. I am emotionally committed to this principle in part because of what I was exposed to at school. If children are not exposed to atrocities and made to think about them, there is a greater likelihood of the past continuing to repeat itself in the future.

But while instilling a sense of empathy and an awareness of the suffering people cause to others is essential, it is not enough. There are some other key principles that children need to learn that can help them be effective in countering others' threats to humanitarian values.

Nobody in their right mind would suggest teaching school children that free will is an illusion. On the contrary, motivating anybody of any age requires giving them the belief that they can achieve what they want. However, it is important to teach children that everything is connected, that things happen for specific reasons, whether willed or not, and that our actions have consequences for the rest of the world and for others' well-being. This is an important message to communicate early on, as it can help children to seek to understand rather than to blame, and to take responsibility in the search for practical solutions.

The basic principles of logical reasoning should also be introduced as part of older children's compulsory education, rather than as part of a philosophy course taken only by a small fraction of university students. This would help ensure that people grow up with a better understanding of the roots of knowledge, including the basis of our assumptions and how logic leads us from assumptions to conclusions we can trust, and a healthier degree of open-mindedness and willingness to think critically. If a population has learned to respect and employ reason, promoting compassionate behavior becomes less of a challenge. Accounts of the terrible things that people have been made to endure speak for themselves, and reason will more easily lead to the search for effective solutions.

Finally, if people are meant to be happy and not simply productive citizens who contribute to the economy, the educational system has a responsibility to teach young people what empirically based, scientific research tells us about happiness. We should help young people to acquire useful techniques and a healthy way of looking at things when they can learn these easily, rather than have them learn it all the hard way as wounded adults in therapy.

16. Making an Impact: Globally Entrenching Compassion

> It is no use saying, "We are doing our best." You have got to succeed in doing what is necessary.
> —Winston Churchill, British prime minister

> Never doubt that a small group of thoughtful, committed citizens can change the world. Indeed, it is the only thing that ever has.
> —Margaret Mead, anthropologist

At the end of the chapter "As Good as It Can Get", I reflected on our room for maneuver in engineering a better future where the worst human rights abuses and forms of intentional suffering are eliminated and humanitarian values are entrenched. If we are to have any chance of approaching this kind of utopia, we may need a new paradigm by which to act. The challenges we face as a species demand an ambitiously scaled response. A succession of small, incremental improvements according to existing schemas may not suffice to preserve a more compassionate future. For all the effort currently expended by dedicated activists around the world, we will need creative ways of exercising greater influence, whether through existing organizations or, very likely, newly founded ones with unique and powerful agendas. And we may have just a narrow window of time to act decisively.

In this remaining chapter, I would like to reflect on how the ideas developed in this book might translate into practice in making an impact. A number of broad, basic principles emerge. Few of these will be particularly startling. But if they were followed more consistently, I believe they would increase the effectiveness of social activism, present and future, aimed at shaping a global society driven by humanitarian values, and also be of potential value to many existing NGOs carrying out more targeted work to relieve suffering on the ground.

THE NEED FOR AMBITIOUS NEW ORGANIZATIONS AND INITIATIVES

A substantial improvement in the prospects for humanity might only be achievable through the emergence of a new type of ambitious organization originating in civil society, possibly operating on a scale not yet seen. An organization that can successfully tap into the expertise and insight of specialists from a range of relevant disciplines, that possesses the necessary drive, creativity, intelligence, influence and organizational skills, and that can set in motion a project that forges a universal global consensus around a defined, common set of humanitarian goals. Something of a humanitarian Manhattan Project, with similarly focused intensity but with peaceful aims. I would see such an organization playing a leadership role as well as acting as a facilitator, allowing ordinary citizens of the world to connect and have greater influence on international politics—not just as voices, but as active agents of change. What would distinguish such an organization from existing NGOs advocating human rights and conflict resolution would be its philosophy and approach, the scale of its ambitions, and the degree of sophistication and innovation with which it made use of existing knowledge.

The relatively new Internet-based advocacy organization Avaaz (www. avaaz.org) is just one example of how there is ample room for innovation. Avaaz still seeks to effect change above all through the traditional exertion of public pressure, but its operational model allows hundreds of thousands of voices to be mobilized very rapidly. Further impetus for change needs to come from ambitious, creative international organizations that, like Avaaz, have a transparent agenda, are perceived as independent, and whose objectives are overwhelmingly shared by the world's populations. The principles contained in the rest of this chapter could have a significant role to play.

TRANSPARENCY IN ADVOCATING UNIVERSAL HUMANITARIAN VALUES

I have been arguing repeatedly why it is so important that universal humanitarian values be promoted. The specific principle that some things—the very worst forms of suffering—should never be allowed to happen needs to be vigorously defended, and the core set of universal humanitarian values should represent the transparent basis of all argumentation used by organizations advocating change, and also the basis for all our future endeavors as a species. Ensuring that actions in favor of a better world are understood as being consistent with compassion and universal values is essential for them to be widely accepted and not viewed primarily as instruments of personal gain.

Trust in the underlying motives ideally requires a human element. While we can spread endless amounts of information and idealistic principles around the globe, behind the information and the advocacy of universal values needs to lie real human empathy, untainted as much as possible by self-interest. During the popular uprising in Egypt in early 2011, the ability of an activist's tears to move a nation as he was interviewed on television attested to the power of the emotional expression of empathy as a force for positive change when it is perceived as genuine.

While compassion as an underlying principle is implied in Western constitutions that guarantee freedom of expression and human rights within their borders, and (very much in principle) in the foreign policy of Western nations that seek to promote humanitarian values abroad, the universal applicability of the values, to the extent that this is true, and the underlying reasoning and emotions that support them are rarely clearly exposed. I believe this is critically lacking. Especially when, in the world of diplomacy, the ends require pragmatic means, the underlying values must always be transparent.

Making Effective Use of Self-Interest

We have to acknowledge human nature in any long-term strategy that seeks stable peace and well-being for our planet's inhabitants, recognizing that some people will always be seeking more, trying to gain higher status than their peers, and fighting to maintain power unless they have a good reason to do otherwise. Pragmatic approaches to change cannot realistically expect that people, whether ordinary citizens or dictators, will voluntarily give up much of what they have already acquired. Even teachings from the ancient Talmud on the subject of charity recognized that people used to a comfortable lifestyle cannot be expected to substantially reduce their standard of living. The success of large-scale initiatives depends on the degree to which they can offer greater sustained happiness for virtually everyone, thereby preempting resistance and reducing the frustration that leads people to commit desperate acts of violence. Although in practice this goal can never be fully reached, this is the kind of thinking we need, whether we are appealing to ordinary citizens to press for change, or trying to persuade dictators and governments to treat their own citizens better.

New initiatives should endeavor to put measures in place that compensate for some people's reduced material gains or losses with other kinds of gains that can convincingly be argued to result in improved quality of life, such as decreased societal tensions and greater cohesiveness, a reduction in crime, a diminished threat of terrorism, greater freedoms and a secure future. This approach relates closely to an economic concept referred to as improving the "Pareto efficiency" of a situation, which means improving at least one person's situation in a way that no one else is worse off. However, to be useful, the concept of well-being must be taken in the largest sense possible to include non-monetary intangibles. It also must take into consideration the value people attribute to *relative* wealth—something that the concept of Pareto efficiency ignores. If everyone else is becoming wealthier, those left behind lose status.

Humanitarian activists will need to take this principle into account as much as possible in their strategic thinking. When it comes to mobilizing people on a large scale, they will have to make it as easy as possible for people to take actions that are consistent with values they in principle agree with, and help them to avoid cognitive dissonance between these values and their lifestyles. Everyone has a legitimate desire to enjoy life. No one wants to become a martyr for the species, unilaterally depriving themselves of pleasure with thanks from no one, a solitary loser in a grand project where almost everyone else comes out ahead. The challenge is to persuade people to help make a difference without giving up their bubble of happiness and meaning. Ways need to be found to combine the two, continuing to appeal to people's own needs and providing incentives to get processes working.

This principle is a practical necessity that is commonly ignored because we cling too rigidly to the ideal of universal values and the notion of human rights as self-evident truths, rather than as drivers of change. People's individual values, whether the security and challenge they get from a high-ranking corporate job or the comfort they derive from religion, are sources of stability and meaning in their lives, and a challenge to these is perceived as a potential threat to their own identity. No sustainable strategy for humanitarian advocacy, whatever the specific target, can expect to exploit indefinitely a feeling of guilt, or expect actions that do not make people feel happier.

Appealing to people's self-interest may appear to be a cynical basis for reducing suffering, but as a practical means towards this end, it needs to be embraced. In fact, when self-interest is understood in a broader sense to encompass psychological well-being, making people feel good about relieving suffering is arguably the most effective, most stable and thus most desirable form of altruism—doing something less out of a sense of duty than because we feel compassion with others and it feels good making others feel good.

On a strategic register, the sophisticated application of game theory can be used to engineer outcomes on the assumption that everyone is pursuing their own self-interest. Bruce Bueno de Mesquita, Professor of Politics at New York University and an applied game theorist, has successfully predicted numerous political decisions and also helped to influence outcomes in the corporate world through the mathematical modeling of human decision-making, based on the principle of self-interest and the collection of solid data on individuals' preferences, degree of passion about an issue and their influence.[95] It is absolutely critical for this kind of approach to be employed as part of any strategy to make the world a more stably compassionate place, incentivizing countries, corporations and organizations to commit sustainably to humanitarian values. There is nothing like participating in a negotiation workshop to stress upon you the degree to which self-interest and the pursuit of specific outcomes drive strategic behavior, and how important it is that compassionate agents learn to play the game wisely.

Furthermore, extending the point I made above, game theory is perhaps less narrowly about self-interest than about people trying to get what they want, which in many cases may really be less about accumulating wealth and power than about making the world a better place—even if there is personal recognition and satisfaction to be gained from it. Many people really care about others' welfare and the fate of the world, and you would have to dig deeply at the evolutionary roots to find the ultimate cause of these feelings in terms of self-interest. Even applied game theorists accumulating expert data on people's motives and political stances may not have access to their deep-down desires, such as for an ideal, peaceful world, and may

---

95 See his book *The Predictioneer's Game: Using the Logic of Brazen Self-Interest to See and Shape the Future.*

not know how strongly these desires would weigh in if properly taken into consideration. Pure egoistic self-interest might often be containable if peace were allowed to dominate and barriers put up to protect it.

While meta-stable situations can evolve or be created in which universal humanitarian values thrive, there is always the danger that uncompassionate agents, whether governments, dictators, extremists or other self-interested groups or people, will gain the upper hand, with the newest technology at their disposal, dominating others and causing them to suffer. A strong, influential, Gandhi-like leader who promotes these values has no way of ensuring an indefinite line of succession of equally strong leaders defending the same values.

For universal humanitarian values to persist stably into the future, there will have to be an intrinsically compassionate system put in place that defends them. This effectively means stabilizing an otherwise non-equilibrium situation by raising the exit barriers, making it sustainably in the interest of all parties, whether individuals, governments or corporations, including those of future generations, to continue to adhere to these values. There are probably numerous ways this might be achieved through creative efforts, all subject to great uncertainty, but the more thought that goes into such initiatives, the greater the likelihood of a positive outcome.

It may even be necessary to implement processes that take on a life of their own. There is a parallel here to research into "friendly artificial intelligence", which aims to ensure that, in case a Singularity occurs, artificial intelligence systems have the right processes engineered in so that they never threaten humans. Without well-designed processes in place, we may be continuously dependent on the values of those in power—whether humans or machines. As a purely speculative idea, if we again consider universal humanitarian values as a meme, we may somehow be able to package it in an intelligent, carefully designed way that allows it to spread spontaneously and sustainably in viral fashion, independent of any single individual though perhaps still dependent on people to provide regular boosts in momentum. There would need to be sufficient advance reflection to ensure that any such processes and the organizations initiating them, driven by humanitarian values, could not readily be hijacked by the self-interest of any officer, leader or group, although the intelligent packaging and putting into motion of processes would still need to come from a collection of human minds who want compassion to win.

A Singularity is still sufficiently far away that it is not clear what specific strategies could be followed now whose effectiveness would persist in several decades' time. But in the meantime, building up a stronger global culture of respect for universal humanitarian values can help ensure that if and when a Singularity occurs, it will be as compassionate as can be.

PRAGMATIC DETACHMENT

In the face of all the intense, preventable suffering going on in the world, there is the urge to grab humanity with one's hands and shout, "What's the matter with you all!?" But one might as well shake one's fist at the stars above or bark at the moon. As I have argued, including in the chapter on determinism, if you want to find solutions to suffering, you have to step outside the system and think objectively and dispassionately about what might actually work.

Blaming individuals and groups of people is a natural human instinct. We become angry at others, and at the world, for not interacting with us in a way that makes us happy. It is an emotional reaction that can help to release tension. It defines the ideas to be targeted or the behavior to be condemned, ensuring that we do not lose sight of our moral compass. When coordinated, it reminds others that an organization has a real human, emotional dimension and is not merely a dispassionate bureaucracy. It can also often serve as a very useful tool for influencing others' behavior and persuading them to assume responsibility. There is certainly a legitimate role for blame in NGOs' documentation of human rights abuses.

But blaming is a double-edged sword. When it encourages defiance, it may be counter-productive as the primary means of effecting positive change. And it encourages people to seek criminals, rather than solutions. This is how the free will paradox rears its head in the most concrete of ways. The notion of individual responsibility is absolutely necessary for the functioning of society and for personal initiatives to improve the world, but a potential distraction in the search for effective, large-scale solutions.

This principle is perhaps nowhere more relevant than to the pragmatic search for peaceful solutions to deadly conflicts. If warring parties can be brought to see the reasons for a conflict from a detached perspective, and to recognize that, if they were in their adversaries' shoes, they would likely act in the same way, they might be more inclined to seek negotiated solutions, even if their adversaries have carried out abominable acts.

Of course, guerillas cannot be expected to transform themselves into philosophers. And even the most detached, objective understanding of events will not persuade parties to a conflict to give up what they consider to be rightful claims to territory according to international law or other criteria. They will still try to get the best deal they can. Neither can the deep emotions that accompany the perception of past wrongs be willed to disappear through words alone. But recognizing the objective causes of a conflict might facilitate reconciliation, including an acknowledgment of the harm one's group has inflicted on others and the search for pragmatic ways to restore goodwill and trust.

Political and religious leaders classically frame the struggle between good and evil as one between people, rather than as the outcome of processes. For example, as Daniel Brook wrote in an article in *Slate*, "in the climate after 9/11...attempts to understand the terrorists were often seen as apologies for them."[96] But if we are to combat hatred, we need to understand the causes and address them. We need to de-personify the notions of good and evil in order to fight evil more effectively. People are also less likely to experience hatred when they feel respected as human beings with needs, regardless of how delusional and paranoiac their misperceptions may be. Recognizing this does not mean condoning violence or lessening the insistence on respect for universal values.

MAKING SYSTEMATIC USE OF FINDINGS FROM A DIVERSE RANGE OF DISCIPLINES

The problems we are facing need to be regarded as one big puzzle to solve, breaking it down and evaluating the actual resources needed, using the best tools at our disposal, including findings from a range of fields. Referring back to the earlier discussion about parallel explanations for phenomena, any hopes we have of significantly improving the world have to be consistent with what we know about the mechanisms of international politics that dictate world affairs, what we know about human nature, and with any other disciplines with predictive value for determining the consequences of our actions.

---

96 Daniel Brook, "The Architect of 9/11," *Slate* (8 September 2009), www.slate.com/id/2227245/entry/2227246.

Where there is money to be made, thousands flock to the scene as if it were a 19th century gold rush. The best talents are recruited, trained in the latest management wisdom and paid handsomely. But where reducing suffering and preserving our planet are concerned, the turnout is more sporadic and the degree of innovation limited. We need far more innovation, constrained only by the boundaries of current technology and knowhow. There is much, much more that can potentially be done.

Humanitarian organizations need to adopt existing best practices from the business world. But there also need to be better and more systematic ways of harnessing and fully integrating the knowledge and latest insights from a wide range of relevant disciplines, including psychology, political science, economics, mathematics, sociology and computer science. As mentioned, it is particularly important that the principles of game theory be applied in engineering outcomes, and that findings from the field of complexity theory be drawn on in order to increase the odds of achieving more stable solutions.

The above is obviously no mean task. Although academics and other specialists are developing increasingly sophisticated models of how humans, technologies and markets operate and interact, this information is so vast, detailed and fragmented that it is difficult for anyone to assimilate it all sufficiently in order to draw all the right conclusions and act on them. Even large corporations with huge resources at their disposal and addressing consumers' explicit needs have difficulty making optimal use of the mounds of data available and sometimes make major strategic mistakes. But if more of the resources already currently available to the humanitarian sector were used to tap more efficiently into the huge pool of current scientific knowledge, it is virtually certain that greater impact could be achieved. And whereas corporations are up against equally determined and resourceful competitors, for many humanitarian issues, the primary opponent is often simply apathy and inertia.

HARNESSING EMPATHY WISELY

Well-meaning parents sometimes tell children with thwarted playground ambitions to try to look at things from their peer's point-of-view. Empathy is a lot to expect of a 5-year-old, but it isn't a spontaneous practice among many adults either. Obtaining a sense of what another person might be feeling often requires an intentional mental effort. In practice, it often needs to be intentionally triggered in order to make people care.

Empathy can be very strong once triggered, but is most often dormant as we go through our daily lives. Others' suffering can seem very intangible, even surreal, if we haven't seen it first-hand, and it often makes only a virtual, cameo appearance in our hermetic urban environments. Given the huge extent of suffering that occurs in the world, it is nonetheless a dilemma for our planet that empathy is activated only under limited circumstances. Suffering happening elsewhere may scarcely encroach on our awareness, and we find ourselves missing the full emotional weight needed to drive change.

It is largely a matter of desensitization. While the degree of violence on television and in films is often condemned for making people more violent, the major problem may be subtly different, in that it desensitizes them to how awful real violence and killing are. The same may apply to the images of real suffering in the world.[97] When we are repeatedly exposed to them, words, images and ideas lose their power to command our attention and interest, to shock us into action. The expression "human rights violations" is not only broad, vague and legalistic, it is also so overused that it does not evokes images of atrocities so much as a breach of signed agreements. And ironically, the greater the number of people affected by suffering, the more we minimize it at the individual level. If the world were nearly free of disease and violence, the rare exceptions would elicit immediate compassion and action. But with endless suffering on a scale far too great to perceive other than abstractly, our responses can lose their emotional component. As that oft-cited quote attributed to Stalin goes, "A single death is a tragedy; a million deaths is a statistic."

Transmitting a lasting sense of the horror of extreme suffering is a major challenge. For example, if one is writing a book, how does one ensure that the impressions conveyed by even graphic descriptions outlast the reading experience and persist long enough to prompt action? How does a filmmaker touch people more deeply than just causing them to spend two hours fidgeting uncomfortably in their seats? Even major Hollywood films that can offer a glimpse of possible future catastrophic scenarios are not taken as much more than sensationalist forms of entertainment and probably have little if any impact on actual behavior. Any medium that really wants to

---

97 See Susan Sontag's book *Regarding the Pain of Others* for an exploration of this issue.

make people understand different states-of-mind in a more concrete, tangible way has to guide them towards actually experiencing them, thereby helping to bridge the perceived gap between people's identities. As suggested earlier on, we need to keep alive an intimate understanding of the horrors of war and of the atrocities committed by humans against others. Helping people to gain a deeper understanding of how our identities overlap and the commonality of subjective experience could also support efforts to promote empathy. Future politicians, business leaders and, perhaps, even computer programmers developing intelligent systems are all people whose sense of compassion will determine the future of well-being on our planet.

Eliciting empathy is sometimes handled rather crudely in the competition for attention exercised by countless humanitarian NGOs, large and small. It sometimes seems like they are scavenging for the last scraps of altruism, using blunt, conventional tools such as posters of starving children—similarly to fishermen depleting remaining fish stocks with large trawling nets. In theory, better orchestration and coordination between NGOs could ensure that resources are used synergistically and that organizations are not actually competing with each other while bombarding their target audiences with stale images.

But even when empathy is elicited, it needs to be linked effectively to action. To press the point, and at the risk of shocking some sensibilities, let me evoke an unimaginably hideous scene. Imagine an infant being skinned alive in front of you by the pitiless soldiers of a fascist regime—a barbarity that, given the extremes of cruelty that humans have shown themselves capable of in even recent history, certainly does not belong to the realm of fiction. The sight would be literally unbearable. Now imagine there was a button a short walk away you could press that would somehow—through a siren or, perhaps, a momentary offer of free beer—immediately cause them to stop. There is no doubt that you would go over to press the button. Imagine now that the horrific scene that began directly in front of you was taken behind a soundproof screen before you were made aware of the button. Presumably you would still find the button and press it. Now imagine that you were told that the whole scene was occurring in a faraway country. Probably you would still look for the button, provided there was nothing else urgent to attend to. Now let's imagine that there were a succession of infants subjected to the same fate, with the button still available to press and end the suffering, one infant at a time. But a friend you hadn't seen for a long time called you and asked you to go to dinner. Would you go, or would you stay to keep pushing the button? Now let's say there was no button, but you had to compose an e-mail for each infant to make its suffering stop. Let's say you had to do some research to find a different address to send for each infant. Let's say your whole family was getting together for a once-in-a-lifetime festivity. What would you do?

This brutal and superficially absurd series of situations illustrates the problem we are faced with in coming to the aid of people who are suffering. Vivid, immediate scenes easily trigger people's altruism response, but when the awareness is vaguer and there are conflicting options to be chosen from, the altruism response becomes weaker, to the point where it may never result in action, regardless of the urgency.

Because empathy is so fragile, it needs to be properly harnessed by linking it to concrete actions with large, sustainable impact that people can carry out, so that the emotion is not wasted. Empathy is a limited resource that we need to use wisely. Where there is a practical means of ending suffering or taking effective action, we need to make it as vivid as possible, but also offer people a "button" they can easily press, ideally in which they put the whole power of their person, delegating their signature, and potentially providing some financial support, to well-thought-out processes that do not depend on their continuous expenditure of time.

To provide a brief anecdote, in early 2009, I was at one point sitting at a beach bar on the Pacific coast of Costa Rica. Latino music was playing as I looked out at the waves breaking beyond the palm trees, a bottle of beer next to me on the wooden table where I was writing. Life was good. And I thought about how, elsewhere on the planet, millions of human beings were living very hard existences, devoid of even the simplest comforts or sense of security. The passport and official identity I am lucky enough to possess afford me great privileges that less fortunate ones do not have. Very little connects my world with theirs. But at that moment, I imagined having a precise set of simple steps to follow on my laptop, setting in motion a process that would cause the life of another human being to improve beyond his or her wildest imagination, with negligible effect on my own material well-being. This is a plausible, theoretically achievable scenario. The question is, what would that simple process be?[98]

---

98 Donors to most charities and humanitarian organizations cannot, in most cases, realistically expect their money to go directly to an individual, but rather to sup-

People can potentially make a highly significant difference to others' lives wherever they are. But while they tend to be enthusiastic about the possibilities of effecting local change, they are less easily motivated when it is remote and intangible, and often doubtful about the real likelihood of effecting sustained, large-scale change. And they are easily distracted by other, more immediate concerns. This is why people need to be given very simple, practical means to contribute resources and support, with defined outcomes that allow them to link their actions to concrete impact. The barrier to action needs to be kept as low as possible. By making it easy for people to have impact, we can harness the power of today's connectivity. We need to move beyond poster children and a website address. This requires a great deal of high-level, creative initiative and planning that, if done well, translates into no greater effort than a limited number of keystrokes or mouse clicks, whether spontaneously or on a regular basis.

People also need to see the results of their actions and of campaigns they participated in, in order to be given a sense of accomplishment, a reinforced sense of being part of a larger whole, and encouragement to continue to participate in the future. When people act and fail to see results, they lose confidence in the usefulness of their efforts. There is a rough parallel to the psychological phenomenon of learned helplessness described earlier, where subjects become depressed and immobile when they learn that nothing they do can help them avoid a painful situation, even if the circumstances change. It is probable that many people are already reluctant to do anything to improve the world because they see their efforts as futile. That can only change when they are made to discover the concrete impact of their actions.

In summary, I believe that the way organizations and individuals call the public's attention to major humanitarian issues could be improved through the use of more sophisticated processes that can convert moments of emotion and empathy into sustained action than can actually increase in momentum. Although people respond generously to acute humanitarian crises and appeals for help, their attention span is short. At moments when their awareness is raised, the long-term role they can play, directly or indirectly, needs to be explained and a refined mechanism needs already to have

---

port programs. But if we could simplify processes and better demonstrate the quantum impact of each additional donation, we would strengthen the connections between us and them.

been put in place in order to harness the full potential of the situation. The buttons need to be ready.

One often hears people say, "It's not our responsibility to save the world." Although sometimes a well-meaning attempt to relieve others of unnecessary anxiety about things they cannot change, what a dangerous meme this is to spread around. Helping to make a significant difference in the world is the price we should each be prepared to pay for permitting ourselves to enjoy life without being incapacitated by an awareness of the scale and intensity of the suffering that persists. It's not enough to claim to be morally unblemished and have neutral net impact on the world.

Those with a spiritual inclination sometimes express the idealistic view that we can change the world one person at a time, through a sort of osmosis, or a chain reaction of goodwill towards others—a version of that popular notion that the flapping of a butterfly's wings can affect the weather on the other side of the planet. The more scientifically inclined tend to have faith in the power of rationalism, of allowing the objective truth about external reality to permeate our collective consciousness and displace fanaticism. But neither of these perspectives on spreading humanism is sufficient. If we can't communicate the right ideas to the right people and engineer effective strategies on a large enough scale, we will not be successful at avoiding widespread suffering and the erosion of human rights and freedom, nor manage to save our species from self-destruction.

We concede too much responsibility to our political leaders and not enough to our own power of imagination. Life and the protection of well-being on this planet are too important to be abandoned to the goodwill of governments. We so easily fall into the pattern of thinking that if they can't improve the world then no one can, overlooking the fact that most government ministers are playing circumscribed roles within defined jurisdictions, and that they are not by nature the sources of the greatest inspirational ideas. In a talk about the extraordinary Brazilian United Nations diplomat and humanitarian Sergio Vieira de Mello, killed while on mission in Iraq, Samantha Power, writer, academic and member of the United States National Security Council, partly paraphrasing Gandhi, said, "If we want to see change, we have to become the change. We can't rely upon our institutions to do the work."[99] Changing the world requires a vision. It requires creativity. And it requires a sense of responsibility.

Any individual who wants to play a contributing role in trying to stabilize a humanistic outcome for our planet should reflect on how they can make a quantum difference, one that just might represent a significant or even a necessary or determining factor in achieving a tipping point towards sustainable change. It should be a powerfully motivating idea to resist the tide of evolution, taming Darwinism and using the intelligence that has evolved to feed back on the world and shape it in a way that reduces suffering to the extent possible. This idealistic achievement would be the ultimate local triumph of meaning over difficult odds, showing that, at least for one of the universe's minute experiments called planet Earth, there can be something approaching sustainable happiness as an outcome. And even in the worst case scenario, if the ultimate goal is never reached, the positive short-term fallout in terms of actual diminished suffering at least makes every endeavor worthwhile.

ORCHESTRATION AND EMOTIONALLY CONNECTING INDIVIDUALS

One of the biggest challenges in effecting change is achieving critical mass. It is unrealistic to expect that very large numbers of people will spontaneously and sustainably decide to behave altruistically, become obsessive about spending their free time and energy helping to relieve misery in the world, and conduct themselves in a way that will have major impact. The reality is that people may not know what they can do, and may not feel sufficiently emotionally engaged or concerned to invest their own time or money. They consider it the responsibility of governments, organizations, or others. They adopt the psychology of crowds, conforming to those culturally closest to them. Most have neither the independence of spirit to think "heretically" nor the will to maintain unusual positions in the face of widespread opposition.

Large-scale change can, of course, sometimes occur spontaneously through a trend that catches on and spreads, or that becomes assimilated into a culture, even without any apparent concerted effort or ambition. Malcolm Gladwell offers some such examples in his bestseller *The Tipping Point*. But spontaneous change may not occur in many places simultaneous-

---

99 www.ted.com/talks/samantha_power_on_a_complicated_hero.html. See also her book *Chasing the Flame: Sergio Vieira de Mello and the Fight to Save the World.*

ly without an external trigger. Urgent, large-scale behavioral change needs at some level to be orchestrated.

There is therefore an essential need to put powerful processes in place to persuade people to act. For initiatives aimed at long-term peaceful stability and well-being, there has to be a serious thought process that addresses the complexity and precedes this change. Without thoughtful orchestration, momentum can quickly recede following an individual, even high-profile, humanitarian initiative, without a tipping point being reached.

Orchestration does not mean top-down planning of all the details and telling large numbers of individuals what to do. For example, in *The White Man's Burden*, William Easterly makes a strong case for the failure of much of utopian, social engineering ideas to achieve much on the ground in relieving poverty. One of the keys to doing so in places like Africa is giving people the opportunity to become economically active and develop diverse, local solutions. But the spreading of humanitarian values requires more than lowering barriers, reducing inefficiencies and allowing self-interest to do the rest. Humanitarian initiatives need to be given as much momentum as possible through a process of coordination and amplification. When a positive outcome depends on a rare event, such as an insightful strategy, measures need to be taken to ensure maximum impact.

Orchestration in the broader sense can include trying to persuade large numbers of people to adopt practical strategies that bear a certain similarity, from voting for a certain candidate to participating in results-oriented campaigns. Orchestration means not leaving individuals to act on instinct alone, and trying to ensure that principles of best practice and empiricism are applied. It means looking at the big picture and trying to ensure that the net effect of people's actions will have the needed amplitude. It means facilitating processes, translated into a branching tree of millions of one-to-one human encounters that build trust and compassion based on transparency and genuine empathy.

On Internet forums, one can observe the degree of detail with which people debate what are, essentially, humanitarian issues, such as the carbon footprint of our diet. Questions such as the effect of eating local, or the extent to which transport plays a role, all attempt to define the optimal diet that will minimize one's personal footprint. The goal is to make a responsible, personal contribution to lowering greenhouse gas emissions, ultimately in order to stave off irreversible climate change, sea level rise, droughts, mass displacements of populations, international conflicts and widespread misery. But when the objectives are so ambitious, personal initiatives need to be part of a concerted effort in order to be effective. In the end, if Bangladesh suffers a similar fate to the mythical, sunken island of Atlantis because the world didn't do enough, your change in diet won't in practice have helped anyone, even though you can still honestly say you made an effort. The point is not at all to discourage any individual from acting in accordance with humanitarian values and trying to live "ethically". But the good intentions need to be translated into real impact, and that requires large-scale changes in behavior.

Keeping people sustainably impassioned about an issue, especially a technical one like climate change, is difficult. To achieve the real impact of widespread behavioral change often requires legislation as a driver. An individual who truly wants to contribute actively to resolving the problem of climate change should, beyond altering their own diet, try to exert pressure on politicians to support laws that will have macroscopic effects, such as the introduction of a carbon tax, inducing changes in people's behavior that will make a real, measurable difference.

Even when any *individual* person's private contribution may be wholly insignificant, millions of people acting together with a shared purpose and approach can effect change, provided there is coordination to ensure concerted mass action. The phenomenon of elections provides a relevant analogy. Except for very rare cases, any individual vote is extremely unlikely to make a difference to the outcome, even though the addition of millions of individual votes can change the course of a country or even the world. If you were thinking rationally about how to make the best use of your time to effect change, you might conclude that you are better off writing a letter to a member of the government than hauling yourself off to the local polling station for an act that, statistically speaking, might be less likely to make a decisive difference than the chance of being run over by a car on the way to vote. But the functioning of democratic movements requires the momentum of masses of people who each see themselves as small agents of change. Even in individualistic societies, we need people to identify themselves with ideals and sometimes to act as part of a larger collectivity in order to change things for the better. Websites on which people pledge to take an action provided that a minimum number of other people do the same are one model to emulate.

Once again, reason desperately needs emotion as an ally. A rational approach to achieving change requires that we appeal to people's sense of being part of something larger and urge them to get caught up in a tide of feeling. In order to improve the whole, you have to get people to feel part of the whole and participate in coordinated actions. Furthermore, while each individual has a role to play as an *agent* of change, the greater the responsibility individuals are encouraged to take as *drivers* of change who serve as sources of momentum and thereby amplify the process, the greater the likelihood of reaching a tipping point.

Let's imagine that repeatedly confirmed scientific analyses indicated that a much more positive outcome for our planet was possible but highly unlikely, as it would require a massive change in behavior on a global scale that would represent a marked shift away from the trends being observed. How could you possibly mobilize huge numbers of people in favor of an outcome that was unlikely to occur, especially when their governments were unwilling to make a courageous case for unpopular measures? You would need to give people "faith" in the possibility of low-probability events happening, focusing on the desired outcome rather than the statistical likelihood, in order to have them act collectively and concertedly. This behavior has something almost religious about it in trying to bring people together around a utopian vision. And yet, if this was the most likely way to yield the change in behavior needed, its necessity could be said to be *scientifically grounded*.

Making people feel part of a larger entity is, admittedly, also the approach that has been used in the past by dictators to commit atrocities against minorities and other populations, appealing to people's primitive, nationalistic instincts and suppressing independent thought. This approach continues to be used for evil purposes today. This is why it is so important that universal values be promoted as aggressively as possible and appealed to, and that people supporting these values be the ones who effect change.[100]

With the Internet, we have the potential to reach, directly or indirectly, virtually anyone in the world, including major decision-makers. There are innumerable clever communication strategies possible that can be concocted by creative people and used to deliver transparent messages that serve

---

100 See Seth Godin's TED talk on creating tribes around shared ideas and values: www.ted.com/talks/lang/eng/seth_godin_on_the_tribes_we_lead.html.

as catalysts of change. The press releases and web-based petitions used by many advocacy organizations are the very tip of the iceberg.

In fact, the huge range of possibilities for orchestrating powerful, creative campaigns with sustained impact has only started to be explored. Given the importance of the outcome, it is almost surprising that the humanitarian sector has not yet exploited these possibilities to a larger extent. This is probably in part because as organizations grow they tend to err on the side of conservatism. But their success will depend on their ability to better harness creativity and existing cross-disciplinary knowledge, and to carefully think through the details.

SUMMARY

As complexity in the world continues to accelerate, ensuring the long-term survival of our species in a way that preserves beauty and meaning and minimizes pain represents both a unique opportunity and a challenge on a monumental scale. A massive, intelligent, creative and coordinated harnessing of both empathy and self-interest in order to promote compassion and universal humanitarian values may be essential if there is to be any hope at all of achieving this goal. The general principles discussed in this chapter, if applied consistently by creative individuals and organizations, may help us to have a fighting chance of succeeding.

17. Epilogue

On 2 October 2009, the sun set forever for Marek Edelman, the last leader of the Warsaw Ghetto uprising of 1943. His life, summarized in an obituary in *The Economist*[101], is in several ways symbolic of the human struggle for self-preservation and connection with others, and it embodies many of the key ideas expressed in this book. Faced with death all around him, imposed on the Jews by the Nazis' barbaric cruelty, the most important thing for Edelman was "just to be alive: not to be one of the naked corpses wheeled past on carts, heads bobbing up and down or knocking on the pavement." He was faced with "a 'terrible apathy'... in which people no longer saw or believed the random horrors round them." And yet love affairs happened, "ecstatic moments of happiness, when terrified and lonely people were thrown together."

Edelman, who stubbornly remained in his native Poland after World War II and refused to express open hatred for the Nazis, declared, "Man is evil, by nature man is a beast. People have to be educated from childhood, from kindergarten, that there should be no hatred."[102] The memory of this low-key hero should serve as an inspiration for those trying to make the world a better place.

---

101 "Marek Edelman", *The Economist* (8 October 2009), www.economist.com/node/14585545.

102 "Marek Edelman", *The Telegraph* (4 October 2009), www.telegraph.co.uk/news/obituaries/politics-obituaries/6259900/Marek-Edelman.html.

For more information on making a difference, please visit the website www.thebattleforcompassion.com.

BIBLIOGRAPHY

Ball, Philip. *Critical Mass: How One Thing Leads to Another.* London: Random House, 2004.

Benatar, David. *Better Never to Have Been: The Harm of Coming into Existence.* New York: Oxford University Press, 2006.

Betancourt, Ingrid. *Even Silence Has an End: My Six Years of Captivity in the Colombian Jungle.* New York: Penguin, 2010.

Blackmore, Susan. *Consciousness: An Introduction.* New York: Oxford University Press, 2004.

Brockman, John, ed. *What Is Your Dangerous Idea?* New York: HarperCollins Publishers, 2007.

Bryson, Bill. *A Short History of Nearly Everything.* New York: Broadway Books, 2003.

Bueno de Mesquita, Bruce. *The Predictioneer's Game: Using the Logic of Brazen Self-Interest to See and Shape the Future.* New York: Random House, 2009.

Chalmers, David, ed. "'Hard' and 'Easy' Problems," *PhilPapers,* http://philpapers.org/browse/hard-and-easy-problems.

Dawkins, Richard. *The Greatest Show on Earth.* New York: Free Press, 2009.

Dennett, Daniel. *Freedom Evolves.* New York: Penguin, 2003.

Deutsch, David. *The Fabric of Reality: The Science of Parallel Universes and Its Implications.* New York: Penguin, 1997.

Diamond, Jared. *Guns, Germs, and Steel: The Fate of Human Societies.* New York: W. W. Norton & Company, 1997.

Easterly, William. *The White Man's Burden: Why the West's Efforts to Aid the Rest Have Done So Much Ill and So Little Good.* Oxford: Oxford University Press, 2006.

Fisher, Len. *The Perfect Swarm: The Science of Complexity in Everyday Life.* New York: Basic Books, 2009.

Fromm, Erich. *The Revolution of Hope: Toward a Humanized Technology.* New York: Bantam, 1968.

Gladwell, Malcolm. *The Tipping Point: How Little Things Can Make a Big Difference.* New York: Little, Brown and Company, 2000.

Glover, Jonathan. *Humanity: A Moral History of the Twentieth Century.* New Haven, Connecticut: Yale University Press, 1999.

Graham, Carol. "The Economics of Happiness," in *The New Palgrave Dictionary of Economics,* Second Edition. Edited by Steven Durlauf and Larry Blume. Houndmills, UK: Palgrave Macmillan, 2008. www3.brookings.edu/views/papers/graham/2005graham_dict.pdf.

Hamilton, Clive. *Requiem for a Species: Why We Resist the Truth About Climate Change.* London: Earthscan, 2010.

Harris, Sam. *The End of Faith: Religion, Terror, and the Future of Reason.* New York: W. W. Norton & Company, 2004.

Hauser, Mark. *Moral Minds: How Nature Designed Our Universal Sense of Right and Wrong.* New York: HarperCollins, 2006.

Joy, Bill. "Why the future doesn't need us," *Wired* (April 2000). www.wired.com/wired/archive/8.04/joy_pr.html.

Hofstadter, Douglas. *I Am a Strange Loop.* New York: Basic Books, 2007.

Koch, Christof. *The Quest for Consciousness: A Neurobiological Approach.* Englewood, Colorado: Roberts & Company Publishers, 2004.

Kurzweil, Ray. *The Singularity is Near: When Humans Transcend Biology.* New York: Penguin, 2005.

Martin, James. *The Meaning of the 21th Century.* New York: Riverhead Books, 2006.

Miller, Geoffrey. *The Mating Mind: How Sexual Choice Shaped the Evolution of Human Nature.* New York: Anchor Books, 2000.

Nagel, Thomas. "What is it like to be a bat?" *The Philosophical Review,* LXXXIII, 4 (October 1974), 435-50. http://organizations.utep.edu/Portals/1475/nagel_bat.pdf.

Orwell, George. *Nineteen Eighty-Four.* San Diego: Harcourt Brace, 1949.

Pearce, David. *The Hedonistic Imperative,* www.hedweb.com.

Pepperberg, Irene. *Alex & Me: How a Scientist and a Parrot Discovered a Hidden World of Animal Intelligence—and Formed a Deep Bond in the Process.* New York: HarperCollins, 2008.

Pinker, Steven. *The Blank Slate: The Modern Denial of Human Nature.* New York: Penguin, 2002.

Power, Samantha. *Chasing the Flame: Sergio Vieira de Mello and the Fight to Save the World.* New York: Penguin, 2008.

Rees, Martin. *Our Final Hour.* New York: Basic Books, 2003. (UK edition: *Our Final Century*)

Rifkin, Jeremy. *The Empathic Civilization: The Race to Global Consciousness in a World in Crisis.* New York: Penguin, 2009.

Safran Foer, Jonathan. *Eating Animals.* New York: Little, Brown and Company, 2009.

Schwartz, Barry. *The Paradox of Choice: Why More Is Less.* New York: HarperCollins, 2004.

Singer, Peter. *Animal Liberation.* New York: HarperCollins, 2009 (reissue edition).

Spier, Fred. *Big History and the Future of Humanity.* Chichester, UK: Wiley-Blackwell, 2010.

Sontag, Susan. *Regarding the Pain of Others.* New York: Picador, 2003.

Taleb, Nassim Nicholas. *The Black Swan: The Impact of the Highly Improbable.* New York: Random House, 2007.

Watts, Alan. *The Book: On the Taboo Against Knowing Who You Are.* New York: Random House, 1966.

Wilber, Ken. *A Brief History of Everything.* Boston: Shambhala Publications, 1996.

INDEX

A

B

C

capitalism/capitalists, 104, 164, 172, 192, 196, 198
categorical imperative, 146
caveman/cavemen, 19, 23
cerebellum, 31
CERN, 137
Chalmers, David, 27, 237
Chamberlain, Neville, 207
chaos theory, 43
Chile, 15
China/Chinese, 60, 90, 145
Chomsky, Noam, 142
climate change, 158, 172, 184, 202, 230-231, 238
Coetzee, J.M., 163
cognitive dissonance, 30, 49, 85, 94, 137, 153, 218
cognitive trap, 48
collider, 137
Colombia, 86
complex systems, 56, 178
complexity, 8-9, 15, 17-21, 31-32, 34-36, 44, 51, 56, 58-59, 76, 78-79, 107-108, 126, 149, 157-158, 161-162, 177-178, 223, 230, 233, 238
complexity theory, 178, 223
compression, 10-11, 85, 94, 119-120, 155
Congo, The, 145
cooperation, 24-25, 59-60, 68, 134, 144, 170, 176-177, 198, 201
Copernican/Copernicus, 2, 92
Costa Rica, 226
Csikszentmihalyi, Mihaly, 100
Cuban Missile Crisis, 156

D

Daily Show, The, 153
Darfur, 145
Darwin Awards, 22
Darwinian, 59, 104, 120, 134, 163, 174
Dawkins, Richard, 11, 19, 117, 237
Deaton, Angus, 102
dehumanization, 49, 51, 53, 72, 123, 158
delayed gratification, 69
Dennett, Daniel, 11, 42, 237
Descartes, 78
determinism/deterministic, 29, 41-44, 49, 52-55, 61, 72, 186, 221
Deutsch, David, 20, 237
Diamond, Jared, 24, 237
Diary of a Bad Year, 163
dictators, 43, 84, 107, 176, 217-218, 220, 232

dukkha, 85

E

Easterlin paradox, 101-102
Easterlin, Richard, 101
Easterly, William, 230, 238
Eastern philosophies, 118
Edelman, Marek, 235
Egypt, 217
emergent properties, 178
Europe/European, 23-24, 108, 122, 128, 137, 145, 185, 188-190, 197, 204
European Union, 197
Evangelism, 116
evolution/evolutionary, 12, 15, 17-22, 24-26, 29, 33, 41, 50, 64, 70, 88, 93, 103, 110, 115, 118, 126, 129, 134, 136, 162, 166, 174, 186, 190, 219, 229, 238

F

Facebook, 109
factory farming, 193
Falkland Islands, 204
Far Side, The, 71, 111
Fifth Element, The (film), 129
Finnish prison system, 188
Fisher, Len, 56, 238
flow (state), 100
foie gras, 90
free market, 105, 107, 192, 196, 198-199
free will, 9, 12, 29, 41-43, 45-55, 57, 59, 72, 100, 186, 212, 221
Fromm, Erich, 158, 238

G

Gaia hypothesis, 158
game theory/theorists, 26, 176, 219, 223
Gandhi, 220, 228
GDP, 106, 195
genetic, 23, 33, 45-46, 60, 64, 69, 87, 111, 164, 183, 186, 198
Geneva Conventions, 206
Germans/Germany, 136, 146, 189-190
Gladwell, Malcolm, 229, 238
Glover, Jonathan, 82, 238
God, 32, 44, 76, 112, 115, 141, 166, 176
Godin, Seth, 232
Godwin's Law, 145
Golden Rule, 146